Almost a Hero

Sir John Meares (1756?-1809)—Royal Navy officer, Pacific explorer and Northwest fur trader. This portrait served as the frontispiece of Meares' *Voyages* (1790), published in London after the Spanish seizure of Meares' ships in Nootka Sound had nearly resulted in war between Britain and Spain.

Almost a Hero

The Voyages of John Meares, R.N., to China, Hawaii and the Northwest Coast

J. Richard Nokes
Foreword by David L. Nicandri

WSU PRESS

Washington State University Press
Pullman, Washington

Washington State University Press
PO Box 645910
Pullman, WA 99164-5910
Phone 800-354-7360; FAX 509-335-8568
©1998 by the Board of Regents of Washington State University
All rights reserved
First printing 1998

Library of Congress Cataloging-in-Publication Data
Nokes, J. Richard.
   Almost a hero : the voyages of John Meares, R.N., to China, Hawaii and the Northwest Coast / by J. Richard Nokes ; foreword by David L. Nicandri.
      p. cm.
   Includes bibliographical references and index.
   ISBN 0-87422-155-2 (alk. paper). — ISBN 0-87422-158-7 (pbk. : alk. paper)
   1. Meares, John, 1756?-1809—Journeys. 2. Explorers—Great Britain—Biography. I. Title.
   G286.M45N65 1998
   910'.9164'092—dc21   98-30762
   [B]   CIP

To the memory of my parents,

James A. and Bernice A. Nokes,

who sacrificed much for their family.

Contents

Illustrations

Acknowledgments

To many historical libraries and librarians go the author's gratitude for their cooperation in searching out rare books, manuscripts, letters and documents of importance to an understanding of the British mariner John Meares and the Pacific maritime explorations and Northwest fur trade of two centuries ago.

The Massachusetts Historical Society produced the hand-written logs of Robert Haswell, John Box Hoskins and John Boit, Jr., concerning the early American voyages to the Northwest Coast of America; the Hawaiian Historical Society and the Archives of Hawaii had records of the early sailing ships that called at the Sandwich Islands and of the Hawaiians who sailed away in those ships; the Provincial Library of Victoria had valuable information on vessels that probed the harbors of British Columbia; the Oregon Historical Society and the Washington State Historical Society libraries provided illustrations and basic information on explorations of the Northwest Coast.

Special appreciation must go to the British Library in London and the Public Record Office in Kew for unearthing early records of the Foreign Office and Admiralty concerning John Meares and the settlement of the Nootka Controversy that almost led to war between Great Britain and Spain in 1790.

Personal thanks to Freeman M. Tovell, British Columbia historian, for his suggestions and contributions, and to Nina Jenkins who found important information concerning the life of Meares in various repositories in London. Also to Robin Inglis, Canadian historian, for casting a critical eye on the manuscript.

Hawaiian contacts who provided valuable information included Herb Kawainui Kane, artist and historian, and Alan Lloyd, Richard W. Rogers and Steve Gould who contributed their own research that was presented to the 1996 symposium on Maritime Archaeology and History of Hawaii and the Pacific, held at the Hawaii Maritime Center under auspices of the Marine Option program of the University of Hawaii. Thanks also go to the State Library of Hawaii for providing access to rare books, to the Bernice Pauahi Bishop Museum's department of anthropology for cooperation in producing records, and to Francis Murphy for some rare documents concerning Spain in the Pacific.

My sincere thanks must go to Glen Lindeman, Editor, Washington State University Press, for his many queries, corrections, research and additions that helped to strengthen the book into a more extensive work than the author had first contemplated. Thanks also to Keith Petersen, WSU Press Editor, for his early support for a work on John Meares. The splendid painting of Meares' ship entering Kawaihae Bay in Hawaii in 1788 was graciously contributed by artist/historian Herb Kawainui Kane, an officially proclaimed "Hawaiian Treasure" for his efforts in preserving Polynesian culture and history. The painting first appeared in Kane's book *Voyagers*. The original is in the collection of Herb and Signe Behring. Praise, too, for David Hoyt for his excellent cover design.

A major contribution came by letter from Colin Johnston, archivist of Bath and Northeast Somerset, England, who provided information concerning John Meares not previously known.

These and many others made important contributions. To all I express appreciation.

And my eternal gratitude to my dear wife, Evelyn, and members of my family for their loving encouragement.

Foreword

by David L. Nicandri
Director of the Washington State Historical Society

Newspapers are sometimes referred to as the first draft of history. J. Richard Nokes, longtime editor of the *Oregonian* in Portland, made his segue to the second draft of history more than a decade ago when increasing attention was being paid to the 1792-1992 "maritime bicentennial" of Robert Gray, George Vancouver and several Spanish explorers including Juan Francisco de la Bodega y Quadra. With a series of articles on Robert Gray that he wrote for his former newspaper, Dick made a place for himself within the community of regional historians. The literary promise inherent in those first attempts prompted the Washington State Historical Society to publish his book length treatment, *Columbia's River: The Voyages of Robert Gray, 1787-1793,* which I had the pleasure of editing on behalf of the Society.

Now, with *Almost a Hero,* the story of John Meares, Dick Nokes turns his attention to another fascinating, if little appreciated, figure in the early maritime history of the Northwest. In this highly readable, entertaining and informative account, Meares, usually a footnote in the backdrop of the explorations that succeeded his, comes dramatically to the fore. Dick Nokes' familiarity with the archival and scholarly resources, places and events of Pacific exploration in the last quarter of the 18th century is exemplary. This allows the reader to safely navigate through the intricacies of overlapping voyages, switched commands, newly named or renamed ships and topographic features with felicity.

The fascinating aspect of Meares' nautical career, and thus the title of the book, is how close he came to being included in the first rank of marine explorers. Indeed, Meares' southward cruise along the Pacific Coast in the summer of 1788 is a tantalizing account of barely missed fame. For example, I could not help but think, now on the verge of the Lewis and Clark bicentennial era, that Meares' experience at the mouth of the Great River of the West, which he missed but Gray found, is the obverse experience of Jefferson's Corps of Discovery. That is, where Meares saw the mouth of the Columbia and took it for a bay in the ocean, Clark saw the mouth of the river and mistook it for the ocean. (Meares also established the exploratory tradition, later followed by Alexander Mackenzie and Meriwether Lewis, of having the company of a Newfoundland dog.) Still, Meares left a substantial mark in regional history, literally via such place names as Cape Disappointment and his own namesake cape on the Oregon coast, and otherwise through his role in the Nootka affair that speeded the ascendancy of English speaking people on the Northwest Coast.

In *Almost a Hero* Richard Nokes properly assays Meares' record in history; that which has been miscast by earlier historians, notably the otherwise estimable W. Kaye Lamb and F. W. Howay. In this book we have the most economical and coherent accounting of the Nootka imbroglio ever published. Thanks to Dick Nokes and Washington State University Press, the historiography of coastal exploration has become clearer.

"The *Felice Adventurer* Bearing into Kawaihae Bay, Hawaii" [1788]. ©Herb Kawainui Kane, Collection of Herb and Signe Behring.

Introduction

I N TIMES OF STORM, the seas break high against the sheer basalt wall of a promontory on the northern coast of Oregon as though trying to reduce it to rubble and sand, while the same gale blowing out of the North Pacific may pour inches of rain onto the virgin forest of an island off the coast of British Columbia. Although hundreds of miles apart, the two landmarks—Cape Meares and Meares Island—have something in common. Both are named for John Meares, a British mariner who piloted sailing ships along the Northwest Coast of America seeking furs and making discoveries, and crossed the Pacific to the Sandwich Islands (Hawaii) and China two centuries and more ago.

This coastline of North America was the last to be probed by European and American sea captains as the Age of Discovery came to a close three centuries after the first voyage of Christopher Columbus in 1492. The voyages to the New World by Columbus, Vespucci, Magellan, the Cabots, Frobisher, Hudson, Drake and various Spaniards such as Balboa, Cabrillo, Vizcaíno and de Aguilar in the 15th, 16th and 17th centuries were the prelude. After them came other mariners of England, Spain, France, Russia and the infant United States who coursed the North Pacific in the late 18th century seeking fame and fortune in their cockle-shell sailing ships.

John Meares was one of the latter. While he attained little in the way of lasting fame and probably even less of fortune, it was not for lack of courage and enterprise. His ambitions were grand; his accomplishments were real, but were denigrated by fellow captains and latter-day historians. Nevertheless, he came close to being a maritime hero. His *Memorial* to Parliament in 1790 was central to a controversy that almost led to war between Britain and Spain.

One looks with little success in libraries for accounts of his exploits. There are books aplenty on James Cook, and George Vancouver. Juan Pérez,

Bruno de Hezeta and other Spaniards have won attention. And, in connection with the bicentennial of the discovery of the Columbia River in 1792, there has been a modicum of interest in the voyages of Boston Captain Robert Gray and his men. These books include this author's work, *Columbia's River: The Voyages of Robert Gray, 1787-1793,* published in 1991 by the Washington State Historical Society.

Except for his own extensive narrative written in 1790,[1] published books concerning the life and adventures of Meares are nonexistent.[2] Historians who have included something of his exploits in works on other individuals generally have demeaned his importance. He deserves better.

Meares was born in England about 1756, and joined the Royal Navy at the age of 15. He apparently considered the old Roman city of Bath his home while he pursued a career at sea.[3] British naval records indicate he served as captain's cabin boy and able seaman on the *Cruizer* for seven months and one day before he was promoted to midshipman on the same vessel. After less than a month he was transferred to the *King Fisher* as an able seaman and served 10 months before he was again promoted to midshipman. He served on a number of other British naval vessels, including the *Captain, Torvey,* and *Triton,* usually in the role of midshipman, until he came before a board considering his application for a commission on September 16, 1778.[4] This, of course, was during his service in the American Revolution when he fought, in his own words, "on the lakes" of Canada.[5] He supposedly "saw action on a number of occasions," including combat against the French.[6]

The examining board a day later found that Meares had "produceth Journals kept by himself in the *Torvay* & *Triton* and certificates from *Capn [Captain]* of his intelligence & etc and is qualified to do the duty of an able Seaman and Midshipman," and thus he met the requirements to be commissioned a lieutenant. His passing certificate was signed by "Ch Middleton," "Ed Le Cras" and "Capn Abraham North." The age of 22 was normal for promotion to commissioned rank for young sailors who were literate and showed a good grasp of seamanship and an aptitude for leadership.[7]

With the signing of the Treaty of Paris in 1783 ending the Revolutionary War, Meares and many other junior officers found themselves with few prospects in the naval service and eventually transferred to the merchant navy. Despite holding the rank of lieutenant, Meares' service was no longer required by the Royal Navy and he could do as he wished until a possible future call-up. He was, in effect, in reserve. He retained the rank of lieutenant and was placed on half pay. (Later, in 1795, after his Pacific adventures as an explorer/merchant trader, he was restored to active duty and promoted to the rank of commander. He served as an impress officer in Ireland before being injured.[8])

Meares' adventurous spirit did not die after his wartime service. He obtained command (or at least passage) on an India-bound vessel in 1785 and sailed to Calcutta to seek his fortune. Meares had become acquainted with the accounts of James Cook's voyages of exploration for Britain in the Pacific, and learned of the possibilities of gaining riches by trading for sea otter and other pelts on the Northwest Coast of America and selling or trading them to the mandarins of Macao and Canton. He also knew that the British parliament after 1745 had offered a reward of £20,000 to the first captain to discover and sail through a Northwest Passage between the Atlantic and the Pacific. The prize had not been claimed.[9]

The legend of a passage between the seas was common in maritime circles during the 16th to late 18th centuries, and Meares became a believer. Its discovery was one of his goals. Such a passage would profit Britain greatly because ships would no longer have to sail circuitous routes around Cape Horn or the Cape of Good Hope to reach the Orient. However, Cook's observation after probing the Arctic ice was that if such a passage ever were found, it would be located too far in the frozen north to have any practical value. Meares, however, believed a practicable route might exist. (Cook's estimation turned out to be accurate. It took the Norwegian discoverer Roald Amundsen a couple of years to sail, east to west, through an icy passage over the top of the world in his ship *Gjoa* in 1903-06. Others followed. A Royal Canadian Mounted Police ship, *St. Roch,* sailed through in 1940 east to west, and in 1944 west to east. In 1969, the super tanker *Manhattan,* escorted by a Canadian ice breaker, sailed from Alaska to the east coast with a cargo of crude oil.[10])

After finding his way to Calcutta in 1785, Meares began his adventurous new career of trying to make a fortune by establishing a fur-trading enterprise in which his ships would obtain sea otter and other furs from Northwest natives and exchange them in China for merchandise that would be of great value in London. His efforts began in 1786, and lasted until 1789, when his quest for gold and glory came to naught because of Spanish intervention in a small harbor on Vancouver Island.

From the beginning, as a master of vessels in the North Pacific Ocean, Meares experienced ill fortune. His dream of establishing a fur-trading empire became a nightmare: scurvy ravaged his crew in Alaska; one of his ships disappeared at sea with all hands, and four other of his vessels were seized by the Spaniards; he almost provoked a war between England and Spain; he failed to find the legendary Great River of the West even though he looked on its tumultuous mouth; and he failed to explore the Strait of Juan de Fuca when the opportunity was at hand.

But, withal, his adventures from Bengal to the ill-charted and mostly unexplored coastline of Northwest America and thence to the Sandwich Islands and to Macao off China's coast were important to history.

According to records supplied by Colin Johnston, archivist for Bath and Northeast Somerset,[11] Meares was honored by the British crown with the title of baronet, and was entitled to be known as Sir John Meares. The honor was apparently in recognition of his maritime adventures on the Northwest Coast of America and his splendid book *Voyages Made in the Years 1788 and 1789, from China to the North West Coast of America* published in London in 1790. Although he married (possibly twice), baptismal records indicate he had no children. The records of Bath Abbey list the marriage of John Meares, "esq of this parish, bachelor," and "Mary Ann Guilliband of St James parish, spinster," on July 8, 1796. Witnesses were Elizabeth Cootes, E. Hammond and Hannah Virtue.

Records of Bath Abbey reveal that Sir John Meares was buried February 6, 1809, and an inscription on a floor slab reads, "Sir John Meares, Bart. died 29 January, 1809 aged 45 years." British naval records state Meares died in 1809; the Bath Abbey records confirm that date and thus this must be the onetime pioneer mariner. These data leave in doubt, however, the date and place of Meares' birth. Navy records show he was commissioned a lieutenant when at "more than 22 years of age" in 1778, which would make his birth date 1756. It also would make him 53 years of age at his death, and not 45 as the inscription in Bath Abbey states. Baptismal records in Bath make no mention of Meares, leading to the belief he was born elsewhere.

Archivist Johnston probed further and found a record of a John Meares and wife who were listed in 1792 as congregants of the Roman Catholic Church of Bath, and that on August 14 of that year a John Meare and Elizabeth Norman were married in that church. Ages were not given. This certainly must be a different John Meares (or Meare). Either that, or Meares must have converted from Catholicism to the Church of England between 1792 and 1796 and his first wife died during the interval.

John Meares was a man of courage, energy and vision who left an indelible mark on the history of the Northwest Coast in an era when Great Britain challenged the Spanish empire's exclusive claims to eastern Pacific lands and commerce.

This is his story.

Notes

1. John Meares [ed. by William Coombe from the papers of John Meares], *Voyages Made in the Years 1788 and 1789, from China to the North West Coast of America: To Which Are Prefixed, an Introductory Narrative of a Voyage Performed in 1786, from Bengal, in the Ship "Nootka"; Observations on the Probable Existence of a North West Passage; and some Account of the Trade between the North West Coast of America and China; and the Latter Country and Great Britain.* (London: Logographic Press, 1790 [reprinted by Da Capo Press, New York, 1967]). Meares' *Voyages* is one of the outstanding accounts of the early coastal fur trade era.
2. (Arthur) Hugh Carrington wrote but never published a biography titled "Nootka Meares"; unpublished typescript, dated 1964, in the British Library, London. Carrington was a Fellow of the Royal Geographic Society.
3. The last will and testament of John Meares, dated January 19, 1809, in the Public Record Office, London, states that Meares lived in Bath.
4. Passing Certificate for Commission of John Meares. September 17, 1778, ADM 107/7, folio 59, Public Record Office, Kew, England.
5. Meares, *Voyages,* 222.
6. *Nouvelle Biographie Generale . . . xxxiv (Mar-Mer)* (Paris: Firmin Didot Freres, 1861).
7. Passing Certificate for Commission of John Meares.
8. Letter, May 12, 1796, John Meares to Evan Nepean, secretary to the British Admiralty: "I beg you will be pleased to inform their Lordships, that since my return from Ireland, for the recovery of my health, after receiving an hurt there, when Employed on the Impress Service, I am now quite recovered, and am ready, and desirous to Serve, wherever their Lordships may think proper to Employ me"; ADM 1/2132, Public Record Office, Kew, England.
9. James Cook in 1778 approached the Oregon Coast just south of 45° north latitude, close to a cape he named Foulweather. He continued his voyage north but mostly at some distance from the Oregon and Washington coast. He spent a month in Nootka Sound, and explored through the Bering Strait into the Arctic Ocean looking for a Northwest Passage. He was turned back by ice at 71° north latitude. See J. Richard Nokes, *Columbia's River: The Voyages of Robert Gray, 1787-1793* (Tacoma: Washington State Historical Society, 1991), 115-18. Spain sent an expedition in search of a Northwest Passage as early as 1532, when Hernando Cortés dispatched Diego Hurtado de Mendoza. All hands were slain by Indians on Mexico's Sinaloa Coast. Other expeditions followed. Warren L. Cook, *Flood Tide of Empire: Spain and the Pacific Northwest, 1543-1819* (New Haven, CT, and London: Yale University Press, 1973), 2.
10. The *Manhattan* was moored for a number of years in the harbor at Portland, Oregon. The *St. Roch* is on display in dry-dock at the Vancouver, BC, Maritime Museum.
11. Colin Johnston, personal correspondence with the author.

"A View of the Volcano, Cook's River; taken from Coal Harbour," in George Dixon, *A Voyage Round the World* (1789). Meares' *Nootka* traded for sea otter pelts in Cook Inlet, September 1786.

Chapter One

Despair and Death on the Northwest Coast

T HE WINTER OF 1786-87 on the Northwest Coast of America was long and severe, and to the British mariner John Meares and his crew of a tiny two-masted snow, the months they spent with their ship frozen in the ice in a cove in Alaska's Prince William Sound were a time of despair and death.[1]

Today, Prince William Sound is known to the world as the site of the grounding of the *Exxon Valdez* in 1989 in which 11.2 million gallons of crude oil spilled into the pristine waterway. While the disaster to the huge tanker took a heavy toll of birds and sea life, the voyage of Meares two centuries earlier brought death to 24 seamen who could not withstand the icy cold and scurvy that beset them in the same sound.

As were other European and American mariners of two centuries ago, Meares was inspired by the accounts of Captain Cook's expeditions into the Pacific, especially his third (and last) during which Cook discovered and named the Sandwich Islands (Hawaii), explored along the American Coast in 1778 in search of a waterway between the Pacific and the Atlantic—the legendary Northwest Passage—and died at the hands of Hawaiian natives.[2]

Meares had little knowledge of the Northwest Coast when he organized his expedition except for the accounts of Cook's third voyage. Cook, in the *Resolution* with its consort vessel *Discovery*, had sailed from Tahiti in late 1777 and on January 18, 1778, sighted the island of Woahoo (Oahu) and a day later dropped anchor in Waimea Bay on Atooi (Kauai). After that discovery, he sailed northeast and intercepted the Oregon Coast near a promontory at 44° and 48' which he called Cape Foulweather for the storm that beset him. His chart of his progress north along what is now the Oregon and Washington coastline is rudimentary, and he missed sighting either the Columbia River (the Great River of the West at 46° 10' north) or the Strait of Juan de Fuca that an English captain, Charles William Barkley, found in 1787.

But Cook and his men did obtain a number of sea otter furs in Nootka Sound and farther north that his sailors later discovered were highly valued in China. This news inspired merchants in London, Boston and Macao to send ships on long voyages to the Northwest Coast to obtain the beautiful furs from the natives which could, in turn, be traded in Canton for merchandise desired in England and America.[3] At times more than a dozen ships, mostly British and American, engaged in the trade. Britain dominated in the early years, but Boston and New York ships later became preeminent. The fur trade lasted for more than 40 years until the sea otter became nearly extinct.

Britain's James Hanna was the first to follow Cook; he found great profit in 1785 ($20,000) and lesser in 1786 ($8,000) in trading with natives for sea otter and other furs that he sold in China. He died before he could mount a third expedition.

A few others also preceded Meares. David Scott of Bombay financed and organized a two-ship expedition under James Strange that sailed late in 1785. Those ships, *Experiment* and *Captain Cook,* were under the command of John Guise and Henry Laurie. Off the northeast end of Vancouver Island, the expedition was the first to find Queen Charlotte Sound which they thought might be an opening to the fabled Northwest Passage.

Nathaniel Portlock and George Dixon, veterans of Cook's third expedition, sailed from London in September 1785 under sponsorship of the King George's Sound Company and were in the Northwest trading waters briefly in 1786 and longer in 1787 with the ships *King George* and *Queen Charlotte,* named for the queen and king (George III) of Britain. Dixon is credited with naming the Queen Charlotte Islands for his ship, and nearby Dixon's Entrance also is named for him. They took 2,552 pelts, worth $54,857, to the China market.[4]

Charles William Barkley was briefly on the coast after sailing from the Sandwich Islands in May 1787 with an Hawaiian girl, Winee (Wynee), aboard.[5] His expedition is recognized as the first to have sighted the long-sought Strait of Juan de Fuca. He entered and named a nearby inlet "Barkley Sound" on the west coast of Vancouver Island.

All of these ships' captains were seeking fortune from the fur trade discovered more or less accidentally by James Cook's expedition, but which already had been pursued for a score of years before then by the Russians along the Alaskan Coast. Meares was as anxious as any to develop the fur trade for himself and Britain. He envisioned establishing a trading post manned by Chinese in the Northwest and enrolling natives to keep it supplied with pelts for ships that went to and fro between China and the West Coast, with stops in the Sandwich Islands for "refreshment."[6]

Meares was a flamboyant almost swashbuckling character and he charmed several Calcutta merchants into joining him in the trading venture across the Pacific Ocean. The partners, known as the Bengal Fur Society, included the governor-general of India, Sir John Macpherson. The partners believed they could circumvent the onerous controls and licensing costs of the South Sea Company and the East India Company which had exclusive rights from the British government to trade in the Pacific (the South Sea) and in India's waters respectively. An English scholar has asserted that at this time the South Sea Company was "naught but a blood-sucking monstrosity."[7] Meares and his partners, whether rightly or wrongly, so regarded it and bent every effort to avoid it. This was especially true of his second voyage.

Also attractive to the British shipmasters was a £20,000 reward offered by the British Parliament after 1745 to the first English ship to discover and sail through a Northwest Passage. At first the reward was offered only to commercial ships, but it was extended to naval vessels as well prior to Cook's third voyage, and Cook was charged with seeking such a passage between the oceans. Meares was a believer in the legendary waterway, even though he said in the Preface to his lengthy narrative that his sea ventures "were Voyages of Commerce, and not of Discovery; and that whatever novelty they may possess, or original information they may bestow, arose out of, and form, as it were, an incidental part of a commercial undertaking."[8]

On January 20, 1786, Meares purchased two vessels, the *Nootka* (200 tons burthen) and the *Sea Otter* (100 tons). Each was classed as a snow. He was the senior officer of the expedition and also master of the *Nootka*. Another Royal Navy lieutenant on half pay and inactive duty, William Tipping, became master of the *Sea Otter*. To round out a crew, Meares frequented the waterfront of Calcutta and signed on 40 European sailors,

THE MARINE CHRONOMETER

In the 18th century, a ship's navigator could determine with relative accuracy the latitude at which a vessel was sailing by taking observations of the sun during the day and of certain stars at night, but determining longitude was a much more inexact matter that remained unresolved until a practical chronometer was developed later in the century. Accuracy in navigating and mapping was critical in this age of expanding European and American sea-going commerce. To find longitude at sea, a navigator needed to relate precisely the time aboard ship with the time at a base location (eventually assigned to the observatory at Greenwich, England). Having a device to determine exactly these two clock times would enable a navigator to fix the geographical distance between a ship's position and England. However, the technical aspects of developing such clocks were formidable, and adverse conditions at sea, such as rolling, pitching decks, temperature and barometric changes, etc., could adversely affect the accuracy of timepieces.

In 1714, the British Parliament had offered an award of £20,000 for the development of a means of determining longitude to within half a degree of accuracy (King Philip III of Spain had offered a reward as early as 1598). A British carpenter, John Harrison, spent nearly his entire lifetime perfecting the marine chronometer, but he was bitterly disappointed on several occasions when his sea clocks, after being tested, were not granted Parliament's award. King George III eventually interceded and obtained a financial settlement for Harrison. Though Harrison is recognized as the developer of the chronometer, the timepiece that Captain James Cook used successfully to chart New Zealand and Australian waters was made by Larcum Kendall and was known as the K1. Captain William Bligh of the *Bounty* also used a K1, and this may well have been the type Meares had aboard the *Nootka*. The K1 was a virtual twin of Harrison's No. 4 marine chronometer, first tested in 1762.

A truly practical chronometer eventually was developed by two Britons, John Arnold and Thomas Earnshaw. The clockmaker to the King of France, Pierre Le Roy, invented the forerunner of the modern chronometer. His achievement was to detach the balance wheel so that it swung with a minimum of interference. Naval ships in World War II used chronometers mounted in gimbals that kept the timepiece level no matter how violently a vessel pitched and rolled in the waves.

[Adapted from Dava Sobel, *Longitude: The True Story of a Lone Genius Who Solved the Greatest Scientific Problem of His Time* (New York: Walker, 1995)] and later in Madras took on 10 Lascars (sailors of the East Indies) for the *Nootka*.[9] Tipping's crew was a bit smaller.

To help finance the voyage across the Pacific, Tipping took a cargo of opium to Malacca for "about" 3,000 rupees. Meares left Bengal on March 2, 1786, carrying a Mr. Burke, the Royal Army paymaster, and his party to Madras for another 3,000 rupees. Meares arrived in Madras March 27 and sailed April 7. The two ships were to rendezvous in the summer on the Northwest Coast if they did not meet before.[10]

When Meares arrived in Malacca on May 23 he was informed that Tipping had already sailed for the Northwest trading grounds. A month later, Meares arrived at a port on Grafton Isle in the Bashee Islands, described by Meares as a Spanish base south of Japan. Here he augmented his supplies by trading iron for "hogs, goats, ducks, fowls, yams, and sweet potatoes," which he hoped would suffice for the duration of the long voyage.[11]

Meares noted that he had a type of timepiece aboard his flagship which "proved of the greatest utility," but he did not name it. Alexander Dalrymple, hydrographer for the East India Company, in the *Journal of the Esther Brig* identified it as a new marine chronometer—a device so precise in keeping time that it helped to determine longitude with good accuracy. A similar device was used with success by Captain Cook, but mariners of other nations were generally not so equipped in those early days.

Meares sailed from the Bashees on July 1 and steered a northeast course past Japan, arriving off the fog-shrouded "Isles of Amluc and Atcha" in the Aleutians on August 1 where he made contact with Russian traders and the natives. He remained two days, then sailed in heavy fog for "Ounalaschka," encountering native whale hunters in canoes.

On one occasion, visibility was so restricted that the crew could hear the surge of the sea on rugged shorelines on all sides but could see nothing. "Every way appeared to be blocked up against us." When the fog finally lifted on August 5, the *Nootka* was surrounded by a snow-covered land "of a tremendous height" with a rocky shore all around.[12]

"When we got round to the South side of the island [unnamed], a Russian came off to us and piloted our ship into an harbour adjacent to that in which Captain Cook refitted."[13] (This must have been Unalaska which Cook's expedition visited on October 3, 1778. The carpenters repaired Cook's ships, and the Russian orthodox priest presented Cook with a salmon pie.[14]) Meares noted that two of his shipmates who went ashore fell into the entrance (a hole in the roof) of the subterranean shelter of a group of natives. The occupants promptly fled the premises. To quiet the resulting consternation, the sailors offered the residents "a small present of tobacco."

On August 27, the *Nootka* arrived in the Shumagin Islands where a large number of small canoes came off. They actually were kayaks, though Meares did not then know that term. Each was occupied by one or two natives seated within a "skin-frock" fastened tightly over the holes and around the waists of the paddlers. Not a drop of water could enter, Meares observed. "These vessels are paddled at a prodigious rate, and go out in any weather."[15]

Proceeding on, Meares obtained his first sea otter skins from natives in Cook's River (today's Cook Inlet which leads into Anchorage, Alaska). The inhabitants here already knew the value of furs from their dealings with the Russians. In *Voyages,* Meares devoted a part of his account to the way the Russians used natives as virtual slaves, compelling them to provide pelts for little more than a few pinches of snuff to which they seemed addicted. The Russians who manned the trading bases seemed little better off. They were kept as long as eight years in this grim land before being relieved.[16]

After quitting Cook Inlet around September 20, Meares and his ship-mates fought a raging storm before entering Prince William Sound. Meares headed for Snug Corner Cove, a refuge found and named by James Cook in 1778.[17]

Shortly, Meares would learn from the Indians that Tipping's ship had been there and gone, presumably back across the Pacific. Meares' men observed some wood which had been fresh cut with "an edge tool" and "also found a piece of bamboo," hardly native to the Alaska Coast. "On the 4th day," natives came alongside in canoes and confirmed that a ship fitting the description of the *Sea Otter* had been there and sailed away only a few days earlier with a good cargo of pelts. The natives indicated they would provide plenty of furs in exchange for metal if Meares would stay the winter. Meares must have congratulated himself that Tipping's successful trading would ensure a good profit for the Bengal Fur Society. (Captain James Strange's two ships also had been in Prince William Sound, and Strange dined with Tipping before the *Sea Otter* sailed away toward Cook Inlet.)

Because he arrived too late in the season to fill out a cargo of the desired skins, Meares was faced with a dilemma: Should he stay the winter on the coast, which no other shipmaster had attempted, or should he sail to the Sandwich Islands more than 2,000 miles away and spend the months in warm comfort?

Knowing from Cook's accounts something of the tropical splendor of the climate and the charms of the women, Meares feared he might lose his sailors to the ambience of the Hawaiian Islands should he seek refuge there. So he decided to risk the rigors of an Alaskan coastal winter, having no real concept of what that might entail. On October 7, he moved his ship east-northeast to a more "commodious" anchorage, as he described it, "about 15 miles" away to the mouth of a creek emptying into the sound. Here fresh water was abundant and salmon ran in the stream. Too, the hillsides and trees appeared to provide better shelter from storms.

He put his sailors to work unrigging the ship and felling trees in the virgin forest to begin construction of a log shelter for a work or trading station. The men began the task with vigor, glad to be on land after a long and taxing voyage. Soon the natives became interested; moreover, they began stealing tools and otherwise harassing the unarmed workmen. On occasion, they even tried to pull nails from the ship's planks with their teeth, so much did they covet metal objects which could be used as tools, weapons or ornaments.[18]

On October 25, the crew ashore felt so threatened that Meares permitted the men to abandon the project and return to the ship. He ordered a cannon filled with grapeshot to be fired into the water near the natives, followed by a cannonball over their heads, causing considerable panic amongst them. But this remedy did not deter them long. Meares decided against firing directly on the natives. He next invited them to come aboard. When they learned that the Europeans coveted their sea otter garments, the Indians cast them off and stood naked.

Thus trading went on. The group of natives exchanged 60 fine otter skins for a moderate number of "spike nails," Meares wrote. Was this taking advantage of these unsophisticated aborigines? Not necessarily. This was still the stone and bone age in these waters, and to the natives metal was a precious item that could be used to good purpose; on the other hand, skins of the sea otter were easy to obtain.

Freezing temperatures set in and snow began to fall. Meares' men already were at work trying to cover the weather deck with spars from the forest as insulation in expectation of severe weather. Nets were erected to prevent boarding by native thieves or possibly a war party. A large Newfoundland dog, named "Towser," prowled about to give warning of any who approached. Ice froze around the hull. For a few days the men enjoyed skating, but soon the snow was so deep that they had to give up that form of recreation.

The work on the deck also had to be abandoned. Before long, the overhead below the deck was covered with hoar frost an inch thick despite three fires which were kept burning 20 hours each day. The heavy smoke made breathing difficult. To keep the fires aglow, fuel was brought from the nearby forest on a sledge dragged through the snow.

Even before this, salmon began disappearing from the stream and the ducks and geese that had been plentiful were flying away south. The natives, too, had gone to winter quarters, though a few garbed in skins, but with legs bare to the cold, came seeking aid. Meares granted them a supply of whale oil or blubber. Snow became too deep for the sailors to hunt game, and the ship was iced in solidly in the cove, although the open sound was not completely frozen over.

The temperature dropped to 26°, then to 20°, and to 14° after the onset of the new year. Daylight this far north was of short duration. The darkness of the cove, surrounded as it was by cliffs and dense forest, caused Meares to write of "the scene of desolation which encircled us.—While tremendous mountains forbade almost a sight of the sky, and cast their nocturnal shadows over us in the midst of day."

The crew members began to fall ill from the cold, scurvy and suffocating smoke that enveloped them below deck. In the month of January, 23 reported sick, including Chief Mate Ross, but he tried chewing pine needles and swallowing the juice. He recovered from scurvy. Meanwhile, four sailors had died.[19] By the end of February, 30 of the men were too ill to leave their hammocks, and another four died. In March, the surgeon and pilot succumbed.

Meares noted in his account: "Having lost our surgeon, we were now deprived of all medical aid." He commented, "too often did I find myself called to assist in performing the dreadful office, of dragging the dead bodies across the ice, to a shallow sepulchre which our own hands had hewn out for them on the shore. The sledge on which we fetched the wood was their hearse, and the chasms in the ice their tombs."[20]

Most of the men refused the treatment Chief Mate Ross found effective, preferring to turn their faces to the bulkhead and die rather than swallow the evil-tasting remedy. "They considered the slightest symptom of the disorder to be a certain prelude to death." (They did not realize that a lack of fresh fruit or vegetation, the source of vitamin C, in their diet was the actual cause of their illness.)

"Fish or fowl was not an offering of the winter here," Meares wrote. "A crow or a sea-gull were rare delicacies, and an eagle, one or two of which we killed, when they seemed to be hovering about, as if they would feed upon us, instead of furnishing us with food, was a feast indeed." The two ship's goats were "reluctantly" butchered which provided broth for the ill for two weeks.

Meares said the ship's stores still held biscuit, rice, flour, and salt beef and pork, but no one cared to eat those items. "The aversion . . . to the very sight of it, would have prevented salutary effects." All the "cordial provisions [sugar and wine, especially] had long been exhausted." The natives who came by appeared to be as distressed as the sailors.

Snow continued to fall in April with strong variable winds. The sick grew worse. Four more Europeans and three Lascars died. By this time, in desperation, a few sailors tried drinking pine juice and revived. But others had "a determination to die at their ease, (according to their manner of expression) rather than be tormented by such a nauseous and torturing remedy."[21] By now, those afflicted had gums too swollen and bloody to chew food. Their legs swelled and their stomachs ached. They remained in their hammocks in exhaustion and despair.

In early May, winter began to relax its grip. The sun was seen a bit longer, fish returned to the streams and the crew of the *Nootka* began to have hope. Natives, who also had suffered from the harsh winter, returned to the anchorage and began providing fish and fowl. Then on a bright day early in the month, Chief Shenoway, headman of the area, aged and nearly blind, came alongside to congratulate Meares on the return of good weather and also to tell him that two ships were at anchor at the mouth of Prince William Sound. Meares' narrative indicates the date was May 17. He was in error. Based on later events, the date more likely was May 7 or earlier.[22] The ships turned out to be the *King George* under Nathaniel Portlock, and the *Queen Charlotte* captained by George Dixon—fellow Britons who had arrived on the Northwest Coast from Hawaii for a second season of trading before taking their cargoes of furs to China.

Rescue seemed at hand and the sailors rejoiced, though Meares later commented that by this time the ice had melted enough so the *Nootka* could almost swing free at her anchorage, and the sick were beginning to recover. But two more men were "added to the number of those whom fate had ordered to take their sleep on this horrid shore."

Twenty-three died during the terrible winter; another died later. Meares also would learn that his second ship, the *Sea Otter*, had been lost at sea with all hands. The size of Tipping's crew is not known exactly, but probably was around 35.

These disasters combined were the worst in the history of sailing ships on the Northwest Coast two centuries ago. Two years later, two Boston ships, the *Columbia Rediviva* and *Lady Washington,* wintered on Vancouver Island with no serious problems, but the climate was milder that far south. During the early coast trade era, most captains chose to sail their ships to the Sandwich Islands rather than risk a winter on the Northwest Coast. Until 1786-87 no captain had attempted to spend the winter on the North Pacific Coast, so Meares might be excused on the basis of ignorance for the resulting tragedy to his crew which ended in death for half of them.

Notes

1. John Meares' account of his first expedition to the North Pacific Coast is titled "An Introductory Voyage of the *Nootka,*—Capt. Meares, from Calcutta, to the North West Coast of America, in the years 1786, and 1787," pp. i-xl, in *Voyages Made in the Years 1788 and 1789, from China to the North West Coast of America* (London: Logographic Press, 1790).

2. J. Richard Nokes, *Columbia's River: The Voyages of Robert Gray, 1787-1793* (Tacoma: Washington State Historical Society, 1991), 111-18.

3. By 1784, official and unofficial accounts of Cook's third expedition had appeared outlining how the Northwest Coast fur trade with China could be prosecuted and with recommendations focusing on Nootka Sound. A number of individuals who sailed with Cook later returned to the North Pacific to make additional discoveries and conduct the fur trade, including four men who later figured prominently in Meares' story— Nathaniel Portlock, George Dixon, James Colnett and George Vancouver.

4. Derek Pethick, *The Nootka Connection: Europe and the Northwest Coast, 1790-1795* (Vancouver, BC: Douglas and McIntyre, 1980), 15. Barry M. Gough, in *The Northwest Coast: British Navigation, Trade, and Discoveries to 1812* (Vancouver: University of British Columbia Press, 1992), 77, states these exact figures and comments that Portlock and Dixon accounted for more than half of the 5,033 sea otter pelts taken to China by 1787. See also, George Dixon, *Remarks on the Voyages of John Meares, Esq. in a Letter to That Gentleman* (London: J. Stockdale and G. Goulding, 1790), 12; reprinted in F.W. Howay, ed., *The Dixon-Meares Controversy* (Toronto: Ryerson Press, 1929), 31.

5. Ralph S. Kuykendall, *The Hawaiian Kingdom, 1778-1854,* vol. 1 (Honolulu: University of Hawaii Press, 1980 [6th printing]), 22; Edwin N. McClellan, "Winee of Waikiki," *Outrigger Forecast Magazine,* April 1950.

6. John Meares was not the only early mariner who desired to establish fur-trading posts in the Northwest. John Boit, a young officer aboard the *Columbia Rediviva,* expressed the same conviction when on the Columbia River in 1792: "This River, in my opinion, wou'd be a fine place for to sett up a Factory." He noted that a post here and another in the Queen Charlotte Islands "wou'd engross the whole trade of the NW Coast with the help [of] a few small coasting vessells": Boit's Log, May 18, 1792. Alexander Dalrymple of the East India Company and entrepreneur Richard Cadman

Etches promoted this trade theory. Others such as Portlock, Dixon and Strange likewise had thoughts along these lines but failed to carry out their sponsors' wishes to establish trading posts; Gough, *The Northwest Coast,* 75, 78, 110-11.

7.   Hugh Carrington, unpublished biography of John Meares titled "Nootka Meares" (1964), Chapter One, 3, in the British Library, London.

8.   Meares, "Preface," vi, in *Voyages.*

9.   Meares, "An Introductory Voyage of the *Nootka,*" i-iii, xxxiv, in Ibid. The *Nootka*'s crew "amounted to forty Europeans, including the purser, surgeon, five officers, and boatswain and ten lascars whom we took in at Madras."

10.   Ibid., ii; Carrington, "Nootka Meares," Chapter One, 8.

11.   Meares, *Voyages,* iii-iv.

12.   Ibid., iv-vi.

13.   Ibid., vii.

14.   William P. Gray, *Voyages to Paradise: Exploring in the Wake of Captain Cook* (Washington, DC: National Geographic Society, 1981), 184.

15. Meares, *Voyages,* viii-x.

16.   Ibid., vii, xi.

17.   Carrington, "Nootka Meares," Chapter Two, 3.

18.   Meares, *Voyages,* xii-xiii.

19.   Ibid., xvii-xviii.

20.   Ibid., xx.

21.   Ibid., xviii, xxi-xxii.

22.   Ibid., xxiii. Carrington in "Nootka Meares" repeats the error.

"Captain Portlock," in Nathaniel Portlock,
A Voyage Round the World (1789).

Chapter Two

Rescue and Controversy

W ITH THE LESSENING of winter's hold and news from friendly natives that two ships had arrived off Montague Island at the entrance to Prince William Sound about 20 leagues away, Captain Meares and the men who had survived the cruel winter gained hope that rescue might be near. Hastily, Meares wrote a letter and asked Chief Shenoway to carry it to one of the ships; Meares outlined the suffering of the crew and the hapless condition of the *Nootka,* and requested that assistance be sent. However, the letter was a long time in delivery.

Earlier, on April 24, 1787, Nathaniel Portlock of the *King George* and George Dixon of the *Queen Charlotte,* fur traders out of London, were visited by natives in five canoes who called out, "Nootka," "Nootka," and pointed up the inlet. The word "Nootka" meant nothing to either captain. They were 700 miles northwest of Nootka Sound and had no knowledge that a vessel of the name *Nootka* was on the Northwest Coast. Portlock commented in his narrative that the natives wore green and yellow beads indicating white men had been in contact with them. He saw trees along the shore which had been cut "by tools of a different kind to those used by the Indians."[1] Had Portlock understood the message the natives were trying to convey, rescue of Meares and his men might have occurred two weeks earlier than it did.

During the natives' visit, George Dixon thought they were saying, *"Nootka Notooneshuck,"* which he interpreted to mean plenty of sea otter. When dogs on his ship began to bark, the natives "called out, 'Towzer, Towzer, here, here,' whistling at the same time, after the manner used to coax dogs in England." Puzzled, the mariners thought that possibly an English ship had been there. Dixon gave small presents to the Indians in the hope they would return with pelts to trade.[2]

Two weeks later on May 8, Portlock noted that two canoes again approached the ships and the natives once more "mentioned the word *Nootka* very frequently; and every time it was repeated they pointed up the Sound: they also mentioned the name of Thomas Molloy. I found they were acquainted with the use of fire-arms, and I rather suppose they have gained that knowledge from the Russians."[3]

Dixon, who in the meantime had left the *King George* and *Queen Charlotte* on an extended trading and exploring excursion in two whaleboats and a longboat, noted on May 6 that he encountered other natives who pointed toward Snug Corner Cove, conveying the message that a ship was anchored there. "This circumstance strongly excited my curiosity."

The next day, Dixon and his men set out for Snug Corner Cove. They found no vessel there, nor any natives nearby (in the previous autumn, Meares had moved his anchorage an estimated 15 miles east-north-east). The party remained overnight in the cove. Next morning, "two Indians came alongside in a canoe" and indicated that a ship was anchored at no great distance. They offered to guide the Britons there for a quantity of beads. Dixon and his men set off in two whaleboats, but in rough weather the guides paddled away shortly after receiving their gifts. He then returned to the longboat in Snug Corner Cove.

In the evening, six other canoes arrived and, again, the occupants seemed to say that a ship was anchored nearby and promised to guide the Europeans to it. Dixon set out in one whaleboat. "At ten o'clock in the evening [of May 8], we arrived in the creek where the vessel I so much wished to see lay [Meares] . . . his vessel was still fast in the ice. The scurvy had made sad havock amongst his people, he having lost his Second and Third Mates, the Surgeon, Boatswain, Carpenter, Cooper, Sail-maker, and a great number of the foremast men, by that dreadful disorder; and the remaining part of his crew were so enfeebled at one time, that Captain Meares himself was the only person on board able to walk the deck."[4] For their part, the *Nootka*'s men welcomed Dixon "as a guardian angel with tears of joy."[5]

Shocked to see fellow Britons in such a terrible state, Dixon assured Meares of "every necessary we could possibly spare." Meares responded, according to Dixon, by saying "he desired me not to take the trouble of sending any refreshments to him, as he would come on board us very shortly in his own boat."[6]

Meares' own account, however, contradicts part of Dixon's statement. Meares advised Dixon of the seriousness of the situation, and told him that the *Nootka*'s longboat was not in seaworthy enough condition to reach the ships "distant near 20 leagues" (such a round trip would require "some days" of sailing and rowing, Meares thought). Dixon replied by saying he could carry Meares to the two ships, but could not assure him of being able to return because Portlock planned to sail very soon. So, instead of accompanying Dixon, Meares addressed a letter, dated May 11, to Portlock who was the commodore of the two-ship expedition. As with the letter entrusted to Chief Shenoway, Meares again described the dire condition of himself, his men and the ship.[7]

Dixon set sail from the cove in his whaleboat at 3 a.m., May 9, and arrived at his anchorage by 4 a.m., May 10. Meares meanwhile decided to follow in his own leaky longboat, reaching the *King George* about 3 o'clock on May 11. By the time he arrived, the longboat "was half full of water." Aboard in addition to Meares were the first mate and five seamen, plus supplies including "two casks of rum, of 50 gallons each, and 12 bags of rice of about 500lb" that Meares hoped to trade for gin, sugar and cheese.[8]

"As soon as we had refreshed ourselves," negotiations between Meares and Portlock began immediately. The latter's account makes no mention of any controversy, but Meares in his narrative insists that his benefactor was less than anxious to provide all the men and items which Meares said he needed. Meares also declared that Portlock took too much credit for the rescue because by the time Dixon arrived, the *Nootka* in a short while might have been able to get underway for the Sandwich Islands. Nevertheless, he praised Portlock for rendering "considerable assistance and service."[9]

Portlock did provide for two of his own sailors to be added to Meares' crew, contingent upon Meares' signing an agreement to pay them each £4 a month. Meares thought the wage excessive because, he claimed, Portlock had paid them only 30 shillings a month. The men also wanted a prime otter skin each, but Meares refused that demand.

Meares noted, "the same evening, at my request, Captain Portlock ordered his carpenter to caulk my long-boat's bottom" and Portlock also accepted Meares' rum and rice in trade for "6 gallons of brandy, 11 of gin, two casks of flour, of 20 gallons each, 10 gallons of melasses [*sic*], and six loaves of English sugar."[10] Meares bid Portlock adieu and set out in his repaired longboat with the two extra seamen aboard.

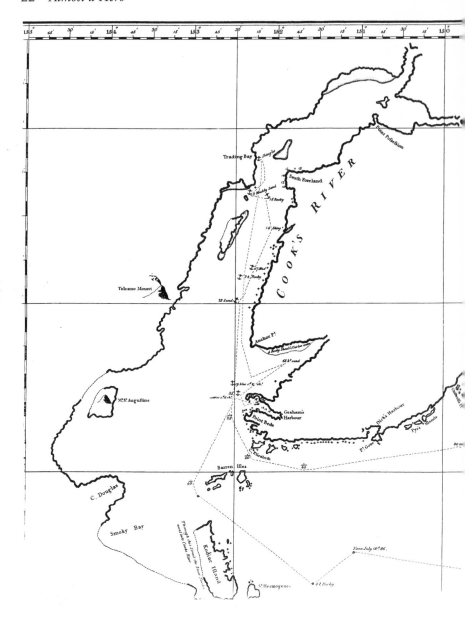

A section of the chart in Nathaniel Portlock's *A Voyage Round the World* (1789). The dotted line is the 1786 track of Portlock's *King George* (which was accompanied by George Dixon in the *Queen Charlotte;* not shown). Solid line is the *King George*'s track upon

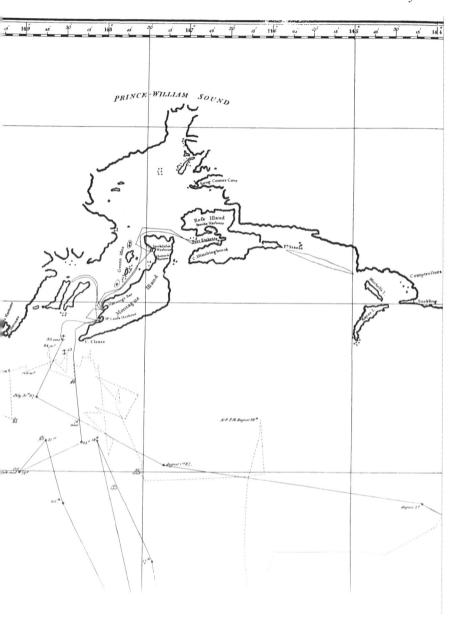

returning from Hawaii in 1787 (again accompanied by the *Queen Charlotte*; not shown).
Captain Dixon in a longboat found Meares' *Nootka* in distress at anchorage, 15 miles east-
northeast of Snug Corner Cove. No similar chart was published for the voyage of the
Nootka, 1786-87.

Dixon realized now that the Indians, from the first contact beginning on April 24, had been trying to tell the two captains about Meares' plight by repeating the word "Nootka." "Neither did we any longer wonder at their coaxing our dogs, and speaking English, as they are exceedingly articulate in their pronunciation, and one of them it seems, had been on board the *Nootka* several weeks." [11]

In a few days, two whaleboats from the *King George* arrived at the *Nootka*'s anchorage with a letter from Portlock asking for such trade items as yellow and green beads, and iron, a spare anvil, pepper and a compass. Meares replied that many of the items were stored deep in the hold of the *Nootka* and could not easily be reached. He sent a compass, pepper, and considerable rice and other articles he thought Portlock might want. [12]

Two weeks later, the ice had melted sufficiently to allow Meares to sail the *Nootka* to an anchorage near the *King George* just inside the sound at "Port Etches" (named for Richard Cadman Etches of London, a sponsor of Portlock). Meanwhile, Captain Dixon in the *Queen Charlotte* had taken leave of Portlock (on May 14) and sailed for Nootka Sound. Upon meeting again, Portlock handed a letter to Meares, dated June 9, 1787, in which he stated he had decided to remain in Prince William Sound to trade with the natives. If the *Nootka* remained, it would "stop a considerable part of the trade." Portlock made a proposition: if Meares would pledge a £500 bond to refrain from trading in the area and let Portlock have 20 bars of iron, and beads, Meares could keep what he already had been given "and what other assistance I have in my power to afford you."

It is apparent no love was lost between these rival captains engaged in the Northwest Coast fur trade. Portlock was trying to eliminate Meares as a competitor even while providing him with the necessities to reach Hawaii or China.

(At this point in his account, Meares interrupted the story of his relationship with Nathaniel Portlock to insert an account of a native girl whom the Indian chief, Shenoway, had brought to the *Nootka* in October 1786. Meares purchased her "for an axe and a small quantity of" trade beads. "She soon made us understand that she was a captive, and had been taken with a party of her tribe, who had been killed and eaten, which was the general lot of all prisoners of war . . . [She had been saved] to wait upon the Royal ladies, who were now tired, or perhaps jealous of her services." She remained on board four months seemingly content, but finally fled in a canoe with natives from a tribe living nearby. [13])

Resuming his account of his dealings with Portlock, Meares said, "impelled by cruel necessity, I agreed to these hard conditions, with a proviso . . . to let me have another man from him, and the probability of a boy," and some supplies "at the Canton price." Portlock promised to send a man, possibly a boy, and some "porter" (a mixture of ale and stout) and other supplies, including chocolate and sugar.

Portlock did order a carpenter to caulk the deck of the *Nootka* and examine her pumps. The carpenter used oakum donated by Portlock. In return, Meares sent 11 fathoms of "old" cable (to compensate for the oakum), but later Portlock demanded 20 fathoms. Meares answered that this was exorbitant, whereupon Portlock sent another demand for more iron and more cable.[14] "Oakum," which figures prominently in the negotiations between Meares and Portlock, was a fiber used to insure the watertight integrity of a wooden ship's hull. Oakum was prepared by picking loose strands of old hemp rope and treating it with tar. It then was pounded or stuffed into the seams between the planks of the hull.

Meares did dispatch more cable and "six stands of arms, some brass musketoons, and the anvil [which Portlock had earlier requested] until we met in China." Portlock at this point said he "could not spare the man," but would trade "20 dozen of porter, and 10 gallons of gin, for a new European 13 inch cable" and give in return, "'an old 9 inch hawser, of 80 fathoms.' I naturally rejected this offer with indignation," Meares replied, but he proposed selling the cable at the same price his sponsors had paid for it. Consequently, Portlock then withdrew his carpenter and the offer of an additional man and boy, "and in other private points was guilty of the most improper conduct," stated Meares.[15]

On June 18, Portlock sent another letter demanding "a security that you will leave the coast immediately on your quitting this Sound." He threatened to take back the two sailors he had provided to Meares, saying that the offering of the men's services "was not to enable you to trade along the coast." He now asked for a bond of £1,000 (instead of £500) in order that Meares would not trade along the coast, but would sail immediately for Canton. Meares signed the bond under protest, replying, "you have used me extremely ill." Meares refused to return the two men, and declared he would repel by force, if necessary, any attempt on the *Nootka*. At the last moment, before Meares sailed on June 21, Portlock attempted to quiet Meares' anger by sending him a "Sandwich Island cap and cloak as a present," which Meares refused.[16]

THE CURSE OF SCURVY

For centuries, sailors on long voyages had been plagued by scurvy, an ailment that caused bleeding gums, swollen limbs, stiffness of joints, slowness in the healing of wounds, and often death. European seafaring nations all sought remedies, but Britain, with its vast fleets of naval and commercial vessels, especially was interested in finding a cure. The lack of vitamin C from a diet deficient in fruits and vegetables was the cause. Vitamin C was unknown in these times, but a Scottish naval surgeon, James Lind, determined citrus fruit would prevent scurvy and in 1753 published his findings.

While Captain James Cook was not the first to learn about remedial measures, he is considered to have been the greatest exponent of instituting the use of citrus fruits such as lemons and oranges, sauerkraut, greens and almost any growing thing to effect a cure or serve as a preventive. Robert Gray of the American ship *Columbia Rediviva* ordered his men to harvest nettles and fresh greens upon their arrival on the Northwest Coast, and he even found that burying stricken men up to their waists brought rapid recovery. Spruce beer, a liquid potion made of the needles of evergreen trees, became a popular remedy. Chewing evergreen needles also was beneficial, as evidenced by Chief Mate Ross aboard the *Nootka* in the winter of 1786-87.

After 1795, the British Admiralty required naval ships to administer lime juice to crews each day. For the past 200 years scurvy has been almost nonexistent in maritime circles.

[Adapted from Daniel J. Boorstin, *The Discoverers: A History of Man's Search to Know His World and Himself* (New York: Random House, 1983)]

While Portlock and Dixon both published narratives in 1789 (under identical titles), only Dixon eventually reported the arguments with Meares in Prince William Sound and over other affairs in and around Vancouver Island, a matter that will be discussed later. However, letters sent between Portlock and Meares which are printed in Meares' narrative throw light on Portlock's views of the controversy.

Despite his seeming harsh attitude, Portlock expressed sympathy for the plight of Meares and his men during the winter—"indeed it must have been a very dreadful one; for before the winter broke up the captain and a Mr. Ross, his chief mate, were the only two persons capable of dragging the dead bodies from the ship over the ice, and burying them in the snow on shore." Portlock also did grant that Meares had provided him with information on several other British ships from India and China that were, or had been, on the coast, "a circumstance that we had no idea of at the time we left England."[17]

Portlock stated he provided "as many refreshments of various kinds as the [long]boat [of Meares] could well carry. We spared him some flour, loaf-sugar, molasses, Sandwich Island pork, gin, brandy, and cheese, and two good seamen, to assist in navigating his ship to China; at which place he was to return them: their names were George Willis and Thomas Dixon, both of whom went on board the *Nootka,* agreeably to their own requests, and not from any entreaty whatever. Besides the above articles, I furnished captain Meares with 150 cocoa-nuts, which I had great hopes would help to recover his people."[18]

Portlock also, at Meares' request, had provided the carpenter to assist in repairs, and also had sent an armourer (blacksmith) and furnished "near two hundred weight of oakum." (Meares' narrative reproduces a letter from Meares to John Henry Cox in Canton, ordering payment of $40 to Robert Horne, carpenter of the *King George,* who apparently made repairs on the *Nootka.*) Portlock also said he had sent a party ashore to cut wood for the *Nootka* and to make spruce beer to counteract scurvy, a remedy that became common among mariners on the Northwest Coast. (Portlock provided a recipe for spruce beer: "to a puncheon of beer three gallons and a half of molasses were added; it was afterward worked with prepared yeast.")

Captain Dixon also was sympathetic to the crew's plight, but blamed Meares for the extent of the sickness on the *Nootka.* Dixon claimed he learned from the *Nootka* crew "that a free and unrestrained use of spirits had been indiscriminately allowed them during the extreme cold weather, which they had drank to such excess about Christmas, that numbers of them kept [to] their hammocks for a fortnight together; add to this, their liquor was of a very pernicious kind, so that there is reason to suppose its effects, when drank to such an extreme, was not less fatal than the scurvy itself."

Dixon continued, "admitting this to be the case, it surely was ill-judged in Captain Meares to suffer such hurtful excesses amongst his people; and I am afraid that a scanty supply of the various antiscorbutics absolutely necessary for these voyages, put it out of their power to check the cruel disorder, so often fatal to sea-faring people."[19]

Meares denied in a letter to Portlock that he had permitted an undue amount of liquor to be consumed, and countercharged correctly that Dixon had had problems with scurvy among his own men. Overindulgence at Christmas time was not uncommon among British sailors, as Captain Cook himself admitted in his log of his voyages in the Pacific.

It was not until June 13 that Chief Shenoway finally brought to the *King George* the letter which Meares had written to parties then unknown, after the chief had advised Meares many days earlier about two ships entering the sound. By this time, of course, the letter served no purpose. Shenoway claimed he had trouble finding the *King George*, which had moved to a different anchorage.

It may be that the differences which arose among the mariners were caused by Dixon's and Portlock's resentment of Meares because he had no licenses from the East India and South Sea companies to trade in the Pacific, but which Dixon and Portlock held because of Etches' sponsorship. In other words, they felt Meares was poaching in their hunting grounds.[20]

When Meares sailed from Prince William Sound on June 22, 1787, he took a heading for Hawaii, but wet weather and fog intervened and illness again affected some of the men. So, after 10 days at sea, he was forced to turn back east, and found refuge "40 leagues distant" in an unidentified inlet which he stated was at 57° north latitude. This would place the anchorage somewhere at or near Baranof Island in Alaska's vast Alexander Archipelago. Meares had on board at this time 24 sailors, "including myself and officers," plus the two sailors from the *King George*. Not all were yet recovered and able bodied, and, indeed, a 24th man would die en route due to the rigors of the winter in the "inhospitable sound."[21]

How large a cargo of furs did Meares finally carry to Canton? Enough to assist him in helping finance a second venture, but the actual number of pelts is uncertain. In his narrative, he did not mention how many he had acquired. Dixon, however, said Meares and Ross, the first mate, had given contradictory estimates of the number of skins they had aboard, claiming 2,000 on one occasion and 700 at another time. Dixon believed Meares and Ross were trying to keep secret the exact number to discourage other traders on the coast. The lower estimate seems more likely to be accurate because the *Nootka* had little time for trading before the severe winter set in. Before the *Nootka*'s arrival in Prince William Sound, the only fur trading that she had accomplished was in and near Cook Inlet where the Russians already were established.

There is no doubt Meares had intended to continue trading during the spring and summer of 1787. The log structure that his men started to build was part of his dream of establishing a permanent trading system on the Northwest Coast. But he was compelled by tragic circumstances and hard-bargaining by Captain Portlock to leave the coast without completing a cargo. Meares never returned to Prince William Sound, although one of his ships under another captain did in the following year (1788).

Notes

1. Nathaniel Portlock, *A Voyage Round the World; But More Particularly to the North-West Coast of America: Performed in 1785, 1786, 1787, and 1788, in the "King George" and "Queen Charlotte," Captains Portlock and Dixon* (London: J. Stockdale and G. Goulding, 1789) [reprinted by Da Capo Press, New York, 1968], 207-08.

2. George Dixon, *A Voyage Round the World; But More Particularly to the North-West Coast of America: Performed in 1785, 1786, 1787, and 1788, in the "King George" and "Queen Charlotte," Captains Portlock and Dixon* (London: G. Goulding, 1789), 146-47 [reprinted by Da Capo Press, New York, 1968] [360 pages, plus an Appendix]). A shortened, 151-page version of Dixon's narrative is accredited to "C. L." and also appeared in 1789; see C. L., *A Voyage Round the World, in the Years 1785, 1786, 1787, and 1788. Performed in the "King George," Commanded by Captain Portlock; and the "Queen Charlotte," Commanded by Captain Dixon* (London: R. Randal, 1789). Also see Barry M. Gough, *The Northwest Coast: British Navigation, Trade, and Discoveries to 1812* (Vancouver: University of British Columbia Press, 1992), 90-91.

3. Portlock, *A Voyage Round the World*, 217.

4. Dixon, *A Voyage Round the World*, 152-55.

5. John Meares, "An Introductory Voyage of the *Nootka*,—Capt. Meares, from Calcutta, to the North West Coast of America, in the years 1786, and 1787," xxxiii, in *Voyages Made in the Years 1788 and 1789, from China to the Northwest Coast of America* (London: Logographic Press, 1790).

6. Dixon, *A Voyage Round the World*, 155. According to a memoir published 45 years later by John Nicol, a crew member of the *King George*, the men of the *Nootka* were "in a most distressing situation from the scurvy. There were only the captain and two men free from disease . . . They could not bury their own dead; they were only dragged a short distance from the ship, and left upon the ice. They had muskets fixed upon the capstan, and manropes that went down to the cabin, that when any of the natives attempted to come on board, they might fire them off to scare them. They had a large Newfoundland dog, whose name was Towser, who alone kept the ship clear of the Indians. He lay day and night upon the ice before the cabin window, and would not allow the Indians to go into the ship. When the natives came to barter, they would cry 'Lally Towser,' and make him a present of a skin, before they began to trade with Captain Mairs [*sic*], who lowered from the window his barter, and in the same way received their furs . . . We gave him [Meares] every assistance in our power in spruce and molasses"; *The Life and Adventures of John Nicol, Mariner* (Edinburgh: W. Blackwood; London: T. Cadell, 1822), 87-89; quoted by Gough, *The Northwest Coast*, 91.

7. Meares, *Voyages*, xxiv (letter to Portlock, xxxiii-xxxiv).

8. Dixon, *A Voyage Round the World*, 155-56; Meares, *Voyages*, xxiv-xxv.

9. Ibid., xxiii. From his remark, Meares obviously was grateful for the assistance rendered by Portlock, but he felt the assistance was given grudgingly.

10. Ibid., xxv.

11. Dixon, *A Voyage Round the World,* 158.
12. Meares, *Voyages,* xxvi-xxvii.
13. Ibid., xxvii-xxx.
14. Ibid., xxviii-xxix.
15. Ibid., xxix-xxx.
16. Ibid., xxx-xxxii, xxxvii.
17. Portlock, *A Voyage Round the World,* 219-20.
18. Ibid., 221.
19. Ibid., 217; and Dixon, *A Voyage Round the World,* 157. Whether or not Meares and his crew overindulged at Christmas time, scurvy was caused primarily by a deficiency of vitamin C rather than an abuse of spirits.
20. Frederick W. Howay, one of the historians most critical of Meares, refers to him as a "poacher"; *The Dixon-Meares Controversy* (Toronto: Ryerson Press, 1929), 11. But, it should be noted, Meares and other traders felt they were entitled to seek furs on the Northwest Coast.
21. Meares, *Voyages,* xxxvi-xxxvii. In addition to the 24 men who died aboard the *Nootka,* add the approximately 35 lost at sea with the disappearance of the *Sea Otter* commanded by William Tipping to realize the tremendous human tragedy that occurred during Meares' first trading expedition to the Northwest Coast.

"A View in the Bay at Woahoo, Sandwich Islands," in George Dixon, *A Voyage Round the World* (1789).

Chapter Three

A Chief of Atooi
and a Girl of Hawaii

D ESPITE PORTLOCK'S PROHIBITION against it, there have been suspicions that Meares and his crew did some trading for furs on the coast before departing for the Sandwich Islands. If so, there is no mention of it in Meares' narrative, and there is no evidence that Portlock tried to enforce the pledge Meares made to pay a surety bond of £1,000 if he violated the agreement. Meares only says that wind, fog and sickness among his people forced him to seek refuge in a sheltered harbor after ten days of sailing from Prince William Sound.

As the *Nootka,* in early July, again poked her prow into the Pacific swells, she encountered fair skies and, before long, brisk northeast trade winds filled her canvas and carried her to the subtropical warmth of the Sandwich Islands. The crew was ecstatic as the peaks of Mauna Loa and Mauna Kea on the island of Hawaii appeared in view. Soon, waving palms could be seen along the shore. Shortly, natives in canoes provided the British vessel with yams, sweet potatoes and pigs. Within 10 days, Meares wrote, his crew was fully recovered from the scurvy. "Every complaint had disappeared from among us."[1]

After first anchoring at an unnamed harbor on Hawaii, Meares visited most of the islands as he sought supplies for his crew and vessel. At every anchorage natives greeted the sailors warmly: "We remained here a month, during which time the islanders appeared to have no other pleasure but what arose from shewing kindness and exercising hospitality to us.—They received us with joy—and they saw us depart with tears. Among the numbers who pressed forward, with inexpressible eagerness, to accompany us to *Britannee,*—Tianna [Kaiana], a chief of Atooi [Kauai], and the brother of the sovereign of that island was alone received to embark with us, amid the envy of all his countrymen."[2]

It must be remembered that visits by European and American sailing ships were still a rarity in these islands where James Cook had landed only nine years earlier. The Hawaiians were seafarers by tradition. Their ancestors had come in double-hulled, open vessels from distant South Pacific islands, sailing without instruments, but guiding themselves by the stars, the flight of birds and sea currents. The first of these ancient explorers had arrived perhaps about 1,900 years ago from islands as much as 2,700 miles away. The Polynesians had the beneficent Hawaiian Islands to themselves until Cook arrived, January 18, 1778, on his way to the Pacific Northwest Coast.[3]

Many Hawaiians later would join the crews of European and American sailing ships, but, at the time Kaiana joined Meares, few natives were known to have yet done so. The very first was Winee (Wynee), a girl, who became the maid of Captain Charles William Barkley's young bride. Winee was aboard the *Imperial Eagle* when Barkley first set eyes on the Strait of Juan de Fuca in 1787.[4]

The Hawaiian chain was not yet politically united, and bloody battles were fought in the late 18th century between the armies of island chiefs seeking to add to their domains. The wars continued until Kamehameha the Great conquered his rivals and unified the islands (except Kauai) in 1795. Kaiana would become a great general under Kamehameha until the two had a falling out, which cost Kaiana his life, as we shall see in a later chapter.

Meares believed Kaiana was a "brother" of the ruler of all of Kauai. Later historians, however, have assumed that he actually was a "brother-in-law" or "cousin" of Taheo (Kaeo-ku-lani), the chief of the island. Two other eminent historians of Hawaiian lineage, Abraham Fornander and S.M. Kamakau, describe him as a "grandson" of Keawe, the "moi" (great chief) of Hawaii, and "son" of Chief Keawe Ahaula (Ahuula), thus his full name was Kaiana Ahaula. In any event, Kaiana was certainly of the "ali'i" (royalty) and could rightfully be considered by white visitors as a chief or prince of Atooi.[5] Meares described "Tianna" as being about 32 years of age and a splendid specimen of a man—muscular and about 6 feet 5 inches tall. He was married and had a young child.

With the island chief aboard, Meares left Hawaii on September 2, 1787.[6] Of the departure from the Sandwich Islands, Meares wrote: "[We were] leaving behind us, as we have every reason to believe, the most favourable impressions of our conduct and character with the inhabitants of them [the islands],—and grateful, on our part, for the generous friendship and anxious services we received from them.—After a very favourouble voyage, carrying the trade winds through the whole of it, we arrived in the Typa, an harbour [on the lower Pearl River] near Macao, on the 20th of October 1787."[7]

The bad luck that had hounded Meares on the Northwest Coast now plagued him again. A vicious storm arose and, because the *Nootka* had only one anchor left, the little ship was set adrift. "We were obliged to run her ashore, as the only means of preservation." Alarmed to see two French warships standing nearby (Meares initially feared that Britain and France might have declared war again), he soon was grateful when French sailors came to the rescue of the endangered British and Lascar crew. Meares does not provide details, but all hands and presumably the cargo were saved.[8] The little vessel was salvaged and later sold.

Kaiana was an instant sensation among the Chinese of Macao. He generally dressed in the western attire of his shipmates, but on some occasions he wore a feathered headdress and a gold and scarlet feathered cloak, which he had taken with him aboard Meares' ship.[9] Kaiana also was befriended by John Henry Cox, a shipping magnate, and other members of the white community in Macao. They saw to it that the Polynesian was richly endowed with gifts which might be of use to him and his fellow islanders when he returned to Hawaii.[10] Historians claim these included guns, ammunition, a variety of domesticated plants and animals, tools and personal items, though a more recent historical summary expresses doubt about Kaiana's being given any weapons.

While the British colony looked after the Hawaiian prince, Meares entered into negotiations with local merchants. In a short time, he arranged an association that provided him with two vessels for a second voyage to the Northwest Coast.

⚓

Two years later in England, with the writing of *Voyages Made in the Years 1788 and 1789, from China to the North West Coast of America,* Meares closed his account of his first voyage to the New World with speculations about the Northwest Passage.[11] This legendary waterway supposedly extended through the North American continent, and would provide an accommodating route for European ships sailing to and from the Orient.

JEFFERSON'S DREAM

"The object of your mission," President Thomas Jefferson wrote to Meriwether Lewis on June 20, 1803, "is to explore . . . the most direct & practicable water communication across this continent for the purposes of commerce."

Jefferson thus expressed his hope that a connection might be found between the upper reaches of the Missouri River and the headwaters of the Columbia River which would provide a water route—at least by canoe or keelboat—between Atlantic and Pacific waters. In effect, such a connection would be a Northwest Passage with the mouth of the Columbia as the entrepôt for ships sailing between America and Asia. Fur traders could ship cargoes of furs across the Pacific Ocean to China and bring back exotic goods via the connecting river systems to markets in the East.

This became the ultimate goal of captains Meriwether Lewis and William Clark when they embarked on their transcontinental journey in the spring of 1804. After their 2 1/2 year trek through mostly unexplored lands, Lewis had to disappoint the president by telling him the navigable portions of the two river systems were 340 miles apart and separated by "tremendious mountains."

[Adapted from Stephen E. Ambrose, *Undaunted Courage: Meriwether Lewis, Thomas Jefferson and the Opening of the American West* (New York: Simon and Schuster, 1996)]

Meares was a believer in such a passage. He thought its opening on the Pacific side was missed by James Cook in 1778 only because Cook failed to examine the coast thoroughly after making his landfall in the vicinity of Cape "Foulweather," just south of the 45th parallel on the Oregon Coast, and while proceeding northward to what is now Alaska. (This conviction had resulted in Meares' taking time out from his fur-trading activities on his second voyage in 1788 to explore along the coast.)

In his account, Meares reviewed the efforts of earlier mariners (both actual and mythical) who searched for a Northwest Passage. He concluded: "The Northern Archipelago, the Straits of John de Fuca, and Cook's River, all stretching to the North East . . . may not these be the very passages? . . . from the Indians themselves we are informed that great waters, free from ice, stretch themselves to the Northward." Meares noted that western Indians had copper which could have come from mines north and east via

Cook's River, Prince William Sound or the Northern Archipelago. "We have seen in their possession masses of considerable weight from the mines, and of extreme fineness. They told us that they went far Northward for it, and found the ore in the earth, scattered about, and, as we understood them, thrown up by a volcano from the sea."[12]

Meares also believed Admiral Bartholomew de Fonte actually had existed, though Meares claimed his correct name was "de Fonta." Today, historians regard this figure and his accomplishments as fictitious. Admiral de Fonte supposedly had found a passage between the oceans. Meares wrote: "[A] Burgomaster Witson [1705]. . . says he had in his possession the original manuscript of the account of . . . De Fonta [on a voyage around Tierra del Fuego] . . . This circumstance goes very far to prove that such a person did exist . . . that if he performed . . . [such a voyage] in 1649 [around Cape Horn], that he might have accomplished the other [sailing through a Northwest Passage] as recited by Purchas, &c in 1640; and the recent discoveries of this very Archipelago serves to countenance this opinion." Meares said he based his belief on information from Alexander Dalrymple, hydrographer for the East India Company. Dalrymple, a highly-regarded maritime figure, supported the Northwest Passage theory.[13]

Meares conjectured that either from Hudson Bay or the southern parts of Baffin Bay, "navigable inlets may be found to communicate with the Eastern Pacific Ocean . . . so that the idea of the discovery of a North West Passage still continues to have a reasonable foundation."[14] Meares held to this belief even after his second, and final, voyage to the Pacific Northwest Coast in 1788. It is one reason why skeptics later scoffed at his narrative as being fanciful, even though a good number of other mariners and cartographers of Meares' era also sought or believed in the legendary opening.

Meares closed the account of his first voyage with the acknowledgment that his consort vessel, the 100-ton *Sea Otter*, was lost. The *Sea Otter* had not arrived in China, nor had any shipmaster encountered the vessel after the James Strange expedition sighted her in Prince William Sound. "I am to lament the fate of our consort the *Otter* Sloop, Captain Tipping.— No tidings have been received of her after she left Prince William's Sound.— We must conclude therefore that she and her people have perished beneath the waves."[15]

Notes

1. John Meares, "An Introductory Voyage of the *Nootka*,—Capt. Meares, from Calcutta, to the North West Coast of America, in the years 1786, and 1787," xxxix, in *Voyages Made in the Years 1788 and 1789, from China to the North West Coast of America* (London: Logographic Press, 1790).
2. Ibid.
3. Peter Buck, in *Vikings of the Pacific* (Chicago: University of Chicago Press, 1959), discusses theories on whence and when came the early Polynesians. Hawaiian historian and artist, Herb Kawainui Kane, in his book *Voyagers* (Bellevue, WA: Whalesong Press, 1991) opines that an early people, the "Menehune," settled in Hawaii "about 1900 years ago, possibly earlier." While Cook is generally credited with "discovering" Hawaii in 1778, studies by Kane, Richard W. Rogers, Steve Gould and Alan S. Lloyd of Hawaii support the theory that Spanish mariners reached the islands as early as the 16th century. These scholars presented their evidence in papers given at a 1996 symposium sponsored by the Marine Option Program of the University of Hawaii, at the Hawaiian Maritime Center.
4. Edwin N. McClellan, "Winee of Waikiki," *Outrigger Forecast Magazine,* April 1950.
5. Meares, *Voyages,* xxxix. S.M. Kamakau, in *Ruling Chiefs of Hawaii* (1961), traces Kaiana's lineage and confirms he was a member of the "ali'i," or royalty. Abraham Fornander, in *An Account of the Polynesian Race* (1982), describes Kaiana as a cousin of the king. Ralph S. Kuykendall, author of *The Hawaiian Kingdom, 1778-1854* (1980) and co-author of *Hawaii: A History from Polynesian Kingdom to American Statehood* (1970), says Kaiana was a high chief of Kauai.
6. Meares, *Voyages,* xxxix. If Meares cruised in the islands for one month, as he stated, and the usual time for a voyage from the Northwest Coast to Hawaii was about 24 days, then Meares must have left his last anchorage on the Pacific Northwest Coast in early July. This means he had spent a couple of days or up to a week at or near Baranof Island while his men regained their health and the fog at sea abated, before continuing on to Hawaii. As already mentioned, some trading for pelts could have occurred, though such activity is not documented.
7. Ibid.
8. Ibid., xl.
9. Ibid., 4-10.
10. Ibid.
11. Ibid., "Observations on the Probable Existence of a North West Passage, &c.," xli-lxvi.
12. Ibid., lvii, lix. George W. Fuller, in *A History of the Pacific Northwest, with Special Emphasis on the Inland Empire,* vol. 1 (New York: Alfred A. Knopf, 1946, 2d ed. rev.), 83-113, provides a review of the search for the Northwest Passage from the 16th century onward.
13. Meares, *Voyages,* lxi-lxii. Alexander Dalrymple, an official of the East India Company, claimed "Admiral de Fonta" actually existed and might have found the entrance to a Northwest Passage between the Pacific and the Atlantic, possibly via Baffin Bay or Hudson Bay. An article concerning this Portuguese adventurer appeared in a London magazine, *Monthly Miscellany or Memoirs for the Curious* (April and June, 1708). Most historians believe the "de Fonte" (the usual spelling) article was a hoax perpetrated by the editor, James Petiver.
14. Meares, *Voyages,* lxv-lxvi.
15. Ibid., "An Introductory Voyage of the *Nootka*," xl. "Intelligence" later received by Meares indicated the *Sea Otter* was "lost off the coast of Kamtschatka"; Meares' *Memorial* to Parliament, 1-2.

"Wynee, a Native of Owyhee, One of the Sandwich Islands," in Meares, *Voyages* (1790).

Chapter Four

Shed a Tear for Winee

D ESPITE THE TRIBULATIONS of his first voyage to the Northwest Coast of America, Meares continued to pursue his dream of establishing a fur trading network that would bring profit to himself and territorial claims and glory to Britain. Within three months of his arrival in Macao, Meares had arranged a partnership with several merchants, and had purchased and fitted out two vessels to replace the unfortunate *Nootka* and *Sea Otter* of his first enterprise.

Like the *Nootka,* the newly acquired ships, the *Felice Adventurer* of 230 tons burden and the *Iphigenia Nubiana* of 200 tons, were classed as "snows"—two-masted vessels similar to brigs and brigantines except for a difference in the rigging.[1] Meares generally referred to them simply as the *Felice* and *Iphigenia* in his narrative, and noted that both had bottoms sheathed with copper. Meares would command the expedition and the *Felice.* He engaged a Scot, William Douglas, to command the *Iphigenia.*[2]

Meares' new associates had interests in India as well as in Canton.[3] In fact, apparently only three of them, Daniel Beale (of Beale & Co.), John Henry Cox and Juan Cawalho (João Carvalho), were residents of China; the others were in India and possibly included his former Bengal Fur Society investors. Meares did not identify them in his narrative except as "several British merchants resident in India" or the "Merchants Proprietors," but he would later name a major harbor on the Northwest Coast "Port Cox" and a Vancouver Island headland "Cape Beale" in honor of the known Canton benefactors. Cox was the only Briton not associated with the South Sea Company permitted to live in Canton, probably because he was a partner of Daniel Beale, a Prussian national. The proprietors schemed ways to avoid the high port costs assessed by the Chinese against foreign vessels, except those of Portugal. They also contrived to avoid the costs and red

NAUTICAL TERMS

Fathom—6 feet.

League—3 nautical miles.

Nautical Mile—1.151 statute miles.

Sloop—a single-masted vessel with sails rigged fore-and-aft.

Brig—a two-masted, square-rigged sailing vessel.

Brigantine—a two-masted vessel with foremast rigged fore-and-aft.

Snow—two-masted like a brig with a short third mast aft for a trysail or with a trysail rigged to the mainmast on a spar.

Ship—a major seagoing vessel with at least three masts, square-rigged; also, in general, any large seagoing vessel.

Longboat, Pinnace, Jolly Boat—small ship's boats used in shallow waters, to go ashore or as work boats.

Double—to sail around a given point, as in doubling Cape Horn.

Sound—to measure the depth of water with a weighted line.

Sound—a large inlet from the sea.

Strait—a narrow waterway connecting two large bodies of water.

tape of being licensed by the South Sea Company and East India Company, which held exclusive British trade rights over Pacific Ocean commerce.[4]

To accomplish these objectives, the partners arranged for Meares' ships to sail under the auspices of João Carvalho, a Portuguese merchant of Macao, in order to fly the Portuguese flag if ever challenged by British ships or officials. They also arranged for titular Portuguese command of the expedition.[5] Meares would pretend to be the supercargo (clerk) of the *Felice* with a Portuguese, Francisco José Viana, as the captain of record. Actually, Meares would be in command.[6] The *Felice* and *Iphigenia* carried Portuguese as well as British papers. We shall see later the complications this scheme caused. The practice of sailing under false colors was not uncommon in those days.

Meares also was provided with a chart and possibly other information derived from Captain Charles Barkley, who only recently had arrived in China after exploring the Northwest Coast from Nootka Sound south to 47° north latitude. Also, as was customary, Meares obtained other documents and information from other sources and captains.

For his crews, Meares selected Europeans who were available, augmented by "China-men." This, Meares wrote in his account, was an experiment: "They have been generally esteemed an hardy, and industrious, as well as ingenious race of people; they live on fish and rice, and, requiring but low wages, it was a matter also of oeconomical [*sic*] consideration to employ them; and during the whole of the voyage there was every reason to be satisfied with their services.—If hereafter trading posts should be established on the American coast, a colony of these men would be a very important acquisition."[7]

Meares had every intention of establishing permanent trading posts, or "factories," on the Northwest Coast, where natives would be encouraged to bring pelts to trade. From the "factories," furs would be shipped to markets in China and exchanged for luxury goods, such as spices, tea, silks and porcelains, which when carried to London would sell at a high profit.[8]

Apparently, hundreds of Chinese were avid to ship out on the British vessels. Meares carefully made his selections, and 50 were chosen. They would have many adventures. Some were experienced in sailing junks on the South China Sea. Others were artisans, such as carpenters and smiths, who later proved invaluable in building a schooner and a headquarters post in Nootka Sound. These were the first Chinese known to visit the Pacific Northwest, and they also were the first to reach Hawaii.

Each ship was loaded with six cows, three bulls, four bull calves and four heifers, goats, turkeys, rabbits, pigeons, and lime and orange trees. It was hoped that these animals and fruit trees would augment the flora and fauna that already existed in the Hawaiian Islands. Possibly, most of this was provided by friends of Kaiana. Meares believed the gifts would make Kaiana the richest inhabitant of his native islands.

Meares described the "prince" as an "amiable Indian" who was held in awe by the Chinese. But Kaiana regarded the Asians with disgust, the captain wrote. Kaiana, who ambled about Macao as he pleased, did not understand how to use coins to purchase goods and often had to call upon a friend, such as Cox, to come to his assistance. He was astonished by the ships of so many nations anchored at Macao and at Whampoa, the anchorage between Macao and Canton on the Pearl River.[9] When Kaiana learned that he was to return to his home islands, and be reunited with his wife and child, he was overjoyed. Apparently, his desire to visit *"Britannee"* had vanished. Meares said that for Kaiana, the thought of home "produced those transports which sensible minds may conceive, but which language is unable to describe."[10]

The two ships were ready for sea on January 20. Before this, Meares had decided to take aboard several other Hawaiian and Native American passengers who had been brought by other vessels and left in China. The small group included Winee (Wynee), the Hawaiian girl whom Captain Barkley's bride had taken aboard as her maid on the *Imperial Eagle* (originally the *Loudoun*). Winee was on the *Imperial Eagle* when Barkley discovered the Strait of Juan de Fuca in mid summer 1787, and when several of his sailors were killed in a native ambush on the northern coast of what is now Washington State a few days later. She is recognized as the first Hawaiian to leave the islands by sailing ship, and the first to visit the Northwest Coast, and thus the first to visit America.

After the long voyage to Macao in 1787, Winee became so ill that Barkley decided to leave her at the port. Meares, however, volunteered to take her back to Hawaii.[11] Little is known about Winee. Meares believed she came from Owyhee (Hawaii, the Big Island), but a recent Hawaiian historian, Edwin North McClellan, claims she was a resident of Waikiki on the island of Oahu. He proposed that a monument be erected on the famous beach in her honor, but such has not come to pass.[12] It was here that the *Imperial Eagle* had arrived, May 25, 1787, en route to the Northwest Coast—the first "haole" (foreign) ship to anchor in Waikiki Bay. Mrs. Barkley (the former Frances Hornby Trevor) was the first white woman to visit the islands, and the Northwest Coast. On this voyage, Mrs. Barkley also is believed to have been the first woman to circumnavigate the globe.[13]

Mrs. Barkley noted that Winee was an engaging young woman of fine character, quick to please, anxious to learn, and an agreeable companion.[14] Spoilum, described by Meares as a famous Chinese artist, painted both Winee and Kaiana. Meares said Kaiana was inordinately proud of his portrait. According to Meares, the artist accurately portrayed Kaiana's face and head, but could not properly depict his fine physique. ("Tianna, a Prince of Atooi" and "Wynee, a Native of Owyhee" are pictured in Meares' *Voyages.*)

Also on board when the *Felice* and *Iphigenia* left anchorage at "the Typa" on Sunday, January 22, 1788, were a "stout man and a boy from the island of Mowee (Maui)" and a native of Nootka Sound who had been conveyed to China by other merchant ships. Captain William Douglas in his account identified the "stout man" by the name Tawnee.[15] Meares gave them little attention in his narrative, but implied that the Northwest native, Comekela, was a somewhat disagreeable character who showed little gratitude for his chance to see the outside world and return to his home country. Kaiana, Winee and Comekela were aboard the *Felice,* whereas the others were with Douglas on the *Iphigenia.* The *Felice* had signed on a crew of 50 men and the *Iphigenia,* 40 men.

Although some had sailed on junks, the Chinese quickly became sea-sick as the *Felice* cleared Whampoa and entered the South China Sea. As the ships sailed together toward the Philippines, Meares soon learned that the *Iphigenia* was a "heavy" sailer—considerably slower than the *Felice.* Eventually, the cattle suffered a "droop," Meares wrote, and he thought best to butcher all, save two cows and a bull and one bull calf and one heifer, and some goats. Winee's decline continued, and Kaiana was con-fined to his bunk with a fever for a few days.

On the *Iphigenia,* scurvy soon made its unwelcome appearance, but the ship was suitably prepared with remedies, such as oranges and spruce beer. Also while in Philippine waters, the *Iphigenia* began to leak. Because of this, as well as the fact that the foremast was sprung so that it needed replacing, the captains decided a port call was required. They charted their course toward the Spanish settlement of "Samboingan" on Mindanao, even though "the hospitality of the Spaniards was always to be doubted." As the two ships boldly sailed through these hazardous, monsoon-swept waters, a careful watch was kept for treacherous currents and winds, numberless shoals and islands, and "Malayan" pirates in powerful fleets of swift "proas," each manned by 50 to 200 sailor warriors.

On the *Felice,* Winee's condition worsened, and Kaiana became a constant attendant at her side. "She every day declined in strength, and nothing remained for us, but to ease the pains of her approaching dissolu-tion, which no human power could prevent . . . She had been for some time a living spectre, and on the morning of the fifth of February she expired. At noon her body was committed to the deep" in a Christian service conducted by Meares. Kaiana grieved so intensely that Meares feared for his life.

"Thus died Winee, a native of Owyhee, one of the Sandwich Islands, who possessed virtues that are seldom to be found in the class of her countrywomen." Before dying she gave "a plate looking-glass, and a bason and bottle of the finest China" to Kaiana, her faithful friend, and "added a gown, an hoop, a petticoat, and a cap for his wife." The remainder of her effects she bequeathed to her family and asked Kaiana to make sure of their delivery to her father and mother. In his brief eulogy in *Voyages,* Meares asked "humanity . . . [to] yield a compassionate tear to the unfortunate Winee!"[16]

Now, the captains again turned their attention to the long voyage ahead. It would be a time of adventure, a time of profit, and a time of missed opportunities.

Notes

1. The terms *snow, brig* and *brigantine* are old-fashioned nautical titles for a family of vessels. A *brig* is a two-masted vessel, square-rigged. A *snow* is two-masted and square-rigged as a brig, but with an additional small mast or spar abaft the mainmast bearing a trysail. A *brigantine* also is two-masted and square-rigged like a brig except the mainmast which is fore-and-aft rigged. The terms *brig* and *snow* were used interchangeably by such early captains as John Kendrick. A *ship,* on the other hand, is firstly any sea-going vessel, but more particularly it is a sailing vessel with a bowsprit and at least three masts, square-rigged, each with lower, top and topgallant members.

2. Hugh Carrington, in "Nootka Meares," Chapter One, 1, claims only "one" of Meares' ships was sheathed in copper without specifying which vessel. One must rely on Meares' firsthand account stating that both were copper lined. Copper sheathing provided additional hull protection, faster sailing, and prevented damage from shipworms. Meares noted that his second in command, Captain William Douglas, "was an officer on board my ship during our first voyage," and "was well acquainted with the coast of America,"; John Meares, *Voyages Made in the Years 1788 and 1789, from China to the North West Coast of America* (London: Logographic Press, 1790), 1-2, 281.

3. Meares, *Voyages,* 1; Carrington, "Nootka Meares," Chapter One, 6. The investors were believed to be employees of the East India Company seeking to profit privately.

4. Carrington, "Nootka Meares," Chapter One, 3; and Barry M. Gough, *The Northwest Coast: British Navigation, Trade, and Discoveries to 1812* (Vancouver: University of British Columbia Press, 1992), 91.

5. According to Warren L. Cook, in *Flood Tide of Empire: Spain and the Pacific Northwest, 1543-1819* (New Haven, CT, and London: Yale University Press, 1973), 137: "Meares and his associates contrived to fly another flag. João Carvalho, a merchant of Macao, was given one share in the venture for his services, and Meares used Carvalho's firm as a front for the true owners. He would reap a double advantage: circumvent the monopoly companies and partake of privileges that the Portuguese enjoyed with Chinese officials, who exacted higher port charges from other nationalities." The name of the Portuguese merchant was spelled variously: Carvalho, Cawalho, Cavalho, etc. Other British ships on occasion sailed under foreign flags: e.g., Charles William Barkley flew Austrian and Portuguese colors on the *Imperial Eagle,* also known as *Loudoun.*

6. Ibid.

7. Meares, *Voyages,* 2-3.

8. The Americans, Robert Gray and John Kendrick, who sailed from Boston in 1787, had the same instructions from their sponsors: establish a fur trade network between the natives of the Northwest Coast and the merchants of China. See author's *Columbia's River* for discussion.

9. Meares, *Voyages,* 4-7, 10.

10. Ibid., 6.

11. Edwin N. McClellan, "Winee of Waikiki," *Outrigger Forecast Magazine,* April 1950.
12. Ibid.
13. Ibid.
14. Ibid. Also see Meares, *Voyages,* 10, 27-28.
15. William Douglas, "Voyage of the *Iphigenia*, Capt. Douglas, from Samboingan, to the North West Coast of America," in Meares, *Voyages,* 293. Tawnee died while aboard the *Iphigenia* and was buried at sea.
16. Meares, *Voyages,* 27-29.

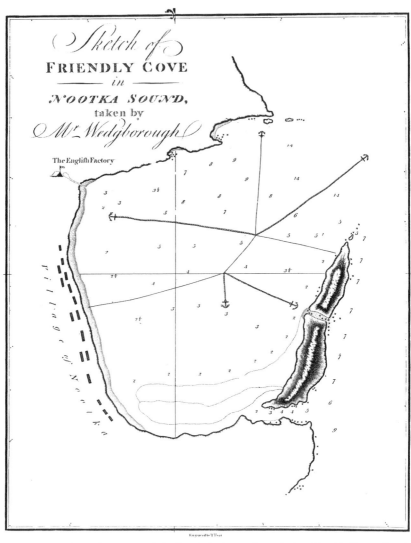

The native village of Yuquot and the "English Factory" are depicted in this illustration in *Voyages*. Friendly Cove is situated on the northern promontory of the entrance to Nootka Sound. The chart is based on a sketch attributed to Mr. S. Wedgborough of the James Strange expedition in 1786.

Chapter Five

Philippines to Nootka

T HE GRAND STRATEGY for the Merchants Proprietors enterprise called
for Meares in the *Felice* to chart a course for Nootka Sound (Meares
still used the British name, King George's Sound), while Douglas in the
Iphigenia, the smaller ship, would sail first to the Aleutians, and then sweep
down the North American Coast, trading as she went, until rendezvousing
with Meares late in the summer either at Nootka or in Hawaii.

The *Iphigenia* was badly in need of repair, and Meares, in the faster
vessel, was impatient to get underway. There was naught but for Douglas
and Meares to make port in the Spanish base at Zamboanga on the south-
western tip of the island of Mindanao in the Philippines, where a new
mast and spars could be obtained and repairs made to the leaks in the
Iphigenia's hull. Surrounded by a generally hostile native population,
Zamboanga had a population of about 1,000, including a small number of
troops who garrisoned a dilapidated prison fortress. The Spaniards initially
treated the visitors well, but one of the Chinese sailors, while ashore with a
timber-cutting party, strayed in the woods and was "seized by the Malay-
ans" and murdered or taken captive.

While Meares had promised Kaiana that he would be returned to his
native Hawaiian Islands, this did not necessarily mean Meares personally
would take him there. Instead, Meares transferred Kaiana and the other
Hawaiians to the *Iphigenia* before setting sail for Nootka Sound in the
Felice, leaving Douglas with the task of taking the islanders to their homeland. The Nootka native, Comekela, remained a passenger on the *Felice.*

(After Meares departed in the *Felice,* it so happened that Douglas
decided against sailing the *Iphigenia* directly from Zamboanga to Hawaii
because of the lateness of the season. His ship was ready for sea on February 19, but he did not leave until the 22nd due to a dispute with the

Spanish governor over trade iron in the *Iphigenia*'s hold. Iron was a valuable commodity in the Philippines and the Spanish governor demanded an exorbitant payment of it from Douglas and jailed two detachments of British sailors and ordered soldiers to board the *Iphigenia*. Douglas astutely resolved the crisis in a few days. The *Iphigenia* sailed northward through the Celebes Sea and the Philippine Sea before crossing the Pacific directly to the northern part of the American Coast. Kaiana's reunion with his people on Kauai would have to wait.)

Having left Douglas at the Spanish port, Meares was underway with the *Felice* on February 11, 1788, with additional livestock, rice, vegetables, and fruit, and within days encountered heavy weather. (The *Felice*'s course over the next three months would take her east between the Philippines and New Guinea, then generally northward through the Caroline Islands and continuing past the Marianas, where more favorable winds would carry her eastward across the North Pacific.) In March a typhoon battered the two-masted snow. Before the blow abated, the remaining livestock save for one bull, one cow and one heifer, perished. All the remaining goats met death in one sudden roll of the little vessel. A fine orange-tree that was in blossom and about a half-dozen cinnamon trees acquired in Zamboanga, along with other plants, also were destroyed.[1]

With a return of good weather late in March, Meares put his craftsmen to work preparing for the summer's duties on the Northwest Coast. The *Felice* was carrying in her hold materials for "the moulds and model for a" schooner and some framing for a "house," both to be built at Nootka. The European type of ship construction was entirely new to the Chinese, Meares noted, but, despite some initial difficulty, he praised his Asian carpenters, and he regarded the Chinese armourers who made trade items as being more skilled than their European counterparts.

In early April, a violent storm again smashed into the *Felice,* in the vicinity of 22° 26' north latitude, 139° 38' east longitude: "The sea soon rose to such an alarming height, that it became necessary to set the fore-sail and scud before the storm, in order to preserve the ship . . . [T]o the leeward of us, we perceived the water to rise many feet above the level of the sea in circles, which formed a beautiful but awful sight . . . [W]e were obliged to perform the . . . dangerous operation, of heaving to in such a high sea, to avoid running into the dreadful vortex before us." Meares called it a "tuffoon" (typhoon). The *Felice* was sailing in waters where typhoons often lash the seas with winds above 100 knots, although not usually at this time of year. It likely was a full gale—bad enough for a small sailing vessel.[2]

⚓

Just as the *Felice* had met with severe storms in the western Pacific off Asia, so did the Britons again encounter heavy weather as they approached the coast of North America. Wrote Meares: "We kept running, during the night, under a press of sail, directly in for the American coast. The whole atmosphere was in a state of illumination, which we attributed to the reflection of vast mountains of snow on the continent: nor were we mistaken; for, on the morning of the 11th of May, the long-wished for land of America appeared, bearing East by South, at the distance of 13 leagues. It consisted of a ridge of mountains, whose summits were hid in the clouds . . . At noon the latitude was . . . 49° 35' North, and King George's Sound bore nearly East of us."[3] Meares sighted a ship and "knew her to be the *Princess Royal*, of London, on a trading voyage for the furs of America," but the *Felice* could not close with her.

That night a terrible storm arose which continued through May 12 and forced Meares to heave to, out of sight of land. After struggling back eastward, on the morning of the 13th the crew "happily anchored in Friendly Cove . . . in four fathoms water." Thus, "after a passage of three months and twenty-three days from China," the *Felice* stood within Nootka Sound and 100 yards off the Indian village of Yuquot.

Meares was not the first European to bring a sailing vessel into the sound; that honor went to Captain James Cook in the *Resolution* and *Discovery* on March 30, 1778. Cook stayed a month and named "Friendly Harbor" for the reception his men received from the Indian residents of Yuquot. Pérez had passed nearby, too, in 1774 and several trading vessels had stopped here beginning in 1785. But Meares was the first who would attempt to establish a permanent base at Nootka. This remote, island-dotted coastal inlet on the west side of what is known today as Vancouver Island was to be at the heart of his scheme to develop a fur-trading empire from which he and his sponsors hoped to gain great profit, and also establish a foothold for Britain in this primitive corner of the earth.

In a short time, the stormy weather returned. Though "a tempestuous gale of wind, with very heavy rain" lashed the sound, Friendly Cove provided a safe haven for the *Felice*. The British ship was welcomed by "a multitude of the natives, assembled on the banks in front of the village." Comekela, who had sailed from China with Meares, had hastily gone ashore and now performed as a village headman in the absence of his brother, Nootkan chief Maquinna, who was visiting another village. "To excite the

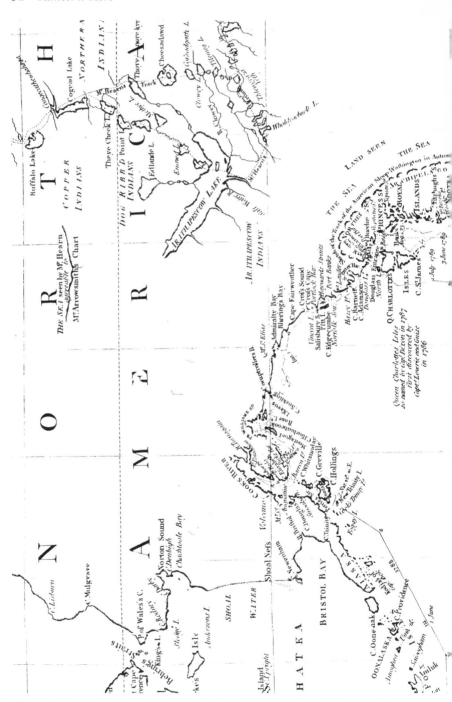

This section of Meares' chart in *Voyages* depicts the routes of the *Felice* and *Iphigenia* in the eastern Pacific, 1788-89.

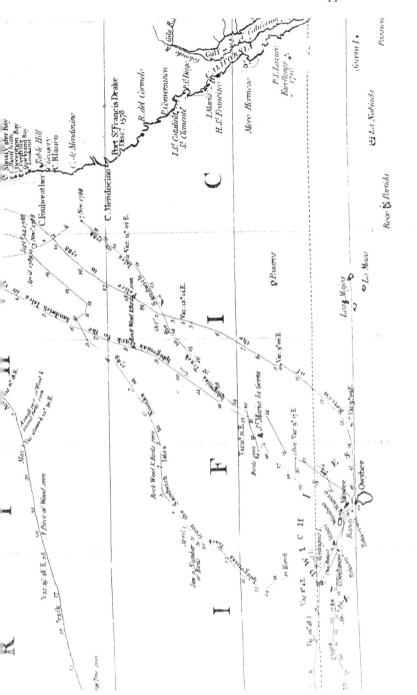

extreme admiration of his country-men," Comekela "was dressed in a scar-let regimental coat, decorated with brass buttons,—a military hat set off with a flaunting cockade, decent linens, and other appendages of Euro-pean dress."[4] The rich suit of clothing had been presented to the chief by some benefactor in Macao. (Such garments were worn with pride by na-tive leaders of the Northwest Coast. Captain Robert Gray's records show that clothing was sometimes preferred over copper, iron or beads by the Indians when trading furs to the white men.[5] Some chiefs went even fur-ther in mimicking the Europeans. An example of this is seen in Chief Cleaskinah of Clayoquot Sound who adopted the name "Hanna" in an exchange of names with British Captain James Hanna in 1786.[6])

The *Felice's* crew, restricted to a monotonous diet of salt meat and biscuit on shipboard, welcomed the natives who paddled alongside bring-ing fresh fish to trade. As for Meares and the officers, they accompanied Comekela ashore and attended a feast that night in his plank house. Such feasts were called "potlatches" where valuable gifts were exchanged.

Meares wasted no time in ordering his crew to begin squaring away the ship after the long trans-Pacific voyage. Chinese and European crew-men pitched two tents not far from the Indian village to be used by "wooders and waterers" and sailmakers, until a building could be erected. "For this purpose a spot was chosen at a small distance from the village, and con-tiguous to a rivulet. The rest of the crew were employed in unreefing the running rigging, unbending the sails, and the other necessary duties of the ship." The site for Meares' "factory" was a small indention of the shoreline located northeast of the Nootka village and separated from it by a brushy, rocky outcrop.[7]

On May 16, Maquinna ("Maquilla" in Meares' account) and subor-dinate Chief Callicum and other men in a dozen war canoes entered the cove. The natives paraded around the ship as they sang "a pleasing though sonorous melody," while beating rhythm with paddles against the gun-wales and making other synchronized gestures with their arms. According to mariners' accounts, this was a greeting custom common in the North-west.

The canoes carried about 18 men each, most of whom were dressed in "the most beautiful skins of the sea otter" from head to ankles. "Their hair was powdered with the white down of birds, and their faces" were painted "with red and black ochre, in the form of a shark's jaw." In Meares' opinion they were "extremely savage" in appearance. The canoes circled the *Felice* twice as the natives called out "Wacush, Wacush," which Meares thought meant "friends."

Maquinna and Callicum came aboard. Meares judged the former to be about 30 years of age and Callicum about 10 years older. Meares gave iron and copper "and other gratifying articles" to the chiefs who doffed their fur robes and "threw them, in the most graceful manner, at our feet." The gesture left the chiefs naked, and the officers promptly gave them blankets.[8]

On May 25 occurred an event that soon would be debated by the diplomats of Spain and Britain, and, ever after, by historians. Did Maquinna sell or grant a tract of land to Meares as a site for his headquarters? Meares' own account is clear on the point: "Maquilla had not only most readily consented to grant us a spot of ground in his territory, whereon an house might be built for the accommodation of the people we intended to leave there [while the *Felice* explored and traded south along the coast], but had promised us also his assistance in forwarding our works, and his protection of the party who were destined to remain at Nootka during our absence. In return for this kindness, and to ensure a continuance of it, the chief was presented with a pair of pistols, which he had regarded with an eye of solicitation ever since our arrival." Other gifts were presented to Callicum and the ladies of the chiefs.[9]

Four years later, however, Maquinna denied in an affidavit to the Spanish that he had sold any land to Meares (he recalled, though, that he had sold land only to Captain John Kendrick of Boston in 1791.)[10] This would become a key point of contention during the ensuing international furor over the Nootka question.

Work on a primitive structure on the site went forward rapidly, with the European and Chinese artisans being assisted by Nootka natives who brought timber from the woods and helped in the construction. The natives were paid with beads or iron at the end of each day. On May 28, the "house" was finished.

The building, according to Meares, would provide adequate quarters and work space for "the coopers, sail makers and other artizans" left behind. Work shops were located on the ground floor, along with a large room to store provisions and an attached blacksmith or "armourer's shop." The upper story included a dining room and bed chambers: "On the whole, our house, though it was not built to satisfy a lover of architectural beauty, was admirably well calculated for the purpose to which it was destined, and appeared to be a structure of uncommon magnificence to the natives of King George's Sound.

"A strong breast-work was thrown up round the house, enclosing a considerable area of ground, which, with one piece of cannon, placed in such a manner as to command the cove and village of Nootka, formed a fortification sufficient to secure the party from any intrusion. Without this breast-work, was laid the keel of a vessel of 40 or 50 tons, which was now to be built agreeable to our former determination."[11]

While the *Felice* was being refurbished and construction of the schooner and house was underway, Meares and his officers traded for sea otter pelts and by June 5 had 140 skins on board. About this time, a grindstone was stolen, and soon after the ship's pinnace disappeared. The Nootka chiefs declared their innocence. Meares took no vengeance, as was usual among other sea captains, and the thefts passed peaceably. Meares noted: "It afterwards appeared, as we suspected, that the boat had been stolen and broken up for the sake of the iron and nails, which were afterwards dispersed throughout the Sound."[12] The Indians left Yuquot village in early June and moved to a bay two miles from the sound, where plentiful fish would provide them with a food supply preserved for the winter.

The consort ship, the *Iphigenia*, still had not arrived at Nootka, but Meares decided to sail to the south before the season was further advanced. He had assigned several officers ashore along with sailors and artisans under the command of Robert Funter. On the eve of departing, Meares paid a formal visit to Maquinna, advising the chief of his plans to be gone three or four months. Meares requested the chief to watch over the men who would remain in Friendly Cove. "He was promised that when we finally left the coast, he should enter into full possession of the house and all the goods and chattels thereunto belonging . . . he was presented with a suit of cloaths covered with metal buttons . . . [and] several presents were made to the ladies of his family . . . [Maquinna] confirmed, with the strongest assurances of good faith, the treaty of friendship which had been already entered into between us." (Despite Meares' promise that the natives later could have the building, Douglas had it torn down and gave some of the boards to Captain Kendrick of the *Columbia*.)

When Maquinna was informed that the *Iphigenia* "was expected in the Sound," he surprised Meares by asking for a letter that he could give to Captain Douglas certifying his friendship. Meares was unaware that the Nootka were cognizant of "the faculty of communicating our thoughts to each other on paper." Maquinna had learned about written words from a

"Mr. Maccay" (John Mackay), a young Irish surgeon who had been left at Nootka Sound by Captain James Strange in 1786, and "who had remained, we believe, upwards of fourteen months among" the Indians. Meares understood that the surgeon's mate had been left "with his own entire consent and approbation." Captain Strange thought "great commercial effects might proceed" if Mackay learned the language and customs, but the captain, failing to outfit a second expedition, never returned to pick him up. Mackay was rescued by the *Imperial Eagle* in 1787. "He was reduced to the level of a savage," according to Meares, who noted that it was a year of famine in Nootka Sound.[13]

Notes

1. John Meares, *Voyages Made in the Years 1788 and 1789, from China to the North West Coast of America* (London: Logographic Press, 1790), 32, 36-37, 85. Regarding Captain William Douglas' resolution of the crisis with the Spanish governor of "Samboingan," see "Voyage of the *Iphigenia*, Capt. Douglas, from Samboingan, to the North West Coast of America," in Ibid., 287-90.
2. Meares, *Voyages*, 87-90.
3. Ibid., 103. These were the mountains of Vancouver Island, where peaks such as the Golden Hinde rise above 7,000 feet.
4. Ibid., 103-04, 108-09; Warren L. Cook, *Flood Tide of Empire: Spain and the Pacific Northwest, 1543-1819* (New Haven, CT, and London: Yale University Press, 1973), 63-64. Yuquot stood on the southeastern tip of extensive Nootka Island, which is separated by narrow sea channels from the west side of Vancouver Island. The insularity of Vancouver Island was unproven at this time. A large island centered in Nootka Sound is named for one of Cook's subalterns, William Bligh, who years later gained notoriety because of the famous *Bounty* mutiny in South Pacific waters.
5. In late summer 1788, Robert Gray noted that Meares earlier had provided a "genteel sute of Clothes" to the brother of Chief Wickananish of Clayoquot Sound; J. Richard Nokes, *Columbia's River: The Voyages of Robert Gray, 1787-1793* (Tacoma: Washington State Historical Society, 1991), 68.
6. Frederick W. Howay, ed., *Voyages of the "Columbia" to the Northwest Coast, 1787-1790 and 1790-1793* (Boston: Massachusetts Historical Society, 1941; Portland: Oregon Historical Society Press, 1990), 67n.
7. Meares, *Voyages*, 112. "The visitor to Nootka today sees that Meares chose a good site—near enough to Yuquot for communication with the aboriginals yet sufficiently distant so as not to interfere with their activities. The place was relatively well sheltered from the weather . . . Timber was available on the beach and in the forest . . . A gently inclining pebble beach afforded an excellent place for beaching and careening small vessels and for conducting those numerous shore activities so essential to keeping a ship seaworthy; Barry M. Gough, *The Northwest Coast: British Navigation, Trade, and Discoveries to 1812* (Vancouver: University of British Columbia Press, 1992), 98.
8. Meares, *Voyages*, 112-14.
9. Ibid., 114.

10. Meares' chief mate, Robert Duffin, also claimed that Maquinna did sell land to Meares. But Maquinna in 1792, when asked by the Spanish about Meares' contention that he had purchased the land, "angrily denounced it as false, declaring he 'had only sold Meares sea otter skins, in exchange for sheets of copper.'" Maquinna called Meares a liar ("aita, aita"). The Spanish commandant at Nootka, Bodega y Quadra, forwarded Maquinna's affidavit to the Viceroy in Mexico with other documents to bolster the Spanish case in the Nootka dispute. Cook, *Flood Tide of Empire,* 138.

11. Meares, *Voyages,* 115-116.

12. Ibid., 119, 123, 127-28.

13. Ibid., 129-32. According to Warren L. Cook, in *Flood Tide of Empire,* 102-03, John Mackay cured Maquinna's daughter of a skin disease and was taken into the chief's lodge. Cook contends Mackay was ordered to guard the furs that the natives had collected and stored for Captain James Strange, but Strange never returned to claim them. A sailor with a similar name (Mackie), possibly the same man, became one of the earliest white residents of the Sandwich Islands. Gough, in *The Northwest Coast,* 82, relates that Mackay "lost Maquinna's protection when he stepped over the cradle of Maquinna's child, a native taboo, and was beaten" and temporarily banned for his indiscretion. When the child died, the ban was extended to exile. Mackay related that human heads were trophies of war used during ceremonial occasions, and witnessed the "brutal killing of more than a dozen captives." See also W. Kaye Lamb, "The Mystery of Mrs. Barkley's Diary: Notes on the Voyage of the 'Imperial Eagle,' 1786-87," *British Columbia Historical Quarterly* 6 (January 1942), 41; George Dixon, *A Voyage Round the World* (London: G. Goulding, 1789) [reprinted by Da Capo Press, New York, 1968], 232-33; and A.V. Venkatarama Ayyar, *James Strange's Journal and Narrative of the Commercial Expedition from Bombay to the North-west Coast of America* (Madras: Government Press, 1929), 22-25, 28.

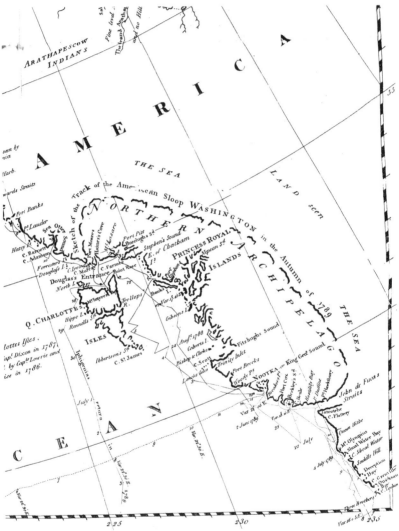

The dotted track indicates Meares' approach to the Northwest Coast in the *Felice*, May 1788, and his explorations along Vancouver Island and the Washington and northern Oregon coastline, June 11 to July 26, 1788. The solid line shows the track of Douglas' *Iphigenia* sailing south from Alaska in 1788; and Douglas' return to Hawaii by doubling the north end of the Queen Charlotte Islands after being released by the Spaniards at Nootka Sound, June 1789. From Meares, *Voyages* (1790).

Chapter Six

No Such River Exists

B EING A BELIEVER that a Northwest Passage really existed, Meares was determined during the summer of 1788 to make an exploratory voyage in the *Felice* south along the coast in search of any rivers or inlets that might lead into such a passage. In particular, he was curious about the report that the Spanish explorer Bruno de Hezeta, in 1775, had paused off the mouth of either a great river or a strait at 46° 10' north latitude. Could this inlet be the entrance to an opening for a passage between the Pacific and the Atlantic, which mariners had sought, off and on, for two centuries?

Others before Meares had entertained similar ideas. For example, Major Robert Rogers, of Rogers' Rangers fame in the French and Indian War (1754-63), dreamed of finding a great western river. He called it "Ouragon" and believed it would connect with, or come close to, the Missouri River system and thus provide a water route between east and west. He never was able to pursue that quest.[1] One of Rogers' officers, Jonathan Carver, did explore westward into the continent's interior, and in his popular published account (1778) he used the word "Oregon" as the name of a great western river known to the natives. But Carver never crossed the Great Plains and Rocky Mountains to glimpse the Columbia or its tributaries.

The legendary stream came to be called the Great River of the West, though it had other names, too. For instance, the crew of a Spanish ship, the *Tres Reyes*, reportedly sighted a large river near the 43rd parallel of latitude in 1602-03. They named it for Martín de Aguilar, the pilot, who died on the voyage. Consequently, the Río Aguilar was sought as the search extended northward. It was a long distance, of course, from where a great river (the Columbia) eventually was found. The identity of Aguilar's river has never been established, but it could have been the Umpqua at approximately 43° north.

Another legendary waterway was the Strait of Anian, supposedly extending between the Pacific and Atlantic oceans. Early maps of the western Pacific identified "Ania" as an area on the northern Chinese coast as well as a waterway. Later cartographers, by guess and imagination, moved "Anian" across the ocean to the Pacific Northwest. The name may have been derived from the accounts of Marco Polo, but another theory traces its origin to a Greek geographer, Anaximander, in the sixth century B.C. The Strait of Anian, supposedly discovered by Admiral Bartholomew de Fonte in 1640, was thought to be north of Vancouver Island, but de Fonte almost certainly was a fictitious character. While the American, Captain Robert Gray, twice thought he might have encountered de Fonte's strait, on neither occasion, of course, was he correct. A Spaniard, Lorenzo Ferrer Maldonado, also supposedly found such a passage, but his report, too, is considered fraudulent.[2]

Meares believed that the British hero James Cook had failed to find a Northwest Passage because adverse weather conditions prevented him from extensively exploring the coast from 45° to 60° north in 1778. Nor had any other mariner of any country made a thorough search, Meares felt. As part of his grand strategy for 1788, Meares intended to probe all of the coastline with his two ships. Douglas in the *Iphigenia* would examine the North Pacific shore from Cook's River (today's Cook Inlet, leading into Anchorage, Alaska) south to Nootka Sound. Meares would sail in the *Felice* from Nootka south along today's Washington and Oregon seacoast. By this "arrangement the whole of the American continent . . . would be explored, with various intermediate places which were not examined by Captain Cook."[3]

The first explorer definitely known to have sailed into these northern waters was the Spaniard Juan Pérez in the *Santiago* in 1774, who explored northward beyond the Queen Charlotte Islands. However, Pérez had sailed some distance out at sea while en route from Mexico, and on the return had hurried south because of scurvy and inadequate supplies without conducting a close examination of the coast.

In 1775, when another Spanish explorer, Bruno de Hezeta in the *Santiago,* arrived off a bay at 46° 10' latitude, he assumed (correctly, as it turned out many years later) that this might be the mouth of some large river or strait. He failed to enter the bay, however, in part because of the ill and weakened condition of his crew, and he never returned to explore this specific area, nor did any other Spaniard in this early period. In addition to naming the northern cape "San Roque," Hezeta named the bay "Bahía de la Asunción" and the southern point "Cabo Frandoso." He did not give a name to the suppositional waterway, but it came to be called "Río de San Roque" ("Saint Roc" by Meares) and the bay later was charted as "Entrada de la Hezeta."[4] Although Hezeta failed to sail into the river's mouth, some historians believe he, and not the American Robert Gray, should be acclaimed its discoverer. Seventeen years later, in 1792, Gray entered the river and sailed upwards of 20 miles to a small bay (Grays Bay) on the north side. He gave the waterway the name, "Columbia's River," for his ship, the *Columbia Rediviva*.[5]

Several British mariners before Meares had investigated the Northwest Coast from Vancouver Island north to Alaska, but no Britons since Cook in 1778 and Captain Barkley on a short cruise in 1787 had explored to the south. Mariners of the late 18th century, in fact, seemed to be more interested in what today is British Columbia and southern Alaska, than the coast between Vancouver Island and San Francisco Bay. Meares thought more attention should be given to the latter area for possible harbors and inlets, and he especially was curious about the reported Entrada de Hezeta.

On June 11, Meares bade adieu to the natives and the carpenters and crew members assigned to remain behind at Friendly Cove and sailed south on an excursion that almost brought him fame, and which did add to the cartographic knowledge of this portion of North America.[6] While the *Felice* proceeded southeast along the Vancouver Island coast on June 13, several canoes approached, "in most of which there were upwards of twenty men, of a pleasing appearance and brawny form, chiefly cloathed in otter skins of great beauty." Two chiefs, Hanna (Cleaskinah) and Detooche, "the handsomest men we had yet seen," came aboard to pay their respects.

Not long after these men left, the principal chief in this area, Wicananish, appeared with a retinue and came aboard. He expertly guided the *Felice* into the vast sound that came to be known by the Indian name "Clayoquot," although Meares tried to name at least a part of it "Port Cox," for his sponsor in Macao, John Henry Cox. The *Felice* came to anchor off what is known today as Meares Island near a village that was "almost thrice as large" as Yuquot, and "from every part of which we now saw the people launching their canoes, and coming off in shoals to the ship, laden with fish, wild onions, and berries, which they disposed of to the sailors for small bits of iron, and other articles."

Invited ashore the next day, Meares was impressed by the "vast area" enclosed in Wicananish's large plank-covered house. Huge carved and painted logs formed the rafters that were supported by great vertical posts set in the ground which also were embellished with strange images. A "most luxurious feast" was in progress with an estimated 800 people in attendance.

Meares gave blankets, two copper teakettles, and other presents to the chief. The universally and much admired teakettles were placed "with great care in the royal coffers." Wicananish, in turn, sent about 50 sea otter pelts "of the most jetty blackness" to the *Felice*. On June 17, the chief produced another 30 fine otter pelts to trade. The Britons reciprocated with presents for the chief and the ladies.[7]

As the *Felice* prepared to embark to nearby "Port Cox," the natives at Clayoquot captured a man from a rival village who was in a party attempting to visit the ship without Wicananish's knowledge. They took the captive into the woods, apparently to be killed. Meares protested, to no avail. The captain had to admit that Wicananish was so powerful and controlled such an extensive territory, "that it was very much in our interest to conciliate his regard and cultivate his friendship."

When Wicananish concluded a lucrative and domineering agreement with other nearby villages regarding the trade with the Britons, he had to give up the much treasured teakettles to the independent chiefs Hanna and Detooche. Meares, having no replacement aboard ship, compensated by providing the powerful chief with six brass-hilted swords, two pistols, and a musket. After trading for another 150 otter pelts, the captain sailed his two-masted snow south out of the sound, and continued meeting with Indians in canoes down the Vancouver Island coast.[8]

On June 29, 1788, the *Felice* "arrived at the entrance of . . . [a] great inlet . . . which appeared to be twelve or fourteen leagues broad." This was the Strait of Juan de Fuca which today forms the boundary between Vancouver Island in the province of British Columbia and the state of Washington. One of the great waterways of the West Coast, it was first viewed in 1787 by the Charles William Barkley expedition in the *Imperial Eagle*, a Briton sailing under Austrian colors. Meares was the second British mariner to view the strait's entrance.[9] No mariner of any European nation had entered the strait as of yet. Later, in 1789, the Spaniard Estéban

José Martínez claimed that he had viewed the strait's entrance while serving as a mate on Pérez's ship in 1774, but he had made no notation of it. Meares, in *Voyages*, accredited Barkley with being here in 1787.

Meares noted that the strait stretched east by north and extended "as far as the eye could" see. At the south side of the entrance (Washington's Cape Flattery), Meares "hove to off a small island [barren Tatoosh Island, on which stood a sizeable Makah Indian village] . . . near which we saw a very remarkable rock, that wore the form of an obelisk . . . In a very short time we were surrounded by canoes filled with people of a much more savage appearance than any we had hitherto seen." [10] The large canoes were manned by 20 to 30 men, dressed in sea otter skins, faces painted red and black, and well armed with mussel-shell tipped spears, and bows and arrows with barbed bone points.

Meares identified the chief here as "Tatootche . . . so surly and forbidding a character we had not yet seen." His face was completely blackened and covered with glittering sand. Tatoosh "informed us that the power of Wicananish ended here, and that we were now within the limits of his government, which extended a considerable way to the Southward." Meares' longboat was unable to find a good anchorage for the *Felice* and the natives appeared threatening, so he did not pause here more than a few hours. "The strongest curiosity impelled us to enter this strait, which we shall call by the name of its original discoverer, John De Fuca . . . [W]e are pursuaded, that if Captain Cook had seen this strait, he would have thought it worthy of farther examination." Actually, Meares was only reiterating the name "de Fuca" that Barkley had given to the strait a year earlier. Though Meares wanted to explore the strait, circumstances "put it out of our power." He did not fully explain what those circumstances were, but probably it was the fear of Tatoosh's warriors whom Wicananish had warned Meares about, and the lack of a good "place of security" for an anchorage.[11]

As Meares sailed south along the Olympic Peninsula, observing Indian villages on the rugged shoreline, he noted "the small river and island of Queenhithe," where six crewmen of the *Imperial Eagle* had perished in an ambush in 1787. At 47° 10' north latitude, Meares sighted and named "Mount Olympus," the highest peak in the Olympic Mountains of northwest Washington. The mountain also had been seen by Pérez in 1774 who had called it "Santa Rosalía."

Farther south, the crew of the British ship sighted a large sound or bay where the water shoaled to six fathoms and "breakers were seen to extend in a direction quite across it, so that it appeared to be inaccessible

"Entrance of the Strait of John de Fuca," in *Voyages*. The longboat from the *Felice* is approaching Tatoosh Island off the northwestern tip of the Olympic Peninsula.

to ships." Meares, hauling off to a safe 16 fathoms, named the sound "Shoalwater Bay" and the land at the south entrance "Low Point." A higher bluff on the north side he named "Cape Shoal-water." He judged the headland to be at latitude 46° 47' north, and the longitude at 235° 11' east. This is believed to be today's Willapa Bay. "Low Point" at the northern tip of the North Beach Peninsula (more commonly called the Long Beach Peninsula) today is known as Leadbetter Point.[12]

Meares again was frustrated by the shallow depth soundings in a second attempt to enter through the shoals running "from shore to shore." "From the mast-head it was observed that" the bay extended inland a considerable distance with arms to the north and east and high mountains behind. "This wild and desolate shore was without inhabitants," he initially observed, but shortly a man and boy came out in a canoe and traded two otter skins, but would not come on deck. "Their eyes ran over every part of [the ship] .. with a most rapid transition . . . as gave us every reason to conclude that this was the first time they had ever been gratified with the sight of such an object . . . [They] replied to us in a language which bore not the least resemblance . . . to any tongue that we had heard." The "fashion of their canoe" also differed from those of peoples to the north. On July 6, Meares made another approach and examined the countryside through his long glass. He could see no opening to the southward that promised a safe harbor from which to trade and to explore with the longboat. The failure to find safe anchorages was doggedly afflicting Meares' exploratory aspirations during the cruise down this south coast.[13]

Later on the same day, a "high bluff promontory" was sighted 12 miles to the southeast "for which we steered to double, with the hope that between it and Cape Shoal-water, we should find some sort of harbour [this bluff must have been North Head, the northern part of Cape Disappointment]. We now discovered distant land beyond this promontory, and we pleased ourselves with the expectation of its being Cape Saint Roc of the Spaniards, near which they are said to have found a good port."[14] Meares was sailing along the Long Beach Peninsula, approaching the basalt cape standing at the north side of the Columbia River. (Today, two lighthouses, North Head and Cape Disappointment, guard the entrance to the Columbia River at this location.)

Meares said he doubled the cape[15] at three miles and had "a perfect view of the shore . . . [W]e did not discern a living creature, or the least trace of habitable life." Meanwhile, shallow soundings and "a prodigious Easterly swell" threatened the *Felice*. To continue his account of this important episode:

After we had rounded the promontory, a large bay, as we had imagined, opened to our view, that bore a promising appearance, and into which we steered with every encouraging expectation.

The high land that formed the boundaries of the bay, was at great distance, and a flat level country occupied the intervening space: the bay itself took a westerly direction. As we steered in, the water shoaled to nine, eight, and seven fathoms, when breakers were seen from the deck, right a-head; and, from the mast-head, they were observed to extend across the bay. We therefore hauled out, and directed our course to the opposite shore, to see if there was any channel, or if we could discover any port.

The name of Cape Disappointment was given to the promontory, and the bay obtained the title of Deception Bay . . . [I]t lies in the latitude of 46° 10' North, and in the computed longitude of 235° 34' East. We can now with safety assert, that there is no such river as that of Saint Roc exists, as laid down in the Spanish charts: to those of Maurelle [Francisco Antonio Mourelle, a Spanish explorer and cartographer] we made continual reference, but without deriving any information or assistance from them.

We now reached the opposite side of the bay, where disappointment continued to accompany us; and being almost certain that there we should obtain no place of shelter for the ship, we bore up for a distant head-land [probably Tillamook Head], keeping our course within two miles of the shore.[16]

Meares certainly had sailed across the outer reaches of the mouth of the Great River of the West and, according to his own statements, in a period of excellent visibility. It is difficult to understand how he could have decided no river existed here without having entered the bay to investigate. Obviously, the shallow soundings near North Head and the breakers caused him alarm. Possibly, wind, tide or storm at sea had made for severe breakers on the bar this day despite the good visibility that he noted. His "Table" of the *Felice*'s route does state that on July 6 as he approached the river entrance the *Felice* encountered strong northerly gales, and "a great sea."[17] It also is true that under any circumstances the river was difficult to see and hazardous to enter.[18] Too, from river level, the extensive surrounding hills could cause an observer to believe this was simply a land-locked bay. Meares was not the first nor would he be the last mariner to miss the mouth of the Columbia.[19] His frustration at not finding a serviceable waterway here clearly is revealed in his assigning the names "Deception Bay" to what is actually the river's mouth and "Cape Disappointment" to the northern headland (the latter designation remains in use today).

Meares' decision to "haul out" would have serious ramifications. In April 1792, also during fair weather, Great Britain's George Vancouver sailed past the bay, having accepted Meares' word that no river existed here as Bruno de Hezeta had suspected. This left the opportunity open for an American, Robert Gray of Boston in the *Columbia Rediviva*, to take the first sailing vessel into the Columbia's mouth, on May 11, 1792. The Yankee's discovery became the basis of the U.S. claims to the great Pacific Northwest region.[20]

Had Meares in the *Felice* entered and explored the long-sought river in 1788, he might have been entitled to the mantle of a maritime hero of Great Britain. Such a discovery could have given Britain additional strong grounds for claiming all of the Northwest Coast from San Francisco Bay to Alaska.

Notes

1. Lewis A. McArthur, *Oregon Geographic Names* (Portland: various editions) presents a full discussion of the historical background for the name *Oregon*.
2. Warren L. Cook, *Flood Tide of Empire: Spain and the Pacific Northwest, 1543-1819* (New Haven, CT, and London: Yale University Press, 1973), 12-13, 29-30.
3. John Meares, *Voyages Made in the Years 1788 and 1789, from China to the North West Coast of America* (London: Logographic Press, 1790), 133.
4. Herbert K. Beals, trans. and annotation, *For Honor and Country: The Diary of Bruno De Hezeta*. (Portland: Western Imprints, Oregon Historical Society, 1985), 86-89.
5. See J. Richard Nokes, *Columbia's River: The Voyages of Robert Gray 1787-1793* (Tacoma: Washington State Historical Society, 1991). Gray's name eventually was attached to the little bay (Grays Bay), a river (Grays River), and a town (also Grays River) on the north side of the Columbia, and to a harbor (Grays Harbor) that he also entered in 1792 on the central Washington Coast. In 1988, he was further honored when a hill inside the entrance to Tillamook Bay was named Captain Gray's Hill.
6. Meares, *Voyages*, 134.
7. Ibid., 135-42.
8. Ibid., 142, 146-47, 150.
9. Ibid., 153; Derek Pethick, *The Nootka Connection: Europe and the Northwest Coast, 1790-1795* (Vancouver, BC: Douglas and McIntyre, 1980), 24-25. The sea-lanes of the Strait of Juan de Fuca extend into Puget Sound and to such major ports as Victoria and Vancouver, in British Columbia, and Seattle, Everett, Tacoma and Olympia, in Washington.
10. Meares, *Voyages*, 153, 169. The "obelisk" seen by Meares may have been the pillar supposedly noted by Juan de Fuca, the mysterious 16th century Greek pilot sailing under Spanish colors in the legendary account of his discovery of the strait written by Michael Lok and published in *Purchas His Pilgrimes* (1625); see Appendix A "Lok's Account of Fuca's Voyage, 1592," in Cook, *Flood Tide of Empire*, 539-43. The story is regarded with skepticism by historians, but de Fuca's name was affixed to the strait by Barkley, in 1787. The claim by the Spaniard Martínez that he had sighted the strait in 1774 when he sailed with Pérez also has been regarded with skepticism, but is not without some support and was used by Spain in its argument with England over Northwest sovereignty.
11. Ibid., 153-56.

12. Meares, *Voyages*, 159, 163; T.C. Elliott, "John Meares' Approach to Oregon," *Oregon Historical Quarterly* 29 (September 1928): 278-87. Elliott, a historian familiar with these waters, contends Meares on the first day actually was off Grays Harbor (at 46° 59' north), and not "Shoal-water Bay" (Willapa Bay). Elliott speculates that during the night the *Felice* drifted south with the current and the next morning was off Leadbetter Point at the entrance to "Shoal-water Bay." Thus, Meares may have been the first mariner to sight Grays Harbor, now a major port in Washington. Captain Robert Gray, however, is credited with discovering "Gray's" Harbor in 1792.

13. Meares, *Voyages*, 164-167.

14. Ibid., 167.

15. It is possible Meares approached the Columbia's entrance over the shallows of Peacock Spit below North Head, and thus he never really "doubled" the promontory (which he named Cape Disappointment) as he claimed. Peacock Spit later lured many a vessel to doom beginning with the U.S. Navy's *Peacock* of the Lt. Charles Wilkes expedition in 1841, the incident that gave the spit its name. See Herman J. Viola and Carolyn Margolis, eds., assisted by Jan S. Danis, *Magnificent Voyagers: The U.S. Exploring Expedition, 1838-1842* (Washington, DC: Smithsonian Institution Press, 1985), 20- 21.

16. Meares, *Voyages*, 167-68.

17. See "Appendix. Table III. Route of the *Felice* from Nootka, or King George's Sound, along the N.W. Coast of America, and back to Nootka," in Ibid. T.C. Elliott in "John Meares' Approach to Oregon," 279, states: "It is incredible that Meares could have 'doubled' the cape . . . or sailed about off the bar on a day of clear weather, and failed to see the prominent physical features on both sides of the river . . . Either the weather was NOT clear or Meares misrepresented the facts in his willingness to discredit the Spaniard Heceta." Elliott, however, does not explain why Meares would want to discredit Hezeta.

18. In modern times, even some of the world's largest vessels—such as the battleship *New Jersey* and the supertanker *Manhattan*—have safely entered the Columbia and proceeded to Portland, thanks to jetties, buoys, pilots, and dredges maintaining a 40-foot-deep channel. Even so, conditions during heavy storms can sometimes keep ships from entering or leaving the river's mouth. The author has experienced difficult conditions twice when crossing the bar. Soon after World War II, I was a passenger on the SS *Mariposa*. The ship had gyrofin stabilizers, but these could not be engaged in the Columbia's shallow waters. As the *Mariposa* rolled heavily, furniture, barrels and the like crashed about the deck and a seaman suffered a crushed leg while trying to corral a wayward article. My second encounter occurred while aboard a 40-foot boat when the owner tried to cross the bar immediately after its reopening by the U.S. Coast Guard. Waves dashed us about handsomely and we feared capsizing. Many a tragedy has occurred at the mouth, earning the title Graveyard of the Pacific for the area from the Columbia River north along the Long Beach Peninsula. Nevertheless, Columbia River ports are among the busiest on the Pacific Coast, and no ocean-going ships have wrecked here in recent years.

19. In early 1778, difficult weather forced the eminent Captain James Cook away from the coast in this vicinity and he passed by far out of sight of the Columbia River and Cape Disappointment. Later, after a cursory investigation of a small portion of the northwest Olympic Peninsula, Cook proclaimed there was not "the least probability" that the "pretended *Strait of Juan de Fuca*" existed; for a discussion, see Barry M. Gough, *The Northwest Coast: British Navigation, Trade, and Discoveries to 1812* (Vancouver: University of British Columbia Press, 1992), 41.

20. See Nokes, *Columbia's River*.

Meares believed an entrance to a Northwest Passage extending to Hudson Bay or Baffin Bay might be discovered east of the "Northern Archipelago." He speculated, too, that suitable navigation could exist via "Slave Lake" or the "River Oregan" which has been incorrectly located here (at lower right) as flowing into the Strait of Juan de Fuca. From Meares, *Voyages* (1790).

Chapter Seven

The Cape Called Meares

O N JULY 6, the same day Meares met disappointment in failing to discover a large river or passage at the Entrada de Hezeta, he continued sailing south along the coast, hoping to find harbors and inlets that might have been overlooked by James Cook 10 years earlier. Noted Northwest historian T.C. Elliott, in appraising Meares in 1928, referred to him as an adventurer whose "reputation for truth and veracity is not considered very good."[1] But there is no cause to doubt the accuracy of Meares' account of his voyage along the Oregon coastline. For example, his description of the scenery closely matches the observations of Robert Haswell, second mate of the *Lady Washington* as she cruised north up the same coastline several weeks after Meares.[2]

Both observed a beautiful shoreline, the finest verdure, distant mountains and white sandy beaches—in all, a joy to see. Wrote Meares: "The face of the country . . . assumed a very different appearance from that of the Northern coast . . . Spacious lawns and hanging-woods everywhere met the delighted eye,—but not an human being appeared to inhabit the fertile country of New Albion."[3] On the other hand, Haswell and the men of the *Lady Washington,* passing by when weather conditions allowed them to see smoke from Indian villages, noted that the Oregon coast was well populated with natives. (Summarizing the weather along the coast in June and July 1788, Meares wrote: "We seldom enjoyed a succession of three days without either fog or rain.")

Meares, and other early mariners, identified the Washington, Oregon and northern California coast as "New Albion," or "Nova Albion." The name was given to an undefined region by Sir Francis Drake in 1579, when he sailed up the coast in the *Golden Hind* and landed at some undetermined place, before proceeding west across the Pacific, homeward bound to England.[4]

"The Country of New Albion. In the latitude of 45 N. when Cape Lookout & the 3 Brothers bore S.S.E. dis^t 8 leag^s," in *Voyages*. The vessel is the *Felice*. These landmarks of the northern Oregon Coast have been renamed Cape Meares and Three Arch Rocks."

Meares next passed a promontory that must have been today's Tillamook Head. Farther south, the *Felice* encountered strong winds and great westerly swells running onshore after Meares had sighted a promising opening which undoubtedly was the entrance to Tillamook Bay—a harbor Robert Gray in the *Lady Washington* would be the first to enter six weeks later on August 14, 1788. According to Meares: "By seven o'clock [on the evening of July 6] we were abreast of this opening, the mouth of which, to our great mortification, was entirely closed by a low sandy beach, nearly level with the sea, which appeared to flow over it, and form an extensive back-water:—beyond it an open champaign country extended to a considerable distance, where it was confined by a boundary of lofty mountains." Meares believed the entrance to the bay was too shallow for his snow to cross. He named the inlet "Quicksand Bay," the entrance "Quicksand Bar," and a headland on the north "Cape Grenville."[5]

Meares continued sailing south with the intention of reaching latitude 45° north, where he thought Captain Cook had begun his voyage north along the coast in 1778. (Cook first caught sight of the Oregon Coast at 44° 33' north. The first geographic point Cook named was Cape Foulweather at 44° 44' 43").

Meares sighted another prominent headland just south of Tillamook Bay which he named "Cape Look-out":

"This cape is very high and bluff, and terminates abruptly in the sea. At about the distance of two miles from it there rose three large rocks, which were very remarkable, from the great resemblance they bore to each other.—The middle one has an arch-way, perforated, as it were, in its centre, through which we very plainly discovered the distant sea.—They more particularly attracted our notice, as we had not observed between King George's Sound and this place, any rocks so conspicuously situated from the land:—their distance from each other might be about a quarter of a mile, and we gave them the name of the Three Brothers."[6]

Inserted close to this entry in Meares *Voyages* is a two-page illustration entitled "The Country of New Albion. In the latitude of 45 N. when Cape Lookout & the 3 Brothers bore S.S.E. dist 8 leags."[7] In this fine view, Meares' vessel, the *Felice*, is shown in the foreground with the cape, the three rocks, a stretch of the shore and the coastal mountains in the background. Meares accurately described this promontory, which, ironically, today is not called "Cape Look-out," but actually is named for him—Cape Meares. The spectacular arched rocks that he described, the "Three Brothers," are now known as Three Arch Rocks and can easily be seen from the Cape Meares light-house. The name he gave to the point, "Cape Look-out," later was be-stowed on another headland to the south. [8]

By accident, in the mid-19th century the name Cape Lookout was affixed to the point 10 miles south of the one Meares had named in 1788. As a result, George Davidson of the United States Coast Survey, in 1857, renamed the original "Cape Look-out" nearer to Tillamook Bay in honor of its discoverer, John Meares. [9]

Meares initially had planned to sail as far south as 45° or possibly 42°, which happens to be the boundary between Oregon and California, but he turned north after reaching 45° 12' on July 7, somewhat short of his goal. He reasoned that by this time he had a good knowledge of the coast and, with the season so far advanced, he feared an "equinoctial" storm might strike ere he could return to Nootka Sound. Autumn, he said, was "a season to be dreaded on this coast." In this, Meares erred. Early fall on the Oregon-Washington coast often is the most benign time of the year. Meares may have been remembering his misadventure in Prince William Sound. Furthermore, "the real existence of the Strait of John de Fuca . . . now renewed its claim to our attention," and he wanted time to have it explored by the *Felice*'s longboat. Also, Meares noted "it was already agreed" a cargo of furs needed to be readied and sent to China on September 20, and he wanted to make certain the vessel being built at Nootka was launched by that date. He concluded, "such were the reasons which determined us to return to the North."

It is apparent from Meares' *Voyages* that in the next three days he made little or no attempt to explore further the Oregon and Washington coast, until he passed north of the Strait of Juan de Fuca to southern Vancouver Island on July 10. For this period, however, Meares made an interesting observation about the region's fauna: "In our passage . . . we saw numbers of sea otters playing in the water with their young ones; but at the ship's approach they quickly disappeared. Once or twice we passed within a few yards of some of them, as they were sleeping on their backs in the sea. At first we took them for pieces of drift-wood, till, on being awak-ened by the noise of the ship, they instantly dived away. We also saw many whales of the spermaceti kind, and seals without number, besides other huge marine animals." [10]

Thus, on the evening of July 10, lookouts espied a large bluff near "Port Cox" in the Barkley Sound vicinity. Meares said the bluff "obtained from us the name of Cape Beale," apparently for his Macao business partner, Daniel Beale. Barkley, however, earlier had given the same name to this feature to honor his ship's purser, John Beale (who was killed in ambush along with five other crew members on the outer Olympic Coast in 1787).[11] It could be that Meares conveniently was merely reinforcing the name given by Barkley, whose charts Meares eventually acquired.

A number of historians have made much of the conjecture that Meares attempted to cheat Barkley of the credit for his discoveries in the *Imperial Eagle* in 1787. The allegations cannot be substantiated. Meares made it plain in his *Voyages* that he knew Barkley had made discoveries in this area first. For instance, Meares' entry for July 12, 1788, in connection with Barkley Sound on the southwest coast of Vancouver Island, states: "This sound had been visited by Captain Barclay [*sic*], of the *Imperial Eagle*, in the year 1787, who named it Barclay Sound." Meares did try to name part of it "Port Effingham" for a British Lord, but the name Barkley Sound has stood the test of time for the large bay. (The *Felice* anchored here, and in the days ahead, as the crew replenished the supplies and went about other duties, many natives came with furs, fish, berries, shell-fish and onions to trade.)[12]

In recognition of Barkley's other previous sightings in the area, including the Strait of Juan de Fuca, Meares also reported in the introduction to his *Voyages:*

> The *Imperial Eagle*, Captain Barclay, we believe, sailed from Europe the beginning of the year 1787 [actually, November 24, 1786]; and not only arrived at Nootka Sound in August [mid June], but explored that part of the coast from Nootka to Wicananish, and so on to a Sound to which he gave his own name. The boat's crew, however, was dispatched, and discovered the extraordinary straits of John de Fuca, and also the coast as far as Queenhythe;—when, after the fatal catastrophe which happened to some of them, this ship quitted the coast, and proceeded to China; having performed the whole of the voyage in twelve months, which employed the *King George* and *Queen Charlotte* [Portlock's and Dixon's ships] upwards of two years. The *Nootka* made no other discovery but that of distress and misfortune.[13]

So far as is known, Barkley did not actually penetrate the strait, nor did he ceremonially claim it for England. Meares, however, did not miss the opportunity to do so: "it may not be improper to mention that we took possession of the Straits of John de Fuca, in the name of the King of Britain, with the forms that had been adopted by preceding navigators on similar occasions." Regrettably, where and when this ceremony occurred is not revealed by Meares, but it apparently was done by his first officer, Robert Duffin, during an exploration of the strait ordered by Meares.[14]

Now that fine summer weather had set in, Meares "embraced the present favourable opportunity to dispatch the long-boat, not only to explore the straits of de Fuca, but to procure, if possible, some knowledge of the people of Shoalwater-Bay. She was, therefore, properly equipped for the occasion . . . and furnished with provisions for a month. The command of her was given to Mr. Robert Duffin, our, first officer, to whom written instructions were delivered, by which he was to govern himself in the conduct of this little expedition." The longboat, with mast and sail, "departed on its voyage of discovery" on July 13, with a crew of 13. These were unlucky numbers for those aboard, because seven days later they returned, much earlier than expected, with a harrowing tale of a vicious fight with the natives.[15]

Several men were wounded, but remarkably none had been killed or captured. Duffin received a barbed arrow in the head, but his thick hat saved his life. Another man was wounded with an arrow in the breast, another in the calf of the leg, and another near the heart, but "the weapon. . . very fortunately fell short of the vital parts." A Chinese and an Italian were two of the wounded. The others were terribly bruised by clubs in the hand-to-hand fighting and by stones cast from the shore. "Even the boat itself was pierced in a thousand places by arrows, many of which remained in the awning that covered the back part of it." The natives had "boarded the boat, with the design of taking her, in two canoes, containing between forty and fifty men, who were most probably some of their choicest warriors. Several other canoes also remained at a small distance, to assist in the attempt; and the shore was every where lined with people, who discharged at our vessel continual showers of stones and arrows." A chief was shot in the head just as he threw an enormously long spear at the coxswain. This seemed to cause a lull, and then an eventual halt to the attack. The casualty total among the natives was unknown, but musket fire undoubtedly took a toll.

"The boat had advanced a considerable way up the Straits of de Fuca, and had entered a bay or harbour; when, as our people were preparing to land for the purpose of examining it, they were attacked by the natives . . . From this station, however, they observed, that the straits to the East North East appeared to be of great extent, and to encrease rather than diminish."

(This could have been Haro Strait leading to the Strait of Georgia, which was explored in 1792 by Captain George Vancouver's ships and by the Spaniards, Galiano and Valdés.)

Despite the early termination of this exploratory effort, the *Felice's* longboat had been "able to communicate some knowledge" of the strait. They had "sailed near thirty leagues up the strait," Meares said, though that perhaps is a bit of exaggeration, "and at that distance from the sea it was about fifteen leagues broad, with a clear horizon to the East for 15 leagues more.—Such an extraordinary circumstance filled us with strange conjectures as to the extremity of this strait, which we concluded at all events, could not be at any great distance from Hudson's Bay."[16]

Was this, then, the entrance to the Northwest Passage? Meares later expressed this belief, though the distance to Hudson Bay was far more than what he "conjectured." On one of Meares' maps of the Northwest Coast in *Voyages,* he shows the "River Oregan" entering the Strait of Juan de Fuca from the east.[17] Could he have thought this would be the link through the continent to Hudson Bay? In this period, neither he nor any other traders knew that a range of mountains (the Rockies) lay between. In another instance, he speculated that a connection of 1,000 miles might lead to Baffin Bay, which he noted had yet to be completely explored.

Whatever Meares believed concerning the Strait of Juan de Fuca at this time, he did no further exploring to see where it might lead, and thus missed another chance to win prominence in history. He was basically a fur trader in search of pelts, and his explorations were secondary to that role. With pressing obligations to meet at Yuquot, he gave up his investigation of the strait, and on July 26 returned to Nootka Sound. The attack on the longboat crew probably was an intimidating factor in this decision.

In hindsight, the expedition to the south fell disappointingly short. It would be left to others to first enter the River of the West, or drop the first anchor in an Oregon or Washington harbor, or explore Puget Sound and the Strait of Georgia. But Meares' voyage along the shores of today's Washington and Oregon did add important knowledge concerning the Northwest Coast.

⚓

When Meares returned to London from the Northwest Coast and China and published *Voyages* in November 1790, he aroused the ire of the rival fur trader, George Dixon, who also had gained some renown as the author of *A Voyage Round the World* (1789). In a kind of "pamphlet war," Dixon[18] tried to discredit Meares regarding a number of issues that mostly can be considered minor and insignificant or simply a difference of opinion. In perhaps the most serious charge, Dixon denounced Meares' statement in *Voyages* that the American sloop *Lady Washington* had in 1789 sailed between what is known today as Vancouver Island and the mainland of North America. Meares' *Voyages* contained several charts showing "A Sketch of the Track of the American Sloop *Washington* in the Autumn of 1789" around the island. (Actual confirmation that Vancouver Island was an insular body of land would not be forthcoming until 1792 with cooperative investigations by the British under Captain George Vancouver and the Spanish based out of Nootka.) Meares' claim, if true, was substantial evidence supporting his belief that the coast which mariners of this period were probing was not the mainland of the North American continent, but part of a great "Northern Archipelago." This was vital to Meares' conjecture about the existence of a Northwest Passage in these latitudes.

George Dixon, however, with some justification discounted this claim as a fabrication. He summed up his argument by ridiculing Meares' map as resembling "nothing so much as a mould of a good old housewife's butter pat." In answer, Meares fired back a broadside[19] contending that the American, Captain John Kendrick, in early 1790 had told an official of the East India Company in Macao of sailing through such a channel in the *Lady Washington*.[20] The official ("Mr. Neville") returned to London in 1790 and passed the report on to Meares, who by this time had completed his last Northwest cruise and, after residing in China for a time, also had arrived in England.[21]

Meares' modern critic, historian F.W. Howay, belittles Meares for not having more substantial evidence before making such a claim, but Meares' charts in *Voyages,* based on whatever information he had, do depict much of Vancouver Island roughly the way modern maps show it. Howay nevertheless said, "without the observed latitudes and longitudes, or the charts, or some other support[,] Meares not only accepted it, he embraced it . . . A strong case can be made out in support of the view that Meares had invented the whole story."[22]

When the official British explorer Captain George Vancouver, who was familiar with Meares' views, arrived off the Northwest Coast in 1792, he sighted the *Columbia* and despatched two officers to find out if her captain, Robert Gray, a former master of the *Lady Washington*, actually had sailed around the island in 1789. Gray denied that he had.

Regarding Gray, however, it is very important to point out that by the *autumn* of 1789, when Meares said the circumnavigation had occurred, Gray was no longer captain of the *Lady Washington*. He and Kendrick had exchanged commands in Clayoquot Sound in July 1789, and Kendrick took over the helm of the *Lady Washington*. It is conceivable that Kendrick may have sailed from Clayoquot Sound through the Strait of Juan de Fuca and then north behind Vancouver Island perhaps to trade with natives near the Queen Charlotte Islands. The truth will never be known, because Kendrick died in Hawaii in 1794 without ever returning to Boston, and any record concerning this incident was lost or has never been found.[23]

In any event, Meares was correct in assuming that north of the Strait of Juan de Fuca, mariners mostly had been probing islands, such as the Aleutians, the Alexander Archipelago, the Queen Charlottes, and Vancouver Island, and not the mainland. The squabble with Dixon[24] did nothing to enhance Meares' reputation with critics and historians.

Notes

1. T.C. Elliott, "John Meares' Approach to Oregon," *Oregon Historical Quarterly* 29 (September 1928): 278.
2. J. Richard Nokes, *Columbia's River: The Voyages of Robert Gray 1787-1793* (Tacoma: Washington State Historical Society, 1991), 48.
3. John Meares, *Voyages Made in the Years 1788 and 1789, from China to the North West Coast of America* (London: Logographic Press, 1790), 168.
4. Robert Ward, in "Lost Harbor Found: Where Sir Francis Drake Really Went in the Pacific," (unpublished typescript, dated 1987, Essex, England), theorizes that Drake paused for repairs in Whale Cove on the central Oregon Coast, that the southern boundary of "New Albion" was at about 42° (the present Oregon-California boundary), and that Drake may have sailed as far north as southern Vancouver Island. Other historians believe Drake landed only as far north as Drake's Bay near San Francisco Bay. Thomas Vaughan, retired director of the Oregon Historical Society, has suggested Drake proceeded to Cape Arago on the Oregon Coast, while Wayne Jensen, Director of the Tillamook County Pioneer Museum, believes markings on rocks at Neahkahnie Mountain indicate he was there in 1579. Much mystery remains. See Nokes, *Columbia's River*, 62-64, *passim*, for a fuller discussion.
5. Meares, *Voyages*, 168-69. In 1988, the Oregon Geographic Names Board named the northern headland "Captain Gray's Hill" on the occasion of the bicentennial celebration of Robert Gray's entrance into Tillamook Bay. Historian F.W. Howay believes that Meares' "Cape Grenville" actually might have been Cape Falcon, located about a dozen miles north.
6. Ibid., 169.
7. Ibid., between pages 160-61.
8. For many years, the lighthouse cast its beam from Cape Meares, warning vessels about the dangerous waters of the Tillamook Bay vicinity. The lighthouse still stands as the centerpiece of Cape Meares State Park, though an automated beacon (Tillamook Light)

has replaced the beam from the lighthouse itself. Nearby is a picturesque community named Cape Meares. The "Three Brothers" rocks that so attracted the Englishman two centuries ago have been designated part of the Cape Meares National Wildlife Refuge. See "Cape Meares" in Lewis A. McArthur, *Oregon Geographic Names* (Portland: Koke-Chapman, 1928).

9. Ibid., 57.
10. Meares, *Voyages,* 169-72. Meares' northward course along the Oregon and Washington coast was farther out to sea. Ten years earlier, weather conditions had forced James Cook away from land when proceeding north along much of this same coastline. Sailing in the winter and spring, Cook's expedition experienced frightful storms. According to Barry M. Gough, in *The Northwest Coast: British Navigation, Trade, and Discoveries to 1812* (Vancouver: University of British Columbia Press, 1992), 9, "The northeast trades defied sailing ships and crews bound north, but they could be the ally of pilots on the way south . . . In consequence, almost all the great European maritime discoveries on the Northwest Coast occurred on southward-bound tracks."
11. Gough, *The Northwest Coast*, 63, 91, 94, 215. In retaliation for the murder of the six men who had entered a coastal stream in a launch from the ship, Barkley's men burned a nearby village; Frederick W. Howay, ed., "Four Letters from Richard Cadman Etches to Sir Joseph Banks, 1788-92," *British Columbia Historical Quarterly* 6 (April 1942): 135.
12. Meares, *Voyages,* 172. In addition, on page 169, Meares noted: "This bay had, indeed, been already visited by the ship *Imperial Eagle*." The widow of Captain Barkley later criticized Meares for not crediting her husband for his discoveries. Some historians have followed her lead.
13. Ibid., "Observations on the Probable Existence of a North West Passage, Etc.," lv. On page lxiii, Meares added regarding the Strait of Juan de Fuca, "Captain Barclay's officers . . . saw every particular which I declare to have seen,—having surveyed these parts in a boat,—though he himself [Barkley] did not go within some leagues of the strait." Historian W. Kaye Lamb points out that Barkley's name was misspelled by both Dixon ("Berkley") and Meares ("Barclay") and the correct spelling for Barkley Sound "was not placed on the official charts until 1901 . . . after the Barkley papers had come to light"; see W. Kaye Lamb, "The Mystery of Mrs. Barkley's Diary: Notes on the Voyage of the 'Imperial Eagle,' 1786-87," *British Columbia Historical Quarterly* 6 (January 1942), 32.
14. Meares, *Voyages,* 173. Meares directed Duffin to "take possession of this strait, and the lands adjoining, in the name of the King and Crown of Britain." See "Instructions to Explore the Straits of John de Fuca. To Mr. Robert Duffin, First Officer of the *Felice*," Appendix III, in Ibid.
15. Meares, *Voyages,* 174-76.
16. Ibid., 176-81. There is conjecture about Duffin's route in the Strait of Juan de Fuca. An earlier hostile encounter with tribesmen had occurred on June 16 after Duffin's longboat left the village of "Nittee Natt" on the north side of the strait. Warriors on the beach fired a shower of arrows at the longboat whereupon Duffin fired one shot from a "musketoon" and hoped he had not killed anyone. Hostilities ceased when the natives returned a stolen half-pike. Duffin moved on to "Hostility Bay" on July 17 where the major fight occurred against a people who claimed "Tatooche for their chief," which would indicate that the fight took place on the south side of the strait. On the other hand, one of Meares' charts indicates "Hostility Bay" as being on the north shore. Suffice it to say the conflict might have occurred west of the Port Angeles vicinity on the Washington side or west of Victoria on Vancouver Island. Duffin's

account in *Voyages* is not definitive. See "Copy of Mr. Duffin's Journal," Appendix IV, in Ibid.

17. Ibid., "A Chart of the Interior Part of North America Demonstrating the Very Great Probability of an Inland Navigation from Hudsons Bay to the West Coast," frontispiece to the chapter titled "Observations on the Probable Existence of a North West Passage, &c."

18. George Dixon, *Remarks on the Voyages of John Meares, Esq. in a Letter to That Gentleman* (London: J. Stockdale and G. Goulding, 1790) [reprinted in F.W. Howay, *The Dixon-Meares Controversy*, 1929.] The pamphlet is dated December 1, 1790.

19. John Meares, *An Answer to Mr. George Dixon, Late Commander of the "Queen Charlotte." In the Service of Messrs. Etches and Company. by John Meares, Esq. in Which the Remarks of Mr. Dixon on the Voyages to the North West Coast of America, &c Lately Published, Are Fully Considered and Refuted* (London: Logographic Press, 1791) [reprinted in F.W. Howay, *The Dixon-Meares Controversy*, 1929.] Meares' response is dated January 1, 1791.

20. In "Observations on the Probable Existence of a North West Passage, &c.," *Voyages*, lxiii, Meares claimed the *Washington* "sailed through a sea that extends upwards of 8 degrees of latitude."

21. Meares, *An Answer to Mr. George Dixon*, 14.

22. Frederick W. Howay, ed., *The Dixon-Meares Controversy* (Toronto: Ryerson Press, 1929), 13.

23. According to Thomas Bullfinch (the son of a sponsor of the Kendrick-Gray expedition) in *Oregon and Eldorado: or, Romance of the Rivers* (New York: J.E. Tilton, 1866), 5-6, "to him [John Kendrick] belongs the credit of ascertaining that Nootka and the parts adjacent are an island to which the name of Vancouver's Island has since been given." In 1786-87, Nootka Sound's forlorn sojourner, John Mackay, had learned from Maquinna's people "the nature of the insularity of Vancouver Island"; see Gough, *The Northwest Coast*, 83. It can be assumed that other Indian informants drew rough maps of coastlines and islands in the sand for inquisitive whites.

24. George Dixon's response to Meares' broadside in the "pamphlet war" was *Further Remarks on the Voyages of John Meares, Esq. in Which Several Important Facts, Misrepresented in the Said Voyages, Relative to Geography and Commerce, Are Fully Substantiated. To Which Is Added, a Letter from Captain Duncan, Containing a Decisive Refutation of Several Unfounded Assertations of Mr. Meares, and a Final Reply to His Answer* (London: J. Stockdale and G. Goulding, 1791) [reprinted in F.W. Howay, *The Dixon-Meares Controversy*, 1929.] Dixon's pamphlet is dated February 12, 1791. Meares chose not to respond in kind.

"The Launch of the *North West America* at Nootka Sound. Being the first Vessel that was ever built in that part of the Globe," in *Voyages*. Note the rocky bluff that separated Meares' "house" from the native village in Friendly Cove. British flags are prominent in this portrayal of the launching, September 20, 1788, as the *Iphigenia, Felice* and the American sloop *Lady Washington* stand at anchor in the harbor. The inaccurate portrayal of Yuquot's houses as European-like in construction and the overly mountainous terrain indicate the artist was not an eyewitness to the event.

Chapter Eight

Mutiny, Launching and Departure

O N JULY 26, 1788, when the *Felice* returned to Nootka from her nearly two-month-long voyage of discovery south along the coast, Meares noted with pleasure that his little schooner being built on the rocky shore was "in frame" with part of the hull planked. The deck was laid "and most of her iron work finished." The British and Chinese artisans, and the natives who were paid to assist them by cutting and hauling timbers from the nearby dense forest, had done their duty to the captain's satisfaction. This would be the first ship built on the Northwest Coast, and Meares wanted the work soundly done. The other consort vessel coming from the Philippines, Captain Douglas in the *Iphigenia,* had yet to arrive at Nootka.

Maquinna had promised "to shew every mark of attention and friendship" to Meares' men, and he had done so. Callicum, who appeared to be fond of the Britons, had provided "fish and other provisions." The house by now had been made secure from attack by "a palisado of strong stakes," and a "fence of thick bushes" in addition to a three-pound cannon.[1]

All seemed well on shore, but trouble soon broke out on the *Felice.* Mutineers led by a "disgraced boatswain, and the best men in the ship," in Meares' words, tried to seize the vessel's arms and First Mate Duffin while the other officers were ashore inspecting the new schooner. The plot was frustrated when those on the beach heard Duffin's cries and rushed 100 yards back to the ship. Duffin, "having fortunately gained the cabin" where the arms were stored, had "placed himself at the door with a loaded blunderbuss," keeping the mutineers from advancing.

Meares and the officers armed themselves and faced the crew assembled on deck. Most of the crew remained loyal, but eight "remained deaf to all our persuasions to return to their duty." Meares gave the mutineers a choice: either be put in irons aboard ship, "or be turned on shore among the savages. They preferred the latter,—and were immediately landed" with all their personal gear.

Even though most of the sailors had stood loyal in the end, one crewman confessed that almost all had signed a paper pledging to take "possession of the ship" from the officers, "quit the coast of America, and steer their course to the Sandwich Islands; from whence they proposed to make the best of their way to some port where they might dispose of their valuable cargo" (by this time the *Felice* had 400 skins in her hold).[2]

Meares seemed understanding of the sailors' action. He believed the mutiny was caused by "the impatience of their passions to get to the Sandwich Islands . . . where they longed to solace themselves in the enjoyments afforded by those voluptuous abodes." Freely translated, this meant the attractive women, the benign weather and the plentiful food of the islands, versus the fog, rain and primitive life of the Northwest Coast.

To relieve the crisis, Meares promised to sail soon for the islands and "the eyes of every one sparkled." The departure from the Northwest Coast was no "less anxiously desired by many of the crew, from the reflection that cannibals inhabited its shores . . . the idea of being eaten by the Americans absolutely haunted the imaginations and preyed upon the spirits of many of our people." Maquinna offered to "put the mutineers to instant death," but the officers ardently refused this request. Meanwhile, the highly respected Callicum, wishing also to assist the officers in punishing the mutineers, took the offenders to his house and worked them as virtual slaves doing "menial services." They also had to give up their clothes, dress in skins and assist their new master in fishing from canoes at sea. Eventually all of the mutineers but the stubborn boatswain, John Green, returned to the *Felice* upon sacrificing nine months pay (which was restored to them on arrival in China by the firm's directors). Meares insisted that the boatswain remain ashore in a rude hut and live as a native.[3]

With the mutiny settled, Meares on August 8 got underway with the *Felice* for Clayoquot Sound to conduct an expected good trade with Wicananish's people. Just before sailing, however, he provided much desired guns and ammunition to the delighted Nootkans, who were "preparing for an hostile expedition against" a more powerful northern enemy which had pillaged an allied village "about twenty leagues to the Northward of King George's Sound." Maquinna's warriors embarked in 20 canoes, with 30 "young, athletic men" to a canoe from the tribe's different villages. Comekela commanded two of the boats. The warriors, with "faces and bodies painted with red ochre, and sprinkled with a shining sand," paddled off singing a war song. "The women encouraged the warriors, in the patriotic language of the Spartan dames,—to return victorious, or to return no more." No whites went along, but Meares reported that the "expedition ended in a most shocking seene [*sic*] of blood and massacre."[4]

After the *Felice* departed Nootka Sound, she encountered the 50-ton sloop *Princess Royal*—Captain Charles Duncan, out of London—sailing off the coast. The two ships closed, and, during a cordial meeting, Meares provided Duncan with some emergency supplies. For the past two days, Meares and his men had had glimpses during breaks in the "thick, misty weather" of the *Princess Royal* at sea off Nootka Sound. The *Princess Royal* remarkably had made her way around Cape Horn and up the American Coast with only a 15-man crew, and while lacking sufficient supplies. Shortly, she probably would be the first European ship actually to enter the Strait of Juan de Fuca, although Barkley and the crew of the *Imperial Eagle* had been the first to sight the strait in 1787. After the meeting with Meares, she sailed south southeast conducting further trade on the coast and sailed for the Sandwich Islands and thence to Macao. A year later, the *Princess Royal* would play an important role in an international crisis involving Meares' ships.[5]

On August 10, the *Felice* entered Clayoquot Sound, briefly encountered some of the *Princess Royal's* men a second time, and dropped anchor in an inlet on an island (which, in 1862, would be named "Meares Island").[6] Chief Wicananish and his people had removed to winter quarters about 30 or 40 miles distant. Meares sent out men in a longboat, who found the chief at a summer village site and exchanged presents with him for 40 prime otter skins. The longboat then conducted two other successful trading excursions between the ship and the chief's "rude[ly] magnificen[t]" and "large and populous" winter village of "Clioquatt." The chief was especially delighted to receive a copper teakettle sent by Meares. Wicananish graciously made a return visit to the *Felice*. In the "brisk trade" for "a considerable quantity of furs," the chief and his people received, among other items, 12 swords, clothes with brass buttons, a couple of muskets with ammunition, "and a great variety of articles . . . purposely manufactured to suit the fancy of the women." With Clayoquot Sound almost deserted and offering little further chance of providing furs that season, Meares ordered the anchor raised and sailed again for his Nootka headquarters, arriving on August 24.[7]

THE SEA OTTER

While Oregon is known as the Beaver State because early nineteenth-century trappers obtained numerous beaver pelts in the interior Pacific Northwest, the fur that brought the early mariners to the coast—a half-century before the covered wagons—was that of the sea otter.

Spain on the southwest coast of North America long had been engaged in the sea otter trade via the Philippines, and the Russians had obtained sea otter pelts from the natives of Alaska and traded them in northern China. While in Nootka Sound in 1778, Captain James Cook's sailors obtained from the natives sea otter pelts which they used as bedding. Later in Macao they learned such furs were in high demand among the mandarins for use as outer garments or for trimming robes. The final accounts of Cook's voyages, published in 1784, told of the demand for these soft furs and aroused the interest of merchants in Europe and, by 1787, in the infant United States. By 1830, sea otters were almost extinct on the Northwest Coast. Because of protective laws in the modern era, they have increased in number, especially in California and Alaska.

Sea otters grow as long as 11 feet, including the tail, but generally are in the 5 foot range. The fur is soft, dense and exceedingly fine. The animals were common along most of the North American Coast, and they were easy prey for native hunters if caught sleeping on the surface among kelp beds, but otherwise they were difficult to hunt. They dive deep for shellfish, their chief source of food.

On August 26, Meares' men were aroused by a cry that a sail was seen in the offing. To their "infinite joy," it was the *Iphigenia Nubiana,* the consort vessel under Captain Douglas which Meares had not seen since sailing from Zamboanga in the Philippines many months earlier. Douglas had decided after his delay for repairs in Zamboanga that he would sail directly to the Northwest Coast instead of first calling in Hawaii to return Kaiana to his home island of Kauai.

When the *Iphigenia* anchored in Friendly Cove on the morning of August 27, Kaiana was filled with joy to see his old mates of the *Felice.* Among the men, Meares said, "there was not a seaman in either ship, that did not love Tianna as himself." Meares informed the Hawaiian that he might sail home with the small vessel then being built on shore. In the days ahead, Kaiana with "a firm and fixed attention" watched the construction of the schooner. Meares encouraged him, so that he might put this carpentering experience to good use in his homeland. The stern English captain appeared to have a great fondness for the happy Hawaiian.[8]

On the same day the *Iphigenia* came into the cove, Maquinna, Callicum, Comekela and their warriors returned triumphantly, giving "the shout of victory." The Nootkans carried in several of their baskets the heads of 30 of the enemy who had been killed in battle, "but the victory was not purchased without some loss on the side of the powers of Nootka." The muskets Meares had lent to Maquinna were returned, but the ammunition had been expended.[9] This may have been the first time guns were used by one group of natives against another on this coast. The white men's firearms already were in great demand in exchange for peltries. Some captains did trade guns for furs, but others refused. Soon these weapons were in more general use among the natives, sometimes to the regret of mariners.

As instructed, the *Iphigenia* had crossed the North Pacific to the Aleutians, and then entered Cook Inlet on the Alaska coast, and from there sailed into Prince William Sound. Thence she had coasted south among the offshore islands, trading for a valuable cargo of furs as she went. Meares said Douglas "had brought us the most indubitable proofs of the existence of the Great Northern Archipelago," bearing out Meares' theory that voyagers up to this time had been mainly among islands and not the mainland coast of North America.[10]

The skins Douglas amassed in trade with the northern Indians in 1788 combined with the 400 that Meares had obtained made "a very valuable cargo" for one ship to carry to China. Meares resolved that as soon as the schooner was launched, he would set sail for Macao in the *Felice*. The *Iphigenia*, meanwhile, would remain at Nootka until the new schooner was ready for sea, after which the two ships would "prosecute the general objects" of commerce. Then the two consort vessels would set a heading for the Hawaiian Islands to spend the winter, before returning to the Northwest Coast early the following spring.[11]

Maquinna and Callicum announced on September 7 that their people soon would move to winter quarters, located 30 miles away (on Tahsis Inlet) "and as many from the sea." The site was better sheltered from the winter storms that swept the coast. Before Maquinna's entourage finally left Friendly Cove, Meares presented fine gifts to the chiefs: muskets, ammunition, blankets, etc. Meares told them he would return the next year "and build more houses" and introduce them to "our manners and mode of living," proof that the Britons planned to establish a permanent colony here. Meares said the chiefs appeared delighted "beyond measure."

"Maquilla thought proper, on the instant, to do obedience to us as his lords and sovereigns. He took off his tiara of feathers, and placed it on my head; he then dressed me in his robe of otter skins; and, thus arrayed, he made me sit down on one of his chests filled with human bones, and then placed himself on the ground. His example was followed by all the natives present, when they sung one of those plaintive songs, which . . . [produced] such a solemn and pleasing effect upon our minds. . . [H]e intended to acknowledge, in the presence of his people, our superiority over him."[12]

Meares returned to the ship in his splendid attire, feeling he was "possessed of sovereign power" over the native people. Was Meares justified in thinking Maquinna had bestowed such authority on him? Meares' *Voyages* presents the only account of the ceremony and Meares may well have misconstrued Maquinna's intent. In any event, the natives had come to covet the metal, guns, tools, gew gaws, and clothing that the Britons could offer. Callicum and others requested, upon the ship's return, to bring them certain items, especially clothing, from the civilized world. The natives' material culture was beginning to change—the first of many far-reaching economic and social alterations destined to follow.

On September 17, the superstructure of a ship was sighted jutting above the horizon—or "hull down," in mariners' terms. The Britons thought it might be the *Princess Royal* in distress, coming back again. Meares dispatched a longboat to assist, but, instead of encountering the little British vessel, it was the American sloop *Lady Washington* commanded by Robert Gray more than 11 months out of Boston. She had started out as consort to the *Columbia Rediviva*, under John Kendrick. A hurricane had separated them off Cape Horn, and the *Lady Washington* had sailed on north without Gray's knowing if Kendrick's ship remained afloat.

Gray intended to seek anchorage in Ship's Cove where Captain Cook's party had found refuge in 1778, but the boat crew sent out by Meares invited the Americans to anchor instead in Friendly Cove near the *Felice*. This Gray agreed to do, and soon he was in conversation with the British captain. They exchanged information about their respective adventures, but from the journal kept by Robert Haswell, Gray's second mate, and Meares' own account, it seems that the two mariners almost instantly became distrustful of one another. Meares wrote:

"Mr. Grey [*sic*] informed us that he had put into an harbour on the Coast of New Albion [Gray discovered today's Tillamook Bay on August 14, 1788], where he got on shore, and was in danger of being lost on the bar: he was also attacked by the natives, had one man killed and one of his officers wounded, and thought himself fortunate in having been able to make his escape. This harbour could only admit vessels of a very small size, and must lie somewhere near the Cape, to which we had given the name of Cape Look-out.

"The master of the *Washington* was very much surprized at seeing a vessel on the stocks, as well as on finding any one here before him; for they had little or no notion of any commercial expeditions whatever to this part of America. He appeared, however, to be very sanguine in the superior advantages which his countrymen from New England might reap from this track of trade; and was big with many mighty projects, in which we understood he was protected by the American Congress. With these circumstances, however, as we had no immediate concern, we did not even intrude an opinion, but treated Mr. Grey and his ship's company with politeness and attention."[13]

For their part, the Americans were convinced Meares and his officers were less than frank concerning the success of their trading on the coast. They believed the number of peltries collected was substantial (which it was), but that the Britons were downplaying their success in the hope of discouraging the Bostonians.[14]

A further grievance would arise a few days later as the *Felice* set sail for Hawaii. Meares had promised Gray he would take letters from the Americans to China, whence they could be forwarded by other ships to Boston. The American owners had as yet no knowledge of the whereabouts of their ships. However, Meares would renege at the last minute when leaving Nootka Sound [and after the Americans had supplied a boat to help tow the *Felice* out of the harbor], by returning the letters to Gray via Captain Douglas. Meares said he could not take the letters because he did not know at what part "of India" he might call. This meant Gray had to wait almost another year before he could dispatch a letter advising his sponsors of his safe arrival on the Northwest Coast. Haswell wrote: "this ungentlemanlike maner [*sic*] of behavior gave us an unfavourable opinion of Captain John Mears."[15] However, the Americans were grateful for the workmen that Meares provided to assist in repairing the damage done to the *Lady Washington* when she struck on the bar of Tillamook Bay.

On September 20 came the great day for the launching of the first ship built on the Northwest Coast. Meares named her *North West America* (or *North-West America*, his spelling differs) in honor of the land where she was built. A sketch of the event appears in Meares' *Voyages* showing the British flag flying from staffs on the new schooner, one of the vessels in the harbor and the workhouse onshore. One historian, Frederick W. Howay, has expressed the thought that actually the Portuguese flag, under which Meares supposedly was sponsored, might have been flying this day. Howay based his supposition on a letter from Gray to his sponsors, saying Meares' ships in Nootka Sound were flying Portuguese colors when the Americans arrived. But Gray's comments did not specifically refer to which flags were displayed on the day of the launching of the *North West America*. Meares makes a point in *Voyages* that he hoisted British colors this day, September 20.[16] The point became important later in connection with the Nootka controversy between Spain and England in 1790.

Maquinna, Callicum and "a large body of" natives came to watch from the shore and from canoes. The occasion was baffling to Maquinna's people. In regard to the Chinese artisans, Meares thought they also "did not very well conceive the last operation of a business in which they themselves had been so much and so materially concerned." The Boston sailors lined the deck of the *Lady Washington* to watch. Kaiana, standing on the deck of the schooner as she shot into the water, shouted gleefully, *"Myty, myty"* (maika'i, maika'i), roughly translated as "wonderful, wonderful" in his native tongue. The schooner's velocity took her nearly "out of the harbour" before she was towed back "to her intended station." Proper arresting gear had not been provided to the tiny schooner that was to figure later in a bizarre international crisis. The Chinese and the Nootkans all were astonished, "as they had never before been witness of such a spectacle."

Thus, the *North West America* was duly launched and now only awaited her fitting out. "A commander [Robert Funter], officers and crew, were immediately selected from the *Felice* and *Iphigenia,* to navigate the *North West America;* and each of the ships sent her proportion of stores on shore, to equip her for sea." Meanwhile, the *Felice* took on board the skins collected by the consort vessel, the *Iphigenia,* and a deck load of spars cut from the adjacent forest that would bring a good price in China.[17]

On the evening of September 24, all of the British officers came aboard the *Felice* to bid farewell before she sailed. Undoubtedly, there was a certain amount of sadness: when would the companions meet again? Tears ran down the cheeks of Kaiana, the royal Hawaiian, as he gave a final embrace to Meares, calling him *"Noota,"* a name given to the captain both in Hawaii and America. Kaiana would sail to his homeland with Captain Douglas, who intended to winter there with the *Iphigenia.* Three cheers floated across the water as the *Felice* raised anchor, hoisted sails and headed out of Friendly Cove to begin a long voyage across the great South Sea.[18]

⚓

At about this point in his narrative, *Voyages,* Meares reviewed his own accomplishments somewhat philosophically. Though feeling "chagrin" at
being on the losing end of the American Revolution "on the opposite side
of this continent," Meares believed some honor was due for "the naval
warfare on the lakes of" Canada in which he had participated. He thought
"it was my good fortune, when a youth, to be enured in such a school, to
the hardships and difficulties of naval life, and to learn there, that temper
and perseverance must be added to professional knowledge . . . I am in-
debted to the rigid discipline which necessarily arose from the continual
action, hazard and conflict of the service [Royal Navy] in which I was first
engaged . . . [D]angers and difficulties form the best school of maritime
education; and he that has been so employed as to have seen every thing,
and so circumstanced as to despise nothing, cannot fail of rendering service to his country."[19]

Notes

1. John Meares, *Voyages Made in the Years 1788 and 1789, from China to the North West Coast of America* (London: Logographic Press, 1790), 130, 181-82, 185.
2. Ibid., 187-89.
3. Ibid., 191-95, 214-15. Robert Haswell of the sloop *Lady Washington* identified the boatswain as John Green, who was taken aboard ship by the Americans. After Meares had sailed for Hawaii, Captain Kendrick returned the boatswain to Captain William Douglas and the *Iphigenia*. Frederick W. Howay, ed., *Voyages of the "Columbia" to the Northwest Coast, 1787-1790 and 1790-1793* (Boston: Massachusetts Historical Society, 1941; Portland: Oregon Historical Society Press, 1990), 57, 83-84.
4. Meares, *Voyages,* 195-97.
5. Ibid., 195, 199-201. The *Princess Royal,* 50 tons burden, may have been the smallest ship of this era to sail around Cape Horn to the Northwest Coast and across the Pacific Ocean to China. Boston newspapers gave that accolade to the American sloop *Lady Washington,* but she was of 90 tons burden. The *Princess Royal,* under Charles Duncan, in 1788 probably was the first vessel actually to enter the Strait of Juan de Fuca. See also, Barry M. Gough, *The Northwest Coast: British Navigation, Trade, and Discoveries to 1812* (Vancouver: University of British Columbia Press, 1992), 93-94.
6. Today, Meares Island is a Canadian national archaeological and historical site and the focus of a land use controversy between timber interests and environmentalists. Here in 1791-92, Captain Robert Gray established his winter quarters called "Fort Defi-ance" and built the sloop *Adventure.* It was the second ship constructed on the coast—the first being, of course, Meares' *North West America* built in 1788. The location of the Americans' Fort Defiance was not discovered until 1966, when Kenneth Gibson of Tofino, B.C., after years of research, uncovered bricks and other evidence such as charcoal and a depression used as a slipway. Gibson described the site as "a deserted little cove overgrown with cedar trees . . . about two-thirds of the way up the eastern

shore of Lemmens Inlet in Adventure Cove on Meares Island, approximately five miles northeast of Tofino." The discovery was confirmed in the same year by historian Edmund Hayes, later president of the Oregon Historical Society, and in 1968 by a team from the University of Victoria. A contemporary artist's depiction of the *Adventure* while under construction aided Gibson in determining the site in Adventure Cove where the sloop was built. George Davidson, ship's painter on the *Columbia Rediviva*, rendered the sketch. It appears in color in Thomas Vaughan and Bill Holm, *Soft Gold: The Fur Trade and Cultural Exchanges on the Northwest Coast of America* (Portland: Oregon Historical Society Press, 1982), 213, and in black and white in J. Richard Nokes, *Columbia's River: The Voyages of Robert Gray 1787-1793* (Tacoma: Washington State Historical Society, 1991), 166. See also *BC Studies,* 4 (Spring 1970), and 16 (Winter 1972-73), and Edmund Hayes, "Gray's Adventure Cove," *Oregon Historical Quarterly* 68 (1967): 101-10.

7. Meares, *Voyages,* 202-06.
8. Ibid., 207-08. According to the *Iphigenia's* log for August 17, 1788: "N.W. a strong gale. At 7 A.M. Captain Meares came off in a canoe, with some of the natives, and piloted us into Friendly Cove, where we remained till the 27th October"; "Appendix, Table VII," in Ibid.
9. Ibid., 208-09.
10. Ibid., 211-12.
11. Ibid., 213.
12. Ibid., 213-14, 216-17.
13. Nokes, *Columbia's River,* 71-72; Meares, *Voyages,* 219-20.
14. Nokes, *Columbia's River,* 74.
15. Ibid., 75; Howay, *Voyages of the "Columbia,"* 50.
16. Meares, *Voyages,* 220. According to Robert Haswell's log of the sloop *Lady Washington,* for September 16, 1788 (original in the Massachusetts Historical Society library): "we found riding here the *Fillis Adventurer* John Mears and the *Efagenia Nubiana* Wm Douglas Commanders fitted from Macao in China and under Portogees Coulers"; Howay, *Voyages of the "Columbia,"* 48. Howay notes these ships actually were British masquerading under the Portuguese flag "to evade the South Sea company's monopoly"; Frederick W. Howay, ed., *The Dixon-Meares Controversy* (Toronto: Ryerson Press, 1929), 5-6.
17. David O. Miller, "'Kaiana, the Once Famous 'Prince of Kauai,'" *Hawaiian Journal of History* 22 (1988): 7; Meares, *Voyages,* 220-23.
18. Meares, *Voyages,* 224-5.
19. Ibid., 222.

"Callicum and Maquilla. Chiefs of Nootka Sound," in Meares, *Voyages* (1790).

Chapter Nine

A Question of Cannibalism

S EA CAPTAINS of this pioneering era were not experts on ethnology, but most of them provided some appraisal of the natives they encountered on the Northwest Coast. Meares, in particular, took time out in the account of his adventures to comment on the life, habitat and customs of those he contacted. Like other mariners, he portrayed the native inhabitants as strong, resourceful and clever, but also often unclean and unattractive, at least according to European standards. But he admired the beauties and bounties of their land.

In reference to the central Oregon coast, he wrote: "To the Southward of 45° there must be one of the most pleasant climates in the world." Regarding "the district of Nootka," Meares explained that winter, which extends from November to March, "generally sets in with rain and hard gales from the South East . . . but it very seldom happens that there is any frost till January, when it is so slight as very rarely to prevent the inhabitants from navigating the Sound in their canoes. The small coves and rivulets are generally frozen . . . The winter extends only from November to March, when the ground is covered with snow, which disappears from off the lower lands in April." This benign winter weather was in sharp contrast to the severe cold and deep snow he and his crew experienced in Prince William Sound in 1786-87. He regarded April and May as spring months with June being the time wild fruits had ripened.

"There are several harbours in the district of Nootka, which are capable of receiving, into perfect security, shipping of the largest burthen. King George's Sound [Nootka Sound] is an absolute collection of harbours and coves, which are sheltered from the violence of all winds. Port Cox [Clayoquot] and Port Effingham [in Barkley Sound] are of the first kind for capaciousness and safety." He conjectured that farther north "there are

sounds and harbours equal to any which have been already described."
Meares thought it remarkable that "during the whole length of our coasting voyage, we did not meet with a single river of magnitude." That is
because, of course, he had failed to sight the Columbia when he sailed
across its very mouth.

He enumerated the edible abundance of nature "on the rocky islands,
and in the woods": strawberries, black currants, raspberries, small red berries like a currant (probably red coastal huckleberries) gooseberries, black-
berries (red and white), leeks, succulent roots, nettle tops, wild wheat or
goose grass, plus roses, and sweet briar "which perfumed the air." He described the vast virgin forests which grew to the water's edge as containing
"black and white spruce, with the pine and cypress [cedar]; and a great
variety with whose form and foliage we were wholly unacquainted."[1]

For personal adornment the natives used red ochre to paint their faces.
Also, their bodies often were daubed with black pigment. "Over the latter
they strew a glittering sand . . . our sailors, at first, took it for gold." The
glitter came from whitish rocks in the bed of rivulets which when pulverized to
a powder "formed the proudest ornament of the Nootkan inhabitants."[2]

For the most part, Meares thought the Nootka natives were "robust
and well proportioned . . . and they have, generally, very fine teeth, and of
the most brilliant whiteness." But he said the limbs of the men "though
stout and athletic, are crooked and ill-shaped." He observed that some of
the native women, normally of dark skin and painted, attained "the fair
complexion of Europe" when they were scrubbed clean. He felt a few had
"features that would have attracted notice for their delicacy and beauty, in
those parts of the world where the qualities of the human form are best
understood." Generally, he thought the women more calculated "to disgust than to charm an European beholder," largely due to their facial painting and other decoration, and the unclean living conditions. He noted,
however, the women of Nootka were "reserved and chaste; and examples
of loose and immodest conduct were very rare among them. There were
women in Saint George's [King George's] Sound, whom no offers could
tempt to meretricious submission."

The men generally wore sea otter skins or garments made from cedar
bark, with bear and other skins sometimes used. "The otter vestment is
composed of two large skins sewed on one side, which form a covering
from the neck to the ancles [sic]; it passes under the left arm, and is tied
over the right shoulder by a leathern thong fastened to the skins, leaving
both arms entirely free from any kind of restraint. This garment . . . wants

nothing but cleanliness to make it a vestment of the most pleasing description." During ceremonial occasions, their entire bodies were daubed with red ochre giving them a reddish hue. When they were dressed for war, "black is a prevalent colour, laid on in streaks, on a white ground." Sometimes they were painted all white or a bright red, sprinkled with glittering sand.

The cedar-bark hat "which they use as a covering for their head, is of a conic form, made of matting . . . ornamented with painted representations of birds and other animals." Men and women wore the same type of hat; the women did not wear otter skins or other furs as did the men, but were well covered with garments made from the inner bark of trees: "Their dresses are made of mats . . . in the form of a shift, without sleeves, which falls down to the ancle [*sic*]."[3]

Meares estimated there were 3,000-4,000 inhabitants in King George's Sound, with 2,000 of them at Yuquot (Friendly Cove) and the remainder in two other villages. Eight additional Nootka villages were situated to the north and south of the sound, but the total of Maquinna's subjects did "not amount to more than ten thousand people;—a very small number indeed to occupy so large a space of country;—but the frequent wars which harass these little states, and the fierceness of battle among cannibal nations, are sufficient to satisfy us concerning the stagnant population of these people."

The other principal chief on Vancouver Island, Wicananish, "lives in a state of magnificence much superior to any of his neighbours, and [was] both loved and dreaded by the other chiefs," such as Maquinna, Detooche and Hanna. He ruled over about 13,000 people: "in Port Cox, four thousand; to the Southward of Port Cox to Port Effingham . . . two thousand; and in the other villages which are situated as far as the mouth of the Straits of John de Fuca, on the Northern side there might be about seven thousand." Meares said "the subjects of Wicananish are a bold, daring people, extremely athletic, and superior in every respect to those of King George's Sound; and, at the same time, not so savage as those of Tatooche," the chief who resided across the Strait of Juan de Fuca (on the island that today bears his name, Tatoosh Island). Meares noted that the Nootka nations were in a constant state of wariness or hostility not only with distant tribes "but even among themselves; particularly" between Wicananish and Tatoosh, the leader of an estimated 5,000 people on the northwest Olympic Peninsula.[4]

As did other mariners, Meares noted that many Northwest natives bound the heads of infants to flatten the skull and make them more attractive as adults in Chinookan society. Meares wrote: "we never observed that any of the infants in such a state of preparation for sugar-loaf heads, suffered any visible pain or inconvenience." Facial hair on the men was light, and hairs were plucked making them beardless until their advanced years when this practice sometimes ceased. Meares also noted the use of the labret, a bone or wooden piece that was inserted into the lip.

When describing the occupations of the Nootka men, Meares noted: "Fishing, and hunting the land or larger marine animals . . . form their principal employments . . . [F]ishing for ordinary sustenance is carried on by slaves, or the lower class of people:—While the more noble occupation of killing the whale and hunting the sea-otter, is followed by none but the chiefs and warriors." In his account, Meares discussed the natives' skill in hunting whales and in taking the wily sea otter and seals, an even more difficult and time-consuming task. He also fully described their canoe-building skills, while regretting that "we had no opportunity of seeing them construct one of their enormous houses." Meares concluded, "the ingenuity of these people in all the different arts that is necessary to their support and their pleasure, is [a] matter of just admiration to the more cultivated parts of the world."

For women, in addition to preparing food, "it is their department to clean the sea-otter skins . . . and it is among their duties to keep watch during the night, in order to alarm the men in case of any sudden incursion of an enemy . . . [Garments] made from the bark of trees, are of female manufacture. They also collect the wild fruits and esculent plants that are found in the woods, or take the shell-fish . . . When the canoes return from their little voyages, they are employed in unloading them of their cargoes, hauling them on the beach, and covering them with branches of the pine . . . On all these occasions, however, the female slaves take a proportionable share of the labour. They have also their conjugal and maternal duties; nor shall we be so unjust as not to mention that the women of Nootka are tender mothers and affectionate wives: indeed we have beheld instances of fondness . . . which mark the influence of those sensibilities that form the chief honour of the female character among the polished nations of the globe."[5]

In their domestic life, "they were . . . affable to each other; and they seemed to entertain something like a very correct notion of right and wrong . . . [I]n their demeanour to each other, we frequently saw those attentions, and discovered those friendly dispositions which leave no doubt as to the amiable qualities they posses [*sic*]." With exceptions, Meares found the Nootka natives to be of friendly disposition toward the white men, but "on the other hand, their sanguinary appetites and cannibal propensities were but too evident; so that we were divided between our regard and abhorrence of the Nootkan people." Callicum and Hanna told Meares and his men that they did not eat human flesh; "at the same time they acknowledged it existed among them [the Nootka], and that Maquilla was so much attached to this detestable banquet, as to kill a slave every moon, to gratify his unnatural appetite."

The two chiefs continued "with every look and expression of abhorrence" in telling Meares that on ceremonial occasions, during dancing and singing around a blazing fire, Maquinna while blindfolded would chase a group of slaves, eventually seizing one of them. "Death instantly follows,—the devoted carcass is immediately cut in pieces, and its reeking portions distributed to the guests: when an universal shout of those who have escaped, declares the joy of their deliverance." Meares initially suspected the validity of this story, feeling it was an attempt to discredit Maquinna and noting that Callicum's pillow was filled with skulls (which perchance were those of relatives or war trophies). However, several "natives assured us that he [Callicum] was an honourable exception to the general disposition of the Nootkan people to human flesh."[6] Meares' description about the ceremonial killing of a slave is similar to an account on the last page of a journal kept by John Box Hoskins, clerk of Robert Gray's ship *Columbia Rediviva*.[7]

Meares said Maquinna himself had confirmed that he consumed human flesh. After Maquinna accidentally cut himself in coming aboard ship and sucked blood from the wound, he licked his lips and patted his stomach, "exclaiming *cloosh, cloosh;* or good, good," and admitted that "a very short time before, the ceremony of killing and eating a slave had taken place even in Friendly Cove." Meares claimed he frightened Maquinna into pledging to abandon the barbarous practice.[8]

Robert Haswell and James Strange specifically state they saw acts of cannibalism. Haswell wrote in his log: "Thes people [Nootkans] are canables and eat the flesh of their vanqushed enemies and frequently of their slaves who they kill in Cool blud[.] they make but little serimoney in owning the fact and I have seen them eat human flesh Myself."[9] Nevertheless, the opinion of historians tilts toward the belief that the natives sacrificed slaves on ceremonial occasions, but did not regularly consume the flesh of unfortunate captives.[10]

THE BRITISH CAPTAIN AND THE NOOTKA WARRIOR

Captain James Strange, commander of one of the earliest expeditions to the Northwest Coast, provides considerable detail about cannibalism among Nootka Sound natives in his account of the voyage that began at Bombay on December 8, 1785, and ended at Madras in May 1787.

In July 1786 while in Nootka harbor, Strange became curious as to the natives' attempts to trade human heads and hands to his crewmen, which also had occurred "when Captain Cook was here." On one occasion when ashore, Strange encountered a famous warrior, Clamata, bearing a basket who approached with an offer to sell a head and hands. Strange avows in his narrative that he was appalled, but decided to show interest. He inquired about what use could be made of them.

Clamata replied, *"they were good to eat"* [Strange's emphasis].

Strange continued, "I seemed to discredit the assertion, with a View to urge him to the commission of that act . . . My hero' now gave me occular demonstration, & very composedly put one of the hands in his mouth, & stripping it through his teeth, tore off a considerable piece of the flesh, which he immediately devoured, with much apparent relish . . . I could not help expressing horror & Detestation at the Act. He immediately comprehended my meaning, & endeavoured to reconcile me to the deed, by assuring me that if I died, or if my Friend, or his Friend Died, he would not Eat us; But the hand he had then Eaten was the hand of his Enemy, whom he had killed in War, & that the Eating of it was a deed acceptable in the Eyes of Heaven, to which he at the same time pointed."

The English captain further remarked: "This kind of Traffic was always Carried on with seeming secrecy, and an apparent fear of being Detected by their Own Countrymen" who might consider the practice "dishonorable." Or, he said, this "secrecy" might be "assum'd with a View thereby to enhance in our Eyes the Value of the goods; For I should observe, they were never purchased, but at [a] most exorbitant rate."

Strange was the commodore of two trading vessels, the *Captain Cook* and the *Experiment,* captained by Henry Laurie and John Guise, respectively, and financed by David Scott of Bombay and others. This early fur-trading enterprise was inspired by the recent publication of accounts from the Cook expedition. Strange considered the commercial aspects of his venture a failure, but thought the voyage provided valuable information for the future development of trade between the Northwest Coast and China. Strange did not attempt a subsequent expedition himself, possibly because the first attempt was not profitable.

[A.V. Venkatarama Ayyar (curator, Madras Record Office), intro. and ed., *James Strange's Journal and Narrative of the Commercial Expedition from Bombay to the North-west Coast of America: Together with a Chart Showing the Tract of the Expedition* (Madras: Government Press, 1929), 27.]

The Hawaiian prince, Kaiana, however, did believe the Northwest natives were cannibals. According to Meares, Kaiana detested this custom and remarked that Sandwich Islanders "may immolate human beings on the altars of their deity, [but] they have not the least idea of making such a sacrifice to their own appetites."[11] (It seems unlikely these were actually the words spoken by a Hawaiian native, but no doubt they were Kaiana's sentiments as recorded by Meares.)

Shortly after Meares bid a final farewell to Nootka Sound late on September 24, the *Felice* and its crew encountered another of the maritime dangers common to this era. On the first evening, September 24-25, the *Felice* labored in a storm of "great violence, accompanied by a very heavy, mountainous sea." Shortly, she sprang a leak and took on water at a fast rate. Four feet flowed into the hold by 4 a.m. when Meares first received the alarm, and the water continued increasing in depth. When the pumps choked on the ship's small-sized ballast, the crew had to bail water by hand through the hatchways while the carpenters frantically tried to repair the pumps, which proved unsuccessful. Meares finally brought the ship to, and the crew with hatchets and axes attacked the spars and booms on deck, jettisoning them overboard. The great weight of timber stored on deck for the China trade had caused the *Felice*'s seams to open up as she rolled and pitched in the heavy seas. To everyone's relief, this action "almost instantaneously felt a good effect . . . [The ship] became light and buoyant, and we pursued our course with renewed spirits and confidence . . . without the intervention of any occurrence worth relating."[12]

On October 17, 1788, the men of the *Felice Adventurer* after a voyage of 2,000 nautical miles across the Pacific, sighted the island of Hawaii. The blackness, fogs and vapors of the great shield volcano, Mauna Kea, cast a gloom over the island belying its paradise-like nature. On the morning of October 18, Meares dropped anchor in the harbor of "Toe-yah-yah Bay" (Kawaihae); and now, in much brighter prospects, the great mountain presented itself as "a sublime object of nature." Among Meares' crew were several Chinese, the first of their countrymen to visit the Hawaiian Islands. (Soon, more Chinese would arrive in the islands aboard the *Iphigenia* and *North West America*. In 1788-89, it is believed at least one of Meares' and Douglas' Chinese jumped ship and remained ashore. In 1794, Captain George Vancouver identified one Chinese residing on the island of

Hawaii as well as several Europeans who also had decided to settle permanently in this mid-Pacific paradise.)[13]

No sooner had the *Felice* anchored than numerous natives in canoes came out with hogs, pigs, taro root, plantains, sugar cane and a few fowls. Meares purchased upwards of 400 hogs and quantities of vegetables. (He later planned to acquire large amounts of yams at Niihau.) The ship's decks were loaded with the animals. Most of the hogs were slaughtered and salted to insure provisions for the long voyage to the China Coast. The remainder was spared to provide fresh meat. Some mariners of the time said Hawaiian porkers did not weather rough seas well and would quickly perish.

Meares sought information on what his protege, Kaiana, could expect when he returned with Douglas in a few weeks. Among the Hawaiians swarming out to the ship, "only one person of rank" appeared. According to the man's information, old "Tereeobeo," who had been chief when Meares last called, had been poisoned and his successor was Kaiana's uncle, "Titeeree" (Kahekili) of Maui. A "very fierce war" then had resulted between the two islands of Hawaii and Maui. Meares told his informant to advise the new chief that Kaiana would return soon, and in hope of assuring Kaiana a friendly reception, Meares arranged to send along several presents to the new reigning sovereign.

By the end of the day, Meares wished to set course for Atooi (Kauai) to inform the natives there about Kaiana's impending return, but while in anchorage off Hawaii "the number of the natives, and the women in particular, were so great, not only covering the decks, where there was any room, but even clinging to the rigging, that we were under the necessity of bribing them with presents . . . to procure their departure. Some of the women took to their canoes, but the greater part plunged into the sea, and swam to the shore."

The *Felice* next anchored in Waimea Bay on Kauai on October 23, having "no other motive for stopping here but to inform Taheo, the sovereign of it, that . . . Tianna would shortly return." No canoes appeared that day and Meares at first thought strong winds prevented them from being launched from shore. The next day, only two men and a girl in a canoe dared to come out to the ship in the rough seas. On coming aboard, the men suddenly embraced Meares' knees while crying out "*Noota, Noota*" and burst into tears as they inquired about Kaiana. Meares learned that the old ruler, "Taheo," was growing infirm and a regent, "Abinui," was, in effect, the ruler of Kaiana's home island. Most alarming, Meares understood the new headman was a foe of Kaiana and threatened "him with instant death" should he return. Civil strife also threatened between other relations of Kaiana and the new ruler.

Meares noted that while in Macao: "We had been informed by one of the vessels which had returned to China from the Sandwich Islands, subsequent to us, that Tianna's brother, Taheo [Kaeo-ku-lani], sovereign of Atooi was become so fearful of the power he might acquire from us, as to meditate his destruction; and that, in all probability, some secret attempt would be made on his arrival to cut him off."

Meares now realized that the new regent was prohibiting canoes (a "taboo") from coming out to the *Felice*. From their anchorage, the *Felice's* crew knew they were being watched and could hear "conchs resounding from the distant hills,—a certain prelude of war." Meares may have been confused about the actual family relationships of the various feuding chiefs, but the warning that Kaiana's life might be in danger because of jealousy of the "mana" (power) he would receive while among white men was apt.

There was no way, of course, to communicate this foreboding information directly to Kaiana and Captain Douglas on the Northwest Coast. In regards to the brave threesome who apparently had risked their lives in coming out to the *Felice,* Meares could do naught but ask them to "inform Tianna's wife and brother of the approaching arrival of that chief, who would shortly return in a situation to support them and himself against the unnatural proceedings of their tyrannic brother, and his inhuman minister." Meares gave them gifts for Kaiana's relatives and for themselves, after which "they took an hasty leave, and paddled swiftly to the shore."

By noon on October 25, "when not seeing a single canoe in motion" along Kauai's shore nor receiving any further intelligence from the island, Meares set sail for nearby Oneeheow (Niihau), arriving at 6 p.m. Here, no taboo kept the people of this small islet from the ship: "we were surrounded by a crowd of natives, among whom were many of our old friends, whom we perfectly recollected, so that the ship was shortly filled with visitors of all ages and both sexes." Included in this happy multitude was an "affectionate islander to whom some of our officers had formerly given the well-known, and I may add, honourable appellation of *Friday"* (from the character of that name in Daniel Defoe's famous novel *Robinson Crusoe* published in 1719). The *Felice* took aboard several tons of yams, which would be a substitute for the *Felice's* bread and flour stores, which were depleted. Though yams were not yet in season, Friday's skillful negotiating, persuasion and bribes (with trade items from the *Felice*) had sent islanders to their fields to dig the largest yams that were available.

In *Voyages,* Meares closed his account of the final days of his last visit to Hawaii with touching poignancy as well as concerns for Kaiana's future: "I am really at a loss how to describe the very marked concern, both in words and looks, that the inhabitants of this island expressed, when they were informed of our approaching departure. Friday, however, remained to the last, and with him I entrusted a letter to Captain Douglas . . . which commission he readily undertook, and faithfully performed . . . The subject of this letter was to inform Captain Douglas of the political state of Atooi, and to recommend such arrangements respecting Tianna, as might tend to reinstate him in his rights, or place him where he might be secure from the menaced injuries of his unnatural brother. Nor was Friday forgotten, whose fidelity and attachment were already known to Captain Douglas, who was an officer on board my ship during our first voyage. I now presented that good fellow with such articles as I well knew would afford him the satisfaction he deserved; when, after securing them in his *maro [malo],* which is a cloth that these people wear round their middle, he plunged into the sea; and as he swam towards the shore, from time to time turned his head towards us, and waved one hand, while he buffetted the billows with the other."[14]

With a fair wind and clear skies, the *Felice* put out to sea for China on October 27, 1788. As the *Felice* ran due west along the Tropic of Cancer, often at the rate of more than 50 leagues a day, relatively little worth noting occurred. In the pleasant weather of the early part of the voyage, the crew's "chief occupation . . . was to dry and air the skins; a certain number being every day got up, spread in the sun, and then re-packed in the casks . . . [W]e had the satisfaction to find that very few of these furs were damaged." Meares entered the stormy South China Sea about the first of December. Upon observing the Chinese mainland a few days later, Meares and the crew encountered a multitude of fishing boats, "a sight of the most pleasing novelty to us . . . We passed by many of them; but they are so well acquainted with European shipping of the largest size, that they did not suffer their attention to be in any degree interrupted by so small a vessel as the *Felice.*"[15]

On the evening of December 5, 1788, "we happily anchored in the roads of Macao . . . when an express was immediately forwarded to Canton, to inform our friends of the safe arrival of the *Felice.*" The voyage from the Hawaiian Islands, with 750 sea otter furs in the hold, had occupied 40 days. Meares hoped for a prosperous trade in the ports of Macao and Canton.[16]

Notes

1. John Meares, *Voyages Made in the Years 1788 and 1789, from China to the North West Coast of America* (London: Logographic Press, 1790), 233-38.

2. Meares noted, "Sir Francis Drake speaks of this shining sand in his account of New Albion." Ibid., 247.

3. Ibid., 249-53.

4. Ibid., 229-31, 267.

5. Ibid., 249-50, 258-66.

6. Ibid., 255-56.

7. John Box Hoskins' original narrative is in the holdings of the Massachusetts Historical Society, Boston. A printed version is included in Frederick W. Howay, ed., *Voyages of the "Columbia" to the Northwest Coast, 1787-1790 and 1790-1793* (Boston: Massachusetts Historical Society, 1941; Portland: Oregon Historical Society Press, 1990). See J. Richard Nokes, *Columbia's River: The Voyages of Robert Gray 1787-1793* (Tacoma: Washington State Historical Society, 1991), 321-22n, for comments by John Box Hoskins (from page 104 of Hoskins' original log). Later, the Spanish also were alarmed about similar accounts regarding the cannibalizing of children and took measures to acquire slave youths from the village; "Captain Kendrick mentioned having been offered a human hand, as well as a chunk of meat from a four-year-old child." For a discussion of these and other credible accounts, see Warren L. Cook, *Flood Tide of Empire: Spain and the Pacific Northwest, 1543-1819* (New Haven, CT, and London: Yale University Press, 1973), 190-91.

8. "We terrified him however into a promise, that no such barbarity should be again practiced by himself, or any others in his territories; and gave him to understand, with the most determined tone and look we could assume, that he himself should not long survive another repetition of it." Meares, *Voyages,* 257.

9. As with the Hoskins narrative, Robert Haswell's logs are in the holdings of the Massachusetts Historical Society, Boston, and published versions can be found in Howay, *Voyages of the "Columbia."* Frederick W. Howay believed, "the established opinion today is that the Indians of the Northwest Coast were not cannibals; and that anything that appeared to be cannibalism was in reality merely formal and a part of some ceremonial. Cook, Ledyard, Meares, Galiano and Valdes, Malaspina, Roquefeuil, and many others entertained the view that these people were cannibals; but not one well authenticated instance of cannibalism has been produced"; Howay, *Voyages of the "Columbia,"* (1941) 66, 66n. Howay, however, did not comment on Robert Haswell's or James Strange's eyewitness accounts. Furthermore, during a feast "Ledyard claims a roasted human arm was produced as part of the fare—a course which the whites did not accept"; Barry M. Gough, *The Northwest Coast: British Navigation, Trade, and Discoveries to 1812* (Vancouver: University of British Columbia Press, 1992), 49.

10. Canadian historian Freeman Tovell in private correspondence said, "The issue of cannibalism among the Nootka, indeed the Northwest Coast, is a tortured one," and quotes Christon I. Archer as having written, "The Indians, especially Maquinna, may simply have wanted to instill fear in their faint-hearted visitors" or may have been making a joke; "Cannibalism in the Early History of the Northwest Coast: Enduring Myths and Neglected Realities," *Canadian Historical Review* 61 (1980): 453-79.

11. Meares, *Voyages,* 210.

12. Ibid., 272-74.

13. Today, 6.2 percent of Hawaii's population claims Chinese ancestry. In 1989, Hawaii celebrated the bi-centennial of the arrival of the first Chinese with special events and fireworks.
14. Meares, *Voyages*, 275-82.
15. Ibid., 282-85.
16. Ibid., 286. At this point in *Voyages,* Meares concludes his personal account of the 1788 trading/exploring venture with these words: "And here I must take leave of the reader, whose kind attention has followed me through this long and various voyage." Captain William Douglas' similar, but shorter, account of the *Iphigenia* follows in *Voyages,* plus detailed tables of the routes of the ships and an extensive appendix of documents, including Meares' *Memorial* to Parliament.

"Tianna, a Prince of Atooi, One of the Sandwich Islands," in Meares, *Voyages* (1790).

Chapter Ten

Kaiana Goes Home

A S SOON AS the fitting-out work was finished on the little schooner *North West America* several weeks after Meares' departure, William Douglas, commanding the *Iphigenia*, ordered all tools and supplies removed from the shore and stowed aboard the two vessels in preparation for sailing. His men tore down the structure Meares' artisans had built on the bank of Friendly Cove and he donated some of the roof planks to John Kendrick of the American ship *Columbia*. Douglas possibly did not know (or did not care) that Meares had promised to turn the building over to the natives.[1] Perhaps this added to Maquinna's distrust of Meares which the chief later expressed to Spanish officials and other traders.

On October 27, 1788, the *Iphigenia* and the *North West America* raised anchors and headed out past Breakers Point (Point Esteban) into the broad Pacific en route to the Sandwich Islands to spend the winter. The voyage proceeded smoothly, though Douglas reported the "scarcity of provisions . . . occasioned a very short allowance."

Douglas' two ships arrived off Maui, December 6, and were greeted by many friendly natives canoeing out from shore with provisions. Kaiana was both hopeful and fearful about returning to the islands, being uncertain about the political situation, his rivals, and whether peace or hostility prevailed. According to Douglas' narrative: "Tianna, whose impatience since the *Iphigenia* left Samboingan, had sometimes broke forth into the violence of anger, and might have been expected, on approaching his native country, to have assumed the shape of the most violent joy, became grave and thoughtful."

As it turned out, the sovereign of Maui, Kahekili, was off visiting elsewhere. However, Kaiana's brother Kaeo-ku-lani (Kaeo), the ruler of Kauai who Meares had believed was infirm, happened to be on Maui. At

Kaiana's request Kaeo-ku-lani came aboard the *Iphigenia,* giving a warm welcome to Kaiana who had been gone for nine months to China and the Northwest Coast on various of Meares' ships. Douglas says "they melted into tears, and almost drew the same from the eyes of those who beheld them." Despite Kaeo's strong display of cordiality, Kaiana was yet fearful of how he might be received on his home island of Kauai and decided to remain aboard the *Iphigenia* as she sailed for Kealakekua Bay on Hawaii.[2]

As the *Iphigenia* and *North West America* proceeded toward "Owhyhee," word of Kaiana's arrival spread through the islands and friends and other relations soon came aboard. Kaiana was so liberally disposed in giving gifts to his relations, reports Douglas, "that if he had not been checked in his generosity, the whole of his treasure would have been at once divided among them." The chief of this district on Hawaii was Kamehameha (known to the mariners as Tome-homy-haw, with variations in spelling), a fierce warrior who was destined to establish the Kingdom of Hawaii over most of the islands in 1795, after many bloody battles with the armies of other island leaders.[3] The king sent Douglas a present, with word that he would visit when the *Iphigenia* anchored in Kealakekua Bay. Great numbers of canoes filled with foodstuffs continued coming out to Douglas' ships to trade.

On December 10, Kamehameha and his entourage came alongside "in a large double canoe, attended by twelve others of the same size, beautifully adorned with feathers." As the king came aboard, the Britons fired a seven gun salute. "After crying over Tianna for a considerable time," Kamehameha gave Douglas a beautiful large fan and two full-length cloaks made from the feathers of the mamo and o'o birds, which today are extinct or almost so. Another cape would be given by the king to Douglas during a later visit that winter. (Five months later at Nootka Sound, Douglas apparently gave Hawaiian cloaks and other Hawaiian mementos to Captain Robert Gray. The Yankee soon passed two cloaks on as a gift to the Spaniard, Martínez, while at sea off Vancouver Island. Shortly afterward, Douglas gave another "long feathered cloak and cap" to Martínez while at anchorage in Nootka Sound.)[4]

Kamehameha "professed the warmest friendship" for Douglas, exchanging names with him which was a custom both in the islands and on the American coast. The captain, however, was worried that the king's forces might attempt to seize Captain Funter's little *North West America.* In firing the *North West America*'s guns in a salute to the king and explaining how she could otherwise defend herself, Douglas made it clear to the island leader that any assault on the small vessel would be costly. When Kaiana told the chief about where and how the vessel was built, Kamehameha requested "that a carpenter might be left at Owhyhee to assist Tianna in" building a similar vessel. This did not happen, but later Douglas had his men mount a small cannon on a double-hull canoe for Kamehameha.

On December 12, the king invited Douglas, Kaiana and Funter ashore, where the captains were ceremonially met by chanting priests and given a feast in the village, while "all the natives were *tabooed* on the occasion . . . confined to their houses." At dusk, the king and his queen returned to the *Iphigenia,* where they considered it "a luxury of no common description to sleep in" Douglas' cot. Two days later, the *North West America* lost her anchor in 30 fathoms of water and had to tie up to the *Iphigenia.* Six native divers made a remarkable attempt to retrieve the anchor. Following a half-hour preparatory ceremony including the consumption of taro root, a chief gave a signal and the men plunged into the sea. Douglas reported four of them remained underwater about five minutes, and the fifth man about a minute longer, but there was no sign of the sixth diver. Finally, after about 7 1/2 minutes, "he was seen near the surface . . .but sinking down again; three of the divers . . . plunged instantly after him, and brought him up, but in a senseless state, and with streams of blood issuing from his mouth and nostrils.—It was some time before he was sufficiently recovered." The anchor was too deep to be recovered, but Douglas rewarded the divers for their efforts.

Meares' *Voyages* states that Douglas and his men were the first Europeans to visit Kealakekua Bay since the famous British navigator James Cook was murdered there in February 1779. (Actually, the *King George* and *Queen Charlotte* had visited there in 1786, and Meares later retracted the claim.) Kealakekua Bay eventually became the principal harbor for traders who paused for recreation and refreshment in the Hawaiian Islands en route between China and the Pacific Northwest. The harbor lies on the southwest coast of the largest island in the Hawaiian chain. Today, a monument to the famous Royal Navy captain stands near the spot where he was killed by the natives, probably largely because the Europeans had worn out their welcome by staying too long and then returning for repairs when one of Cook's ships was damaged in a hurricane. Cook's three voyages of discovery into the wide expanses of the Pacific Ocean proved inspirational for mariners from Britain and other European nations as well as the Americans who followed in the late 18th century.[5]

⚓

During a period of squally weather, Douglas decided to find safer anchorage. On the order to haul up the *Iphigenia*'s anchor on December 19, Douglas' men found the line had been cut. At the moment of this discovery, Kamehameha and his chiefs "secretly quitted the ship and paddled hastily to shore," leaving little doubt about who was to blame for the sabotage. Douglas sent Kaiana to the king with word "that if the anchor was not found, his town should be blown about his ears." Kaiana returned with several swimmers who, repeating the preparatory ceremony, dived to 20 fathoms for up to four minutes and successfully attached a rope to the loose anchor. When Douglas set sail the next day, Kamehameha and several chiefs unabashedly came aboard the *Iphigenia*. Upon saying his final farewell, the king departed "attended by upwards of an hundred canoes."

Kaiana decided to remain on Hawaii. Kamehameha had provided the prince with a royal welcome and promised a large tract of land where, according to Douglas' narrative, "he would live in a state of honour and security, which the reigning distractions and jealousies of the government of Attooi would have denied him."

As Douglas left Owhyhee on December 20, Kaiana took "a most affectionate leave" of the entire crew after frequently entreating Douglas to bring his wife and family from Kauai. The prince's treasures, which included a wide array of tools, fabrics, carpets, China-ware and iron, were distributed among five canoes. As Kaiana left the *Iphigenia* "accompanied by a numerous train of his relations in their respective canoes," the Britons showed their deep respect by firing a seven gun salute in his honor.[6]

Kaiana became one of Kamehameha's important and trusted lieutenants. A warrior with his own army, Kaiana supported Kamehameha in wars with other chiefs. Some years later, the two had a falling out for reasons that are unclear. Some Hawaiian historians believe the great chief became suspicious that Kaiana, a handsome fellow which Kamehameha was not, had become involved with Kamehameha's favorite wife, the beautiful Kaahumanu. Others say this is in error; instead, each became suspicious of the other's loyalty.[7]

Before the rift, Kaiana had brought his wife and family to the Big Island of Hawaii and generally lived a life of luxury with numerous commoners serving as their personal retinue. After supporting Kamehameha loyally in several early battles, Kaiana became conscious he no longer was loved by his chief. He rubbed noses with his wife, who decided to remain loyal to Kamehameha, and departed the monarch's encampment on Molokai.

In the climactic battle on Oahu in May 1795, Kaiana and his warriors had switched sides and fought beside Kalanikupule, chief of Oahu, in a losing cause. Different tales are told about how Kaiana died. The most credible version is that at Nuuanu Pali he was backed up to a rocky wall, fighting valiantly, when an enemy warrior thrust him through with a spear. Another version is that he was killed by a cannonball. Or, he could have been forced over the sheer "pali" (cliff) with other island defenders. Nuuanu Pali today is a popular tourist attraction and guides will advise that bones of those who perished in the famous battle still lie on the rugged slope.

So ended the colorful life of the "Prince of Attooi" who had sailed with Meares in the *Nootka* to China, then with Douglas in the *Iphigenia* to the Pacific Northwest, thence back to his beloved homeland to tell of the wonders he had seen. But now his life was forfeit in a losing cause. He is regarded by some historians as being the most famous Hawaiian among the westerners who visited the islands in those early days. He had seen the world, knew foreigners and could speak some English. He served as Kamehameha's official greeter. For example, he was the first chief to greet Captain George Vancouver in 1792. Vancouver later came to distrust Kaiana.[8]

Some accounts have blamed Kaiana for the capture of the small sloop *Fair American* at Kawaihae Bay on Hawaii in early 1790 and the murder of four of the five-man crew, but this is in error. The instigator was the chief Kameeiamoku who was retaliating for being insulted by Simon Metcalfe, the American captain of the *Eleanora*. Ironically, Simon Metcalfe's son, Thomas, was the captain of the *Eleanora*'s little consort, the *Fair American*, and lost his life in that action.

Associated with the incident was a separate tragedy perpetrated shortly before by the father, Simon Metcalfe, off the island of Maui. The *Eleanora*'s boat was stolen by natives who murdered the sailor standing guard. In response, Metcalfe persuaded the villagers of nearby Olowalu to bring their canoes out to the *Eleanora*, whereupon the crew fired the ship's guns into the assembled multitude killing at least 100. This incident became known as the Olowalu massacre. Four years later, Simon Metcalfe, another son and the entire *Eleanora* crew were murdered by Haidas on the Northwest Coast. In later years Kamehameha successfully used the *Fair American* as a gunboat in his wars with other chiefs. Assisting him were John Young and Isaac Davis (the sole survivor of the *Fair American* attack), sailors from

Metcalfe's ships who had, in effect, been kidnapped by Kamehameha and lived out their lives in the islands as honored citizens.[9]

⚓

After December 21, 1788, when Douglas had left Kamehameha's small fiefdom on Hawaii and proceeded to Maui, the natives again attempted to cut the *Iphigenia's* cable. For this action, Douglas says, "one of them received a very severe correction." Off Oahu, again anchors were cut but retrieved after Douglas threatened the otherwise cordial sovereign that "his town should be laid in ashes." Despite mostly friendly interactions with the islanders, Douglas' narrative reveals some undercurrents of discord and aggression as indicated by the several incidents regarding the anchors.[10]

On their arrival at Kauai, Douglas and Funter learned that Kaeo and his retinue had retreated inland "dreading the effects of Tianna's anger, who, they had been informed, was on board one of the vessels, and had tabooed every thing on shore." Three days later, Kaeo returned to the bay after a messenger told him Kaiana was staying on Owhyhee. Several canoes came out to the ships with provisions, but the islanders demanded exorbitant prices (word of which also soon passed to nearby Oahu when the Britons returned there to get more foodstuffs). Douglas claimed this situation arose primarily at the prompting "of a boy, whose name was Samuel Hitchcock, who had run away from Captain Colnett" and became "a great favorite with Taheo himself."

Thus, it is in Douglas' narrative that mention is made of possibly the first permanent white resident of Kauai and the Sandwich Islands. Douglas relates that the young Samuel Hitchcock was such a favorite of the regent that when a native stole the boy's "maro" (malo, loincloth), the chief ordered the culprit captured in the mountains where he had fled. The man's "eyes were torn from their sockets, a pahoo [dagger] was then driven through his heart, and his flesh stripped from the bones, as a bait for sharks." Though cordial relations developed with Kaeo, Douglas was warned to be aware that a poisonous powder might be being sprinkled about the ship, on clothes, or provisions. Though Douglas doubted that the natives would do this, he took preventive measures. The alarm proved false.

When Douglas next returned to Oahu, the inhabitants demanded powder and shot, an indication of the hostility existing among the island sovereigns. Arriving at Hawaii a second time, Douglas had a friendly reunion with Kaiana and Kamehameha. Here, Douglas was informed that

Titeeree (Kahekili) "the sovereign of Mowee, Ranai, Morotoi, and Woahoo" had joined with the king Taheo (Kaeo) of Kauai and a chieftain on the weather-side of Hawaii in a pact against Kamehameha and his headmen, including Kaiana. Furthermore, Kaeo reportedly "had been furnished by the Captains Portlock, Dixon, &c. with a quantity of arms and ammunition, on an express condition that he would not afford any supplies whatever to Captain Meares and his associates." (This statement by Douglas irked George Dixon, further prompting him in London's pamphleteer war following the publication of Meares' *Voyages* in 1790.) At the chieftain's request, Douglas supplied the king and Kaiana with firearms and ammunition, and ordered a carpenter to mount a swivel gun on one of Kamehameha's largest canoes.

Douglas returned to Oahu again for wood and provisions, and then to Kauai for water. Mutiny broke out among some of the crew, probably at the realization that they would soon leave this mid-ocean paradise. Mr. Viana, the titular Portuguese captain of the expedition, broke up a knife fight between sailors while ashore and took them aboard ship. When Douglas ordered punishment for one of the men, named Jones, the accused shouted out "the most horrid execrations" and ran for the fore-top where loaded blunderblusses were kept in case of an attack. Douglas "fired a pistol over his head, and threatened him with a second discharge if he proceeded another step." It became evident several other crew members supported Jones' mutinous actions. Jones was given the choice of either punishment or immediate banishment ashore. He chose the latter and probably became one of a group of foreigners who lived in the islands.

In heading for Niihau that evening and the next day, Douglas and his officers were alert to other mutinous plans, but, regardless, on the night of March 15 the quartermaster and two sailors escaped ashore in native canoes that had come alongside. Supposedly, their desperate plan was to set the *Iphigenia* afire, but they were "prevented in their diabolical enterprise." Friday, the native of Niihau, arranged for the apprehension and return of the two seamen, "but the quarter-master, who was the ringleader in the mischief, could not be brought off on account of the surf, and was therefore left behind," also to join the foreign group.

The *Iphigenia* and the *North West America* had remained in the islands for nearly four months to avoid the winter storms of the Northwest Coast and for "refreshment." As Douglas took on a last load of yams from Niihau, he noted they still lacked some necessary supplies and the *North West America* was without an anchor. Consequently, Douglas thought it best to ignore instructions to head northward, and instead charted a course directly for the North American Coast where he expected to meet with Meares and a ship from China. On March 17, 1789, Douglas set sail for Nootka Sound to begin what he hoped would be a spring and summer of profitable fur-trading.[11]

But a time of crisis lay ahead.

Notes

1. According to a letter from "Robert Gray and Joseph Ingraham to Don Juan Francisco de la Bodega y Quadra" written in 1792: "On the arrival of the *Columbia,* in the year 1788, there was a house, or rather a hut, consisting of rough posts, covered with boards, made by the Indians; but this Captain Douglas pulled to pieces, prior to his sailing for the Sandwich Islands . . . The boards he took on board the *Iphigenia,* and the roof he gave to Captain Kendrick, which was cut up and used as firewood on board the *Columbia*"; Frederick W. Howay, ed., *Voyages of the "Columbia" to the Northwest Coast, 1787-1790 and 1790-1793* (Boston: Massachusetts Historical Society, 1941; Portland: Oregon Historical Society Press, 1990), 476. Kendrick also may have used the boards to help build a chimney on his ship; see Nokes, *Columbia's River,* 79.
2. William Douglas, "Voyage of the *Iphigenia,* Capt. Douglas, from Samboingan, to the North West Coast of America," in John Meares, *Voyages Made in the Years 1788 and 1789, from China to the Northwest Coast of America* (London: Logographic Press, 1790), 334-37.
3. Ibid., 336-37. David O. Miller, "Kaiana, the Once Famous 'Prince of Kauai,'" *Hawaiian Journal of History* 22 (1988): 15; "The indisputable outcome [of the battle of Nuuanu Pali, 1795] was that Kamehameha triumphed . . . By that victory, Kamehameha secured his rule over all the islands from Hawai'i to O'ahu." He was to gain dominion over Kauai by diplomacy at a later date (1809).
4. Douglas, "Voyage of the *Iphigenia,*" 337; "Extract of the Journal of the *Iphigenia,*" Appendix No. XII, [2, 5] in Meares, *Voyages* [also in Meares' *Memorial* to Parliament, April 30, 1790]; and Warren L. Cook, *Flood Tide of Empire: Spain and the Pacific Northwest, 1543-1819* (New Haven, CT, and London: Yale University Press, 1973), 148. During his months in the islands, Douglas received several feather capes and caps and other feathered items. Gray had yet to visit Hawaii and the robes and other Hawaiian souvenirs he presented to Martínez must have come from Captain Douglas. Hundreds of robes, made from the feathers of the mamo and o'o birds primarily, were presented by members of the ali'i (royalty) to early ship captains. The Bishop Museum in Honolulu has preserved a large number; a magnificent golden cloak worn by Kamehameha is on permanent display.
5. James Cook's two ships arrived in Kealakekua Bay on January 17, 1779. Cook was treated as a god (possibly the god Lono). After his two vessels sailed away and then returned for repairs, he was killed in a struggle with natives on the shore when attempting to recover a stolen boat by trying to entice a chief to go aboard the *Resolution* where he would be held hostage. Some historians believe the Lono theory is not credible. The memorial marker to Cook was put in place by Captain George Anson Byron of the HMS *Blonde* in 1825. The present obelisk was erected in 1877, followed by an underwater plaque in 1928 at the sesquicentennial celebration of Cook's arrival

in the islands. Probably more books and articles have been written about Cook and his explorations than any other Pacific mariner.

6. Douglas, "Voyage of the *Iphigenia*," 337-43.
7. Miller, "Kaiana, the Once Famous 'Prince of Kauai,'" 14.
8. Ibid.
9. There are several versions of the tragedies involving the Metcalfes. A recent account appears in Herb Kawainui Kane, *Voyagers* (Bellevue, WA: Whalesong, 1991), 101-02. The first reports appeared in a British publication, and in a Boston newspaper, the *Columbian Centinel*, in 1791. See also Nokes, *Columbia's River,* 110-11, and A.P. Janson, *The Olowalu Massacre and other Hawaiian Tales* (Norfolk Sound, Australia: Island Heritage, 1977).
10. Meares had a similar experience at Niihau in 1787, and fired a four-pound shot over the natives' heads to warn them against trying to steal the *Nootka's* anchor; see F. W. Howay, ed., *The Dixon-Meares Controversy* (Toronto: Ryerson Press, 1929), 40-41, 86-87.
11. Douglas, "Voyage of the *Iphigenia*," 345-58.

"A Young Woman of Queen Charlotte's Islands," in George Dixon,
A Voyage Round the World (1789).

Chapter Eleven

Setting the Stage at Nootka

INSTEAD OF CRUISING to the Aleutians and Alaska as during his first voyage in 1788, Douglas sailed directly from the Sandwich Islands to Nootka Sound. He was anxious to be first on the trading grounds that spring in accordance with Meares' orders. Douglas must have suspected the Americans might have wintered over somewhere on the Northwest Coast. He could not be certain because John Kendrick, commander of the expedition which had sailed from Boston in 1787, had deliberately delayed making a decision on where to stay the winter until after the British ships had left Nootka in the autumn of 1788.

Consequently, Douglas was disappointed, but not completely surprised, to encounter the Yankees when the *Iphigenia* arrived at Friendly Cove on April 20, 1789. He met with Kendrick and his officers who came alongside in a boat and informed Douglas that a few days before the *Columbia Rediviva* had moved to an anchorage eight miles away, in a tributary known today as Kendrick Arm. The sloop *Lady Washington* under Robert Gray was gone on a six-week voyage of trade and discovery to the south (Gray returned three days later, having penetrated 20 or so miles into the Strait of Juan de Fuca and also procuring "about 300 sea otter skins").

Douglas anchored, as in the previous year, near the native village of Yuquot and set the crew "unbending the sails and getting the top-gallant masts and yards down on deck." The next day, April 21, as the men cleared the hold, Douglas recorded sad news: "departed this life Acchon Aching, a seaman; he was delirious from the time of his fall from the cross trees till he died; interred the corpse on shore." This is the first record of an Asian, probably a Chinese, dying and being buried on the Northwest Coast.

Macao and Canton

John Meares and the other traders of this era did not always have an easy time exchanging sea otter pelts for merchandise in the south China ports of Macao and Canton. The process was a complicated one and often vexing. The value of the skins was set solely by the Chinese, and could vary widely. In some seasons the market was closed, and the trader had to leave with his pelts. This happened to James Colnett in 1791. He took his furs to London. John Boit, captain of the sloop *Union,* in 1795, said he received $100 less for a fur than did Robert Gray in 1792.

The brigs, snows and sloops from the Northwest Coast were permitted no nearer to the Canton market than 12 miles downstream at Whampoa. Here the furs were off-loaded and taken by sampans to storage sheds in Canton. Bribes had to be paid to various officials, and especially to the "compradore," a middle man, and the "hoppo," an official from the customs office. Even so, traders found the Chinese officials fair in their appraisal of sea otter and other pelts.

Some agents, such as the American acting consuls, advocated in tough market times that the captains "smuggle" their furs through Macao instead of going through official channels in Canton. Even though the Chinese put dollar values on the pelts, most often the furs were exchanged for goods that would be desirable in London, Boston and New York. Captain Gray of the *Columbia,* for example, brought back casks of tea, porcelains and silk to his home port of Boston, as did Captain Boit.

[Adapted from Thomas Vaughan and Bill Holm, *Soft Gold: The Fur Trade and Cultural Exchanges on the Northwest Coast of America* (Portland: OHS Press, 1982); J. Richard Nokes, *Columbia's River: The Voyages of Robert Gray, 1787-1793* (Tacoma: WSHS, 1991); John Boit, *Log of the Union,* ed. by E. Hayes (Portland: OHS Press, 1981); and Kenneth S. Latourette, *The History of Early Relations between the United States and China, 1784-1844* (New Haven: Yale, 1917).]

On the 24th, a sail was seen in the offing and Captain Robert Funter and the *North West America* arrived at noon after Douglas sent out the longboat, as was customary, to assist the schooner in entering the harbor. Funter and Douglas had separated at sea while sailing from Hawaii. In Friendly Cove, refurbishing of the *Iphigenia* continued aboard ship and ashore, and the little schooner was hauled up on the beach to repair leaks in her hull.[1]

The two captains expected to be joined any day by Meares in the *Felice* in accordance with Meares' plans, and then they would establish a trading post in Nootka Sound and possibly in other Northwest harbors. But unbeknownst to the Britons in Friendly Cove, circumstances in China, India and London had changed. The Portuguese merchant Carvalho, who had been a silent partner of the Meares enterprise, had gone bankrupt and the Portuguese governor of Macao, with whom Carvalho had special favor, had died. As a result, the Meares interests had thrown their lot in with James Colnett and the Etches brothers of London by an agreement dated January 23, 1789.[2] In a quick turnaround, former competitors now were partners, having seen the benefits to all of a combined effort on the Northwest Coast instead of cutthroat rivalry. (Portlock and Dixon had been sailing for Etches' King George's Sound Company in 1787 during their controversial encounter with Meares in Prince William Sound.)

It would be Meares' lot in the new scheme of things to remain in Macao as the directing manager of the new trading enterprise known as the "Associated Merchants Trading to the Northwest Coast of America."[3] In this new arrangement,[4] Meares' ships no longer needed to fly Portuguese flags to escape the wrath of the East India and South Sea companies. The Etches brothers had proper licenses from the two shipping monopolies until 1790 and, moreover, already had other ships engaged in the trade. James Colnett was one of their captains and would be in overall command of the new firm's ships on the Northwest Coast.

The Associated Merchants sold the *Felice* and acquired the two-masted *Argonaut* in Calcutta and put her under the command of Colnett. He also would be in overall charge of the *Princess Royal*, as well as Douglas' *Iphigenia* and Funter's *North West America* when he arrived on the Northwest Coast. The latter two vessels, their captains not knowing of the changed circumstances, still flew Portuguese flags when they arrived in Nootka Sound from Hawaii. The confusion caused by Portuguese flags on ships appearing to be British would complicate the controversy that soon threatened to engulf Europe in war. The *Argonaut* and the *Princess Royal,* sailing from China, would be flying the Union Jack.[5] On the latter vessel, Captain Thomas Hudson now replaced Meares' former competitor in Northwest waters, Captain Charles Duncan.

Meanwhile, at Nootka Sound, as soon as the little *North West America* was repaired, replenished and given an additional two men and a second officer, she sailed under Funter on a trading expedition to the north on April 28. Gray in the *Lady Washington* left two days later. Thus, only Douglas' *Iphigenia* and Kendrick's *Columbia* were present when, to the Britons' and Americans' surprise, a Spanish warship, the *Princesa*, 26 guns, sailed into the sound on May 6 under the command of Estéban José Martínez, an experienced coastal mariner keen to uphold Spanish claims in the North Pacific. Responding to reports of foreign encroachment, he had pledged his life as forfeit should he fail his country on this assigned mission.[6]

Martínez bore orders from the viceroy of New Spain, Manuel Antonio Flores, directing his expedition to prevent the Russians or British from obtaining a foothold at Nootka Sound. In sending warships north, Spain fully intended to protect her claim to the Northwest Coast. As it turned out, the Russians were making no overtures at this time to expand this far south despite rumors to the contrary which officials in Mexico were taking seriously. (Later, Russia did establish outposts in California and Hawaii, but never at Nootka.) However, Great Britain fully intended to pursue a right to trade in the North Pacific.

⚓

Spain's pretension to the eastern Pacific as a private domain dated to the expeditions of Columbus, to Balboa's first sighting of the "Southern Sea" in 1513, to Magellan's discovery of a strait that connected the Atlantic and the Pacific in 1520, and to the discoveries of other Spanish navigators and adventurers over the course of many years. In addition, three papal bulls in 1493 had divided the "New World" between Spain and Portugal, and the Treaty of Tordesillas in 1494 provided for a division between Spain and Portugal of all lands as yet unclaimed by other nations. Other international agreements, such as with the British in the Treaty of Madrid (1670) and the Treaty of Paris (1763), prohibited foreign vessels from entering and trading in Spanish waters in the New World. These factors, Spain believed, entitled her to an exclusive possession of territory and commerce from Cape Horn to Alaska.[7]

Spain soon would make it known that her mariners had explored as far as 55° north. Spanish officials and diplomats would contend that Juan Pérez in the *Santiago* "discovered" Nootka Sound in 1774 while coasting southward (Martínez had been an officer aboard the *Santiago*). The British, however, chafing under Spain's aggressive posture on the seas, would argue that Pérez had not entered the sound, but only anchored briefly off the entrance and did some trading with the natives before sailing away due to adverse tides and weather conditions. James Cook, the British position held, was the real discoverer of Nootka Sound. His expedition not only had entered the inlet in 1778, but spent four weeks there repairing the *Resolution* and *Discovery,* exploring portions of the vast sound, and making cultural observations and establishing good relations with the natives, especially at "Friendly Harbor." Neither nation, to this time, had ceremonially taken possession of the area.[8]

That the natives had lived along the coast thousands of years did not much bother the European claimants. The Russians kept a toehold in Prince William Sound while maintaining their system of trading posts in the Aleutians, Alaska and on the Asian Coast. The Spanish would not be able to attempt to enforce a claim north of 60° in the Russian sphere of interest.

In 1788, Martínez in the *Princesa* and Captain Gonzalo López de Haro in the snow *San Carlos* had scouted northward to Alaska and the Aleutian Islands, meeting with Russian traders and becoming alarmed at the Muscovites' reported plan to expand down the North American Coast. During the voyage, Martínez provoked his crews almost to the point of mutiny. On their return to New Spain, Martínez provided viceroy Flores with the alarming information that Russian traders soon might be extending operations south to Nootka. The Spanish expedition itself, however, had not approached Nootka Sound during the voyage. Despite bad blood between Martínez and López de Haro, the viceroy ordered them to embark at the earliest date in the same vessels to forestall any plans of either the Russians or British to establish a base at Nootka Sound.[9]

⚓

During the first week after the Spanish arrived, Douglas, Kendrick and their British and American officers established cordial relations with Martínez and his command, including several Spanish padres sent to attempt to Christianize the Indians. The padres, captains and officers in turn dined together aboard the *Princesa, Columbia* and *Iphigenia,* and Martínez spent several days on Kendrick's ship anchored several miles away at "Moweena" (on Kendrick Arm). Douglas, who was ill and often bedridden in this period, wrote in his journal on May 8, "waiting with great impatience for the arrival of the *Felice."* The English still expected to see Meares' sail in the offing, but since so much time had now passed Douglas feared some accident might have occurred.

The Spanish, although somewhat suspicious of the Americans, considered them no threat, at least for now. At first Martínez also seemed tolerant of Douglas and the *Iphigenia* in these waters, but his attitude changed with the arrival on May 12 of the *San Carlos*, captained by Gonzalo López de Haro. Possibly the addition of her 16 guns strengthened Martínez's resolve.

On the morning of May 14, Martínez demanded to see Douglas' papers, which were in Portuguese, a language neither Martínez nor Douglas understood. Douglas and Viana were arrested while Spanish officers and 40 or 50 men boarded the *Iphigenia* and hoisted Spanish colors. The Britons' supplies, cannons, trade goods, equipment, the captain's log, papers, charts and most every moveable object were seized by the Spaniards while the British crew was taken aboard the two Spanish warships. The charge: the Britons without license and carrying illegal instructions had violated Spanish sovereignty and illegally entered territory that Spain regarded as her own.

Martínez's interpreters, the Spanish-speaking padres, supposedly advised him that Douglas' papers in Portuguese directed the *Iphigenia* to seize English, Russian or Spanish ships on this coast and bring the captives to Macao for examination as pirates. Martínez expressed horror, but Douglas responded by saying "they had not interpreted the papers right." Douglas told his captors he had read an English version of the papers while in Macao and understood that such action would be authorized only if he were attacked by a ship of another nation, was able to defend himself, and had superiority over them. However, again Martínez's "padries and the clerk read the papers over, and said they had interpreted" correctly. Present with Douglas was the Portuguese "capitan de ruse," Francisco José Viana, but for an unknown reason he did not intervene to clarify the instructions.

Rightly or wrongly, Douglas felt the American Kendrick was privy to and partly an accomplice in some of Martínez's actions against the British. In the days ahead, Douglas continued arguing his case and attempted to be as much of an obstructionist as circumstances would allow in a continual mental chess game with the Spanish commander. On the 15th, Douglas reports, he "was ordered, at ten o'clock at night (although I was very unwell) to turn out, and carry my bed on board the Spanish snow, it both raining and blowing at the time. Here I remained for some time without a soul to speak to." Douglas secretly got word to Maquinna and his chiefs requesting the Indians to warn the *Felice* and *North West America* about the situation should their sails appear in the offing. In turn, the Nootka chief offered to whisk Douglas away in a canoe if the opportunity arose. The British captain chose not to attempt an escape. Meanwhile, the

Indians shifted their village four miles to the north to avoid being drawn into the dispute.

Martínez now put men to work building a military settlement for 200 residents near the Indian village and established "Fort San Miguel" on little Hog Island at the entrance to Nootka Sound to ward off any potentially hostile Russian or English expeditions. Other cannon emplacements were erected at another strategic point by the harbor as well. With due ceremony, Martínez and his men took possession of Nootka Sound for the Spanish empire as Boston, British and Asian mariners looked on.

The British crew was held in two groups on the Spanish vessels and preparations were made for taking half of them to Mexico in irons, which Douglas claimed were being manufactured by Kendrick's American blacksmith. The other half of Douglas' crew eventually would be under British officers aboard the *Iphigenia* with Spanish officers in overall command. Douglas, too, would be sent to San Blas. He complained that Martínez "robbed me of in as gentle a manner as he possibly could, by letting me know he must have my gold watch, my sectant, my stove, and all my charts; likewise all my long feathers, cloaks and caps, that Tianna and his relations presented me with; even my shoes and boots, and very bed cloaths went." Martínez's reply when Douglas protested was "some of those things could be got at Mexico."

By this time, the Spaniards had careened the *Iphigenia* and were expending considerable labor and materials in refitting her, which, as Douglas had claimed, was badly needed after rough service at sea for more than a year. Gradually, Martínez came to the realization that he did not have enough men to sail his prize to San Blas, since Douglas' European and Asian crew steadfastly stood by their captain in refusing to cooperate with their captors nor sail under the Spanish flag. Martínez's own actions had placed him in an untenable situation, and he now needed an alternative plan that would yet meet the purposes of the viceroy's directives.

On the 22nd, the date when the captives were "to proceed instantly to St. Blas," Martínez's interpreter, when reading Douglas' papers again, came up with the understanding that Douglas' orders did indeed call for him to respect the ships of other nations unless he were attacked. Thus, in a surprise turnaround, the interpreters now claimed "the papers very good." Martínez now recanted the arrest orders. He dropped charges against Douglas and several days later released the British seamen and the *Iphigenia*, which, ironically, had been refitted at the Spaniards' expense. On May 24, with American officers as observers, Martínez presented the Scot with a paper to sign stating the British had been well treated. This Douglas refused to do (and he later vehemently denied the validity of Martínez's various claims in the document). At an impasse, however, two days later Douglas felt he had no choice but to sign the document (as well as another similar letter on June 1, of which no translation was provided to the British captain). Martínez stipulated that if the viceroy later ruled the taking of the *Iphigenia* was valid, the firm of the Portuguese merchant Carvalho would pay a proper forfeit.

The pretension that the *Iphigenia* was a Portuguese ship was a thin disguise, as Martínez must have suspected. But Captain Douglas convinced the Spaniard of his honorable intentions. He pleaded that his only desire was to make necessary repairs to the ship and replenish his supplies so he could sail to China. With that assurance, Douglas was allowed to requisition what Martínez thought were only enough supplies, equipment and armaments to allow the *Iphigenia* to reach Hawaii and Macao. Douglas, giving verbal assurances to both the Spanish and Americans he had no intentions of trading along the coast, was allowed to depart on June 1.

With Martínez, Kendrick and other American officers aboard, the *Iphigenia* passed the Hog Island fortification. When Spanish soldiers fired a five gun salute the disgruntled Douglas "begged to be excused" from returning it claiming a shortage of ammunition. After the Spanish and American officers left to go ashore at 3 o'clock, the *Iphigenia* stood to the southwest flying Portuguese colors as though headed for Hawaii and China.

But on June 2 Douglas noted, "having got out of the hands of my enemies . . . [and] knowing it would be a length of time before the Spaniards could have their snow ready which they intended to send to the Northward, and being of opinion they would not permit Captain Kendrick to sail before she was ready, the interval was therefore mine. I had no idea of running for Macao with only between sixty and seventy sea-otter skins which I had on board. My people had been accustomed to short allowance; I therefore gave orders, at midnight to . . . stand away to the Northward." Douglas intended to turn a profit for his proprietors. He also hoped, unsuccessfully as it turned out, to encounter Captain Funter at sea or the consort from China before they fell into Martínez's grasp at Nootka.[10] Though the *North West America* was somewhere to the northward and expected to be returning to Nootka, Douglas missed meeting Funter.

A week later, on June 8, Robert Funter and his small crew of a dozen Britons and Chinese[11] reentered Nootka Sound in the *North West America*.

The little schooner's hull was barely keeping them afloat due to shipworm damage. Out of supplies and having eaten nothing but fish for 20 days, they nevertheless had conducted a successful trade northward to the Queen Charlotte Islands acquiring over 200 sea otter pelts. Two Spanish launches came out to assist them, and upon entering the harbor Funter saw the two Spanish warships instead of the *Iphigenia* or the expected consort from China.

In a progression of events similar to the seizure of Douglas and the *Iphigenia,* Martínez invited Funter and Chief Officer Thomas Barnett aboard one of the warships to dine as guests the first evening. The next day, June 9, Martínez boarded and searched the *North West America*, demanded papers, and seized the ship and arrested the British and Chinese crew on much the same charges as before. The valuable cargo of pelts was unloaded and the crew transferred to the Spanish warships. Martínez intended to keep Meares' little vessel in his possession and use it for trade and exploration. By now, the Spanish captain realized that great profit could be gained in the sea otter trade. The Spaniards beached the *North West America* and carpenters began patching the hull and making other repairs.[12] Never again would she fly the Union Jack. Such was the fate of Meares' little *North West America*, the first vessel built on the Northwest Coast.

In his narrative, Douglas provides details of his cruise to the north and thence to Hawaii and China. After changing course on June 2, the *Iphigenia* proceeded north beyond Vancouver Island and into Hecate Strait between the Queen Charlotte Islands and the North American mainland. This was a region through which Douglas had sailed south the year before. When a heavy fog cleared on the morning of June 6, the crew observed "a great number of sea-otters playing round the ship." Passing considerably northeast of the Queen Charlottes, Douglas entered the eastern part of Dixon Entrance, identified as "Douglas's Entrance" on the maps in *Voyages*. The next day they were at 54° 45', west and north of the present-day Canada/Alaska border. Here they made the first contact with native traders coming out in a canoe, and at 6 p.m. dropped anchor by a village standing on a "high rock" having the appearance of a fort. The British obtained several sea otter pelts at the village which Douglas named Fort Pitt in recognition of the British prime minister, William Pitt. (His father of the same name was prime minister earlier, but is better known in English history as the

Earl of Chatham. British mariners named features on the Northwest Coast for both men.)

On June 8, Douglas hoisted anchor, proceeded westward and by noon was in "Buccleugh's Sound" at 54° 35' north, which Douglas described as having "several arms and branches, some of which take an Easterly direction, and run as far as the eye could reach." The description in *Voyages* fits the southern labyrinth of today's Alaskan panhandle and the Alexander Archipelago, including Prince of Wales Island. Douglas believed correctly that by taking "one or two" of the northerly branches, a vessel could circumnavigate the huge island.

The next day, doubling the southwest end of Prince of Wales Island and its offshore isles, Douglas entered an inlet he called "Port Meares" at 54° 57' north.[13] Douglas claimed it was the best anchorage "he had seen on the coast of America.—The entrance of it is not more than half a mile from shore to shore, off which an island is situated about a mile in circumference; so that a vessel may lay there in a state of security from all winds.—At the bottom of this cove, which is about two miles from the entrance, there is a fine sandy beach." Here, for several days, Douglas obtained furs as well as fish and oil from the natives and was able to do "some necessary repairs to the ship and rigging."

An alarm arose on June 17 when rival chiefs of two villages in the harbor began preparing their men for war over some disagreement. The crew no doubt was relieved when "a very bloody conflict, to all appearance, was prevented, by the interposition of the women, which, after a very loud and angry debate, that lasted upwards of an hour, produced a reconciliation between the hostile parties.—One of the chiefs, attended by his canoes, paddled around the *Iphigenia,* and chaunted a song as an acknowledgment . . . that he had not taken part in the dispute; while the other party were received at the village of their tribe, by the women and children, with the tuneful acclamations of welcome or of triumph."

This was one of several instances noted by early mariners in which women on the Northwest Coast appeared to hold sway over the men. Douglas also tells of an incident in 1788 farther north when a woman in a canoe became enraged at a chief in another canoe. For nearly half an hour, she beat the man with a paddle until Douglas, wanting to put an end to the fray, had a musket fired over their heads. Not deterred, the woman stepped into the humiliated man's canoe and, after speaking at length, cut him across the thigh with a knife. Douglas finally brought the affair to an end. He noted, "not one of the men dared to interfere."

On June 19, they weighed anchor and sailed south across the open-sea expanse of Dixon Entrance arriving after sunset, June 20, at "McIntire's Bay" on the north end of the Queen Charlotte Islands (Graham Island). On June 21, the *Iphigenia* stopped two miles from the village of a chief, "Blakow-Coneehaw," whom Douglas had met the year before. The chief immediately came aboard while 200 villagers "formed a chorus of the most pleasing melody." Blakow-Coneehaw honored the Scottish captain by exchanging names "after the manner of the chiefs of the Sandwich Islands," according to the passage in *Voyages*.

In the evening of June 22, several women warned Douglas "that if he or his crew should fall asleep, all their heads would be cut off, as a plan had been formed by a considerable number of the natives, as soon as the lights were out . . . [they would] make an attempt upon the ship." As predicted, after the ship doused its lanterns a canoe came from behind nearby rocks. The gunner fired a small cannon over the canoe and other sailors discharged several muskets "which drove her back again with the utmost precipitation."

Next morning, Blakow-Coneehaw delivered a long harangue on the beach. When the ship's longboat went ashore to cut wood and fill water casks, "forty men issued from behind a rock" showing a thimble and a few other trifling things they had stolen from the ship. However, realizing the sailors "did not intend to molest them, they gave a very ready and active assistance" in gathering wood and hauling water. The old chief came aboard in ceremonial regalia, which, according to Douglas' curious description, included "four skins of the ermine hanging from each ear, and one from his nose." He told Douglas that the assault the night before had been made by people from another village, and if attempted again they should "be killed as they deserved.—He added, that he had left his house, in order to live along-side the ship, for the purpose of its protection, and that he himself had commanded the women to give that information which they had communicated." The captain and the chief held each other in friendly esteem.

The *Iphigenia* moved anchor across the channel on June 23 to the "great wooden images" of the populous village of "Tartanee" at 54° 18' north, and for several days the crew continued to purchase skins and provisions. Some cultivation was in evidence at Tartanee, particularly in one spot where garden seed had been planted, probably by Captain Gray of the *Lady Washington* who, Douglas noted, "had fallen in with this tribe, and employed his considerate friendship." Douglas added to the garden by planting beans. The natives here showed an affinity for European cooking and frequently refused to trade until they had partaken of a meal on board the *Iphigenia.*

As Douglas steered out of "Cox's Channel," the natives briskly bartered pelts for "coats, jackets, trowsers, pots, kettles, frying-pans, wash-hand basons, and whatever articles of a similar nature" the officers and crew could dispense with. By now, the Britons' small stock of normal trade items was almost depleted. The Indians rejected "chain-plates" which Douglas had ordered made up; the brittle iron broke when the natives tried to work it. Douglas now especially regretted the seizure of much of his trade iron and other goods by Martínez's men at Nootka.

When the *Iphigenia* reached the open sea on June 28, it had been nearly a month since Douglas had left Friendly Cove. After a successful trade in that time and with 760 prime sea otter and other skins now in the hold, he set a course from the Queen Charlottes for Owyhee, not knowing that Meares' *North West America* had been seized and another newly arrived Associated Merchants' ship, the *Princess Royal*, was being detained by the Spaniards.

The *Iphigenia* herself faced a grave threat three weeks later after arrival on July 20 in Kealakekua Bay on the island of Hawaii. Contacts with Kamehameha's people seemed normal enough at first. However, several chiefs with the probable approval of Kamehameha plotted to take the ship. Each chief was assigned to dispatch a ship's officer in a surprise attack, "which being compleated, a signal was to be given for the natives, who lay in their canoes, to get on board, and to throw all that remained alive into the sea.—The vessel was then to have been pulled in pieces, and carried up into the mountains, in order to prevent any suspicions of what had happened."

After the conspirators came on board, Douglas began suspecting mischief upon seeing the chiefs armed and learning that the queen had secretly left the ship. Believing it best not to alert the crew and thus precipitate an incident, Douglas "determined to try a more tranquil method; and, under various pretences, got a pistol from one of the chiefs, and a dagger from another, and being armed himself, he waited with impatience for the arrival of Tianna . . . In a very short time that chief came on aboard." Taking Kaiana into the cabin and locking the door, Douglas demanded information, whereupon "Tianna threw himself upon the floor, in an agony of distress . . . laid the whole blame on the king, and recommended that he should be instantly put to death. Captain Douglas jumped on deck, with a loaded pistol in each hand, which had such an effect on the chiefs, who were assembled there, that they quitted the ship in an instant." Kaiana "with tears and lamentations" said he had refused to participate in the plot and sent a servant to give warning, but the chiefs had watched the man closely preventing him from conveying the message.

The Britons desperately needed provisions and Kamehameha provided "an humiliating apology" blaming his subordinates, and presented gifts including magnificent feather cloaks and helmets. Soon trade was renewed for hogs, fruit and "bass-rope" to replace the ship's cordage which was in a "miserable state." Douglas might have remained longer at Kealakekua had it not been for the plotters among the ali'i. He set sail on July 27 for the other islands after leaving letters for Meares and Funter should either of them arrive at Hawaii.

Douglas reported: "Tome-homy-haw, to the last, intreated forgiveness, and expressed the deepest concern for the alarm which he and his chiefs had occasioned; and Tianna, with all the sensibility of an honest and ingenuous mind, continued to lament it.—Indeed, such was their conduct and behaviour when the moment approached for the *Iphigenia* to depart, that there can be no doubt but that British ships will hereafter find in this island, all the comfort, protection, and friendship which Tome-homy-haw and Tianna may have it in their power to procure them."

The *Iphigenia* anchored on July 28 at Oahu in "Witetee Bay" (Waikiki). Every article of trade being exhausted, the blacksmiths began cutting up rudder chains to exchange for provisions. After cruising to other islands for yams and other foodstuffs, and filling the ship's casks with water from unspoiled streams, the *Iphigenia* raised anchor for a last time in this mid-Pacific paradise and on August 10 took the breeze due west on a course for China.

The voyage toward the setting sun was uneventful and the trade winds held. As was common in this latitude when heading west, the *Iphigenia* sailed straight along the Tropic of Cancer as had Meares in the *Felice* a year earlier. On October 4, 1789, Douglas sighted the Asian coast, and the next day the well-traveled snow "came to an anchor in the roads of Macao."[14]

Much had happened in the year since Douglas last saw Meares at Nootka Sound on September 24, 1788, shortly after the launching of the *North West America* and when Meares set sail for China in the *Felice*. Now, for the first time, Douglas could report to Meares what he regarded as Spanish treachery in Nootka Sound. Though the *Iphigenia* had left Friendly Cove before the other ships arrived and their crews were seized and arrested, Douglas' preliminary account would help set Britain on a course that would become an international crisis. Before long, the American ship *Columbia* would arrive in Macao with later accounts of events at Nootka Sound provided by British officers and sailors who had been released by Martínez.

Notes

1. William Douglas, "Extract of the Journal of the *Iphigenia,*" Appendix No. XII, in John Meares, *Voyages Made in the Years 1788 and 1789, from China to the Northwest Coast of America* (London: Logographic Press, 1790) [also in Meares' *Memorial* to Parliament, April 30, 1790].

2. Warren L. Cook, *Flood Tide of Empire: Spain and the Pacific Northwest, 1543-1819* (New Haven, CT, and London: Yale University Press, 1973), 143-44, 162. "The subsequent union of Meares's Associated Merchants and Etches's King George['s] Sound Company . . . was at once a marriage of convenience and a realization by the rivals that each could profit by the other's advantageous arrangements on either side of the Pacific"; Barry M. Gough, *The Northwest Coast: British Navigation, Trade, and Discoveries to 1812* (Vancouver: University of British Columbia Press, 1992), 95.

3. "Mr. John Etches and captain Mears fortunately meeting at Canton in 1788 . . . agreed to form a joint concern and copartnership . . . John Etches returned to Europe [to handle arrangements from there] . . . Captain Meares was to remain at China, for conducting the commerce and preparing the equipment in that quarter for the American coast, and also for expediting a promising attempt of opening a commercial intercourse with the Japanese islands, and for completing a treaty entered into with Tyana, a prince of the Sandwich islands, who had accompanied captain Mears to China, for the purpose of disposing of the island of Oneehow, and for granting admission to all British ships to those islands"; "Argonaut" [John or Richard C. Etches], *An Authentic Statement of All the Facts Relative to Nootka Sound; Its Discovery, History, Settlement, Trade, and the Probable Advantages To Be Derived from It; In an Address to the King* (London: J. Debrett, 1790), 12-13. The Etches' account was not entirely accurate, particularly in respect to "Tyana."

4. Included among the partners were "John Meares, John Henry Cox, Richard Cadman Etches, John Etches, William Etches, William Fitzhugh, Henry Lane, and Daniel Beale"; Frederick W. Howay, ed., *The Dixon-Meares Controversy* (Toronto: Ryerson Press, 1929), 3.

5. Cook, *Flood Tide of Empire*, 143.

6. "I offer to carry out this commission," he declared, "sacrificing my last breath in the service of God and king if Your Excellency so desires." Martínez to Flores, the viceroy of New Spain, December 5, 1788, quoted in Ibid., 129.

7. Ibid., 46-47, 100, 129-33.

8. Ibid., 63-65; Gough, *The Northwest Coast,* 43-53; and John T. Walbran, *British Columbia Coast Names, 1592-1906* (Ottawa: Government Printing Bureau, 1909), 359. Two silver spoons stolen from Pérez' ship in 1774 were found in native hands by Captain Cook's crew in 1778, which was further proof that the Spanish had been off Nootka Sound four years before. Lt. John Gore, one of Cook's officers, presented the spoons to Sir Joseph Banks, president of the Royal Society, and they subsequently disappeared. According to Walbran: "The sound was discovered and named Nootka,

by Captain James Cook in April, 1778, though the Spaniards unfoundedly claimed priority of discovery in 1774, under the name of San Lorenzo [de Nuca]. . . Cook first named the inlet King George's sound, afterwards changing the name to Nootka under the impression it was the Indian name," which it was not specifically. Because of communication difficulties between the English and the natives (the Mowachaht, or Nuu-cha-nulth) the whites named the sound Nootka, an approximation of a native term meaning "to go around" the harbor or island.

9. Cook, *Flood Tide of Empire*, 129-33.

10. Douglas, "Extract of the Journal of the *Iphigenia*"; Cook, *Flood Tide of Empire*, 151-58; and Gough, *The Northwest Coast*, 127-32. Martínez, while commander at Nootka, held the rank in the Spanish Navy equivalent to lieutenant junior grade.

11. When the *North West America* was launched in September 1788, the crew consisted of "Robert Funter master . . . Peter Henry, Robert Davidson, and John East, quartermasters . . . Thomas Thistlewood [Littlewood], William Graham, and John Clarke, mariners, all subjects of the crown of Great Britain; and also assisting, a native of China, a carpenter, and Assee and Aehaw, mariners of the same country." Before the vessel's seizure by the Spanish, Douglas had added two of his "best men" and second officer Thomas Barnett to the crew. See "Deposition of the Officers and Men of the Schooner *North-West America*," Appendix No. X [also in Meares' *Memorial* to Parliament, April 30, 1790], and Douglas, "Extract of the Journal of the *Iphigenia*," in Meares, *Voyages.*

12. Cook, *Flood Tide of Empire*, 160; and Gough, *The Northwest Coast*, 132-33.

13. Canadian historian Frederick W. Howay attempted to locate Port Meares, so named by Douglas in his journal, in Cordova Bay; see Howay, ed., *The Dixon-Meares Controversy*, 68 fn. 32. This may be incorrect in relation to the latitudes recorded by Douglas. In general, for the month after he left Nootka Sound, Douglas largely confined his fur-trading to the northern parts of the Queen Charlotte Islands, particularly in "Cox's Channel," and also visited the southern Alexander Archipelago where a waterway on the west side of Prince of Wales Island is named Iphigenia Bay for his ship. The *Iphigenia* proceeded as far north as 54° 57' off Prince of Wales Island.

14. William Douglas, "Voyage of the *Iphigenia*, Capt. Douglas, from Samboingan, to the North West Coast of America," in Meares, *Voyages*, 361-72. This concludes Douglas' 88-page account of the years 1788-89. A clue that Meares or his assistant Coombe might have composed Douglas' journal or a part of it in *Voyages* from Douglas' notes is seen in the mention of the letter that Douglas left in Hawaii, which reads: "after having left letters for myself [Meares] and Captain Funter in case either . . . should touch at Owyhee"; Ibid., 371. The journal subsequently refers to Douglas and his ship as "they." On the other hand, the 9-page "Extract of the Journal of the *Iphigenia*," Appendix No. XII, of *Voyages* [also in Meares' *Memorial* to Parliament, April 30, 1790] covering events at Nootka, April 20 to June 2, 1789, appears unchanged from Douglas' hand.

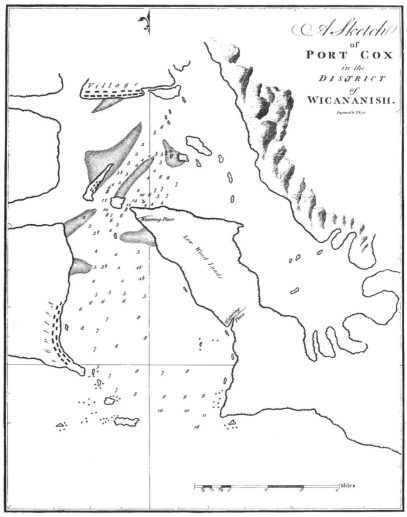

The harbor's name honored John Henry Cox, sponsor and merchant of Canton. In the summer of 1788 Meares concluded a trading agreement with Wicananish, the powerful chieftain of southern Vancouver Island and the Clayoquot Sound region. From Meares, *Voyages* (1790).

Chapter Twelve

The Arrest of James Colnett

WILLIAM DOUGLAS and the *Iphigenia* were sailing on the broad Pacific west toward the Hawaiian Islands when Captain James Colnett, coming from Macao in the *Argonaut*, arrived off the entrance to Nootka Sound on July 2, 1789. Colnett had been preceded by two weeks by Captain Thomas Hudson in the *Princess Royal*, also under Colnett's overall command and on her third trading venture to the Northwest Coast.

Reaching the entrance to the sound at dusk on June 15, Hudson had become alarmed at seeing two strange launches coming out to meet him, and he put the little *Princess Royal* into a state of defense. Surprised to be greeted by Spaniards, Hudson opened a friendly discourse and claimed he was exercising a mariner's right to enter a port to repair and refit his ship after a stormy 116-day voyage. Robert Funter, captain of the *North West America,* came aboard with the Spaniards with word that his ship and the *Iphigenia* had been taken, though the latter had been released.

Hudson's papers appeared in order and the Spanish commodore, Martínez, allowed the pelts he had seized from the *North West America* to be transferred to the *Princess Royal.* He warned Hudson once he left not to return to any harbor south of Prince William's Sound. Hudson then prepared three letters which he hoped would be passed on to Captain Colnett on his arrival. Two of the letters were written with the consent of the Spaniards and each contained a veiled warning about Spanish aggression. A third letter was written in secret to be handed over to Maquinna for conveying to Colnett.

Hudson departed Nootka Sound on July 2, the same day Colnett in the *Argonaut* arrived off-shore. Colnett sighted the *Princess Royal* at a considerable distance in the fog, but did not close with her or make positive identification. The *Princess Royal* traded for sea otter furs on the coast despite Martínez's warning.

At this point, Colnett, was unknowing of the crisis in the sound. However, Robert Duffin, chief mate of the *Argonaut,* later wrote that Chief Comekela (the native who had returned from Macao with Meares in 1788) came out to sea in a canoe to try to convey the fact that British ships had been taken, but Duffin and others conjectured that this activity involved some of Etches' ships, not suspecting Spanish intervention. (Duffin is the source for this assertion.[1])

Unlike the *Iphigenia* and the *North West America* which had displayed the Portuguese flag, the *Argonaut* and the *Princess Royal* flew the Union Jack. As already related, Colnett had become a partner in the new Associated Merchants enterprise formed by the Meares interests and the Etches brothers, who held licenses from the East India and South Sea companies. Meares remained in charge in Macao and Colnett was to command the firm's flotilla of four ships and fulfill Meares' dream of building a permanent headquarters in Nootka Sound and of establishing a trading enterprise between the Northwest Coast and China. This was not to be; the Spaniards saw to that.

With the *Argonaut* becalmed off the entrance, two boats came out of the darkness on July 3 with Martínez and Spanish troops in one and the American, Captain Gray, and several sailors in the other. Martínez was dressed in common clothes and was not immediately recognized as a naval officer. He was greeted with some suspicion when he climbed aboard until his rank was established. Like earlier Britons coming to the sound, Colnett was shocked to meet Spaniards. Though statements would be exchanged between Colnett and Martínez concerning rival Spanish and English rights, all appeared friendly for a time. Colnett brushed aside the first letter from Hudson handed to him by Martínez. The missive contained the warning that "Funter's schooner," the *North West America*, had been "taken" by the Spaniards.[2] The Yankee contingent also tried to tell Colnett about the tense situation, but the British commander accepted Martínez's offer to be towed into the harbor.

In his journal, Colnett maintained that he instructed Chief Mate Duffin to see that the *Argonaut* was anchored near the mouth of the harbor where departure would be easy. He then went below deck for a convivial time with Martínez. To his "Mortification," when he went topside Colnett found his vessel was "in the Centre of the Cove" under the 16 guns of the Spanish packet boat *San Carlos* and was being made fast to the *Columbia* and the Spanish flagship *Princesa*, 26 guns. Colnett had only two swivel guns ready for action; his 12 cannon were stored in the hold.

Colnett then received from Richard Howe, clerk of the American ship *Columbia*, a second letter written by Hudson that again said the Spanish had made a prize of Meares' *North West America*. Colnett still did not take much alarm. He later wrote, "As neither of the letters I receiv'd gave one any apprehension I gave up all thought of Suspicion." He learned later that Hudson gave a third letter with a stronger warning to one of the friendly chiefs which was not at once delivered. Colnett claimed it "would have saved my ship had I received it."[3]

In retrospect, it is difficult to understand Colnett's failure to take alarm from the first two letters. While Hudson's words were cautious for fear of arousing Spanish ire, just the fact he wrote that British vessels had been seized should have warned Colnett to beware Martínez's intentions. He apparently did have some misgivings because early the next morning, Spanish lookouts saw him in a longboat closely examining the harbor and fort. Was he looking for a way to depart? Martínez no doubt feared so when he was awakened and the matter reported to him. But the evening before had gone well between the two as they "drank freely" till late aboard the *Argonaut.*

After breakfasting aboard the *Princesa,* the captains exchanged visits. Colnett offered to share supplies with the Spaniards and consented to transfer a boatswain to Martínez when the latter identified him as a native of Spain (actually, of British-held Gibraltar). The cordiality soon ended. Having previously sent word of his intended immediate departure, Colnett went aboard the Spanish flagship a little later and was greeted by Martínez, a Spanish priest, Spanish officers, and some American officers, possibly Joseph Ingraham and either Kendrick or Gray. Martínez had yet to see Colnett's papers and demanded them. The latter, an officer of the Royal Navy on inactive duty, offered excuses and resisted the order. An argument began escalating and the Americans discreetly departed.[4]

Martínez claimed he had orders from His Catholic Majesty to seize all British ships that he might encounter in waters claimed by Spain. Colnett responded that he had his king's permission to be in these waters with the purpose of founding a colony. Both were stretching the truth. Martínez had orders from the viceroy of New Spain to discourage British and Russian ships that might be encountered in the Nootka area, but no directive to seize them unless attacked. Colnett's authority came only from a lengthy letter of instructions signed by John Meares on behalf of the Associated Merchants.[5]

In a footnote in his published journal, Colnett complained that his first mate, Robert Duffin, had presented to Martínez "a paper in Portuguese which he said signified that he [Duffin] was the proper Captain and after the Vessel was captured he made no secret of declaring in Public he was as much Captain as I was, which was the Sole cause of all our following Misfortunes and detention in the Country." Duffin's papers must have been derived from 1788 when Meares' ships carried Portuguese documents. Here is an instance when Portuguese papers on a British ship added an element of confusion to British and Spanish relations. To compound the communication difficulties, Duffin reported that Martínez's "linguist spoke English very imperfectly."

Colnett claims he placed his own papers on the table and repeatedly entreated Martínez to read them, but Martínez refused to do so with the remark they were forged. According to Martínez's account, Colnett waved a piece of parchment and said it was his passport but did not offer the document for examination.[6]

In the heated argument, Colnett said he intended to sail immediately. Martínez refused to grant permission. Colnett then insisted he would attempt to leave even if the Spanish forced him to strike colors. By this time both men had lost their tempers. According to Martínez, Colnett had slighted the Spanish flag and authority; as the Englishman ranted he placed "his hand two or three times on his sword . . . as if to threaten me in my own cabin," while also calling the Spanish commander a "God damned Spaniard." Another source said it was Martínez "who laid hand on his sword."[7] Martínez ordered Colnett arrested.

Colnett, however, claims Martínez "flew out of the Cabin instantaneously, and unexpectedly three or four Sailors enter'd with muskets. One was presented Cocked to my breast, and another snatched my hanger [sword] from my side, and the third Collared me and Tore my Shirt and Coat. Stocks were ordered to put both legs in; but an Officer that had been in the British navy, but at this time belong'd to the American ship, Advis'd them not to put me in the Stocks. I was confined a close prisoner in the Cabin."[8]

A company of armed Spaniards went aboard the *Argonaut*, captured the crew and raised the banner of Spain on July 3. Colnett complained later that the Spaniards plundered the British ship, taking copper sheets and other goods, supplies and equipment including personal items such as pistols and a fowling piece from the captain's cabin. The charge was similar to that voiced by Douglas concerning his treatment.

The frenzied confrontation eased somewhat at daybreak on July 4 as the *Columbia* began firing a federal salute of 13 guns (for the 13 states) in observance of the thirteenth anniversary of American Independence. The American captains were hosts for a banquet attended by Spanish and American officers, padres, and British officers who no doubt were none too enthusiastic about the celebration. The Spanish fort, the *San Carlos* and the Yankee ships exchanged further cannonades throughout the day. This was the first Fourth of July celebration on the West Coast of America.

Meantime, the confiscated *North West America* had been refitted by the Spaniards at Nootka Sound by June 20. The little schooner, renamed the *Santa Gertrudis la Magna*, remained thereafter in Spanish hands (and shortly was rebuilt again and given another name, *Santa Saturnina).* She proved especially useful for exploring in the shallow bays and intricate waterways of the Northwest Coast. Martínez had sent the *Santa Gertrudis la Magna* south to investigate the Strait of Juan de Fuca, which he claimed to have seen in 1774 while with Pérez. On July 5, the vessel had returned, having confirmed Martínez's observation years earlier.

Colnett became so depressed in early July that he twice tried to commit suicide, saying his life and career were ruined and he would be executed. Once he tried to leap over the *Argonaut*'s gunwale, but was restrained by Spanish sailors and British officers. He later crawled out of his cabin window and splashed into the water, alerting a Spanish launch. He was rescued when someone grasped his hair, then revived by sailors who pumped water from his lungs. During this period his journal is filled with complaints concerning his treatment and that of his men. According to Duffin, Colnett appeared to be in a better state of mind by mid July.

On July 12, Thomas Hudson brought the little *Princess Royal* back from a short but successful trading expedition and attempted to probe the outer reaches of Nootka's entrance without entering to see if the *Argonaut* were there. He thought, correctly, that Colnett had arrived on the same night (July 2) the *Princess Royal* had left Nootka. At dusk Hudson was reconnoitering in a small boat when he was captured. He was forced to surrender his armed and manned vessel in the harbor the next day, July 13, under threat of being hanged. Another British vessel and distraught captain were in Spanish toils.[9] Hudson, recently from Macao, made it known that the Portuguese merchant, Carvalho, had gone bankrupt, which gave

Martínez enough excuse to take the *Princess Royal* as security for payment of the provisions he had provided to Douglas when the *Iphigenia*, supposedly owned by Carvalho, had departed for Macao. A sizable flotilla of two Spanish, two American and three captured British vessels now were anchored in Nootka Sound.

On the afternoon of this same day, another incident occurred that hardened the feelings of the natives against the Spaniards. The friend of the Britons, Chief Callicum, became alarmed at reports given him by *Argonaut* crewmen who were briefly allowed ashore. Callicum came out in a canoe to the *San Carlos* and protested Martínez's actions. Captain López de Haro tried to appease the chief with gifts. Martínez, who happened to be aboard, appeared and seeing Callicum leaving with his wife and child, called him back. Callicum loudly defended the English, and shouted insults at Martínez calling him in Nootkan words, a "rogue" and "thief." Infuriated, the Spaniard grabbed a musket and tried to fire it at Callicum. The gun misfired. A crewman standing nearby fired his musket. The shot killed the chief and his body fell into the water. The murder was perpetrated in full view of Callicum's wife and child. Natives and Europeans alike, including many of the Spaniards, were horrified.[10]

The Spaniards now held captives from three ships. Among the prisoners were numerous British and European sailors and officers, but also included were many Chinese (including 29 who were with Colnett),[11] as well as a scattering of Hawaiians, Lascars, Malays and Filipinos. The captives were relatively well treated with some freedom of movement aboard the various ships and occasionally even ashore. Martínez utilized the skills of the Chinese artisans in construction projects.

On July 14, the *Argonaut,* while flying Spanish colors, sailed on the morning tide for San Blas, Mexico, under commander José Tobar and a Spanish prize crew and with Colnett and other prisoners aboard. The Britons were locked up at night, but allowed freedom during the day. With Tobar went despatches from Martínez to the viceroy explaining his reasons for taking such drastic actions against the British. Basically, Martínez perceived that the British company was trying to establish a colony in what Spain contended was its sovereign territory and he had acted to forestall the plan. (Martínez would detain the *Princess Royal* at Nootka until July 27 when she, too, sailed for Mexico with a prize crew under José María Narváez. Among the prisoners were numerous Chinese. On this voyage, the disarmed *Princess Royal* was escorted by Captain López de Haro in the *San Carlos.*)

The two American ships under Kendrick's command sailed from Nootka on July 15, the day after the *Argonaut* had left for San Blas. Martínez had arranged for Robert Funter's small *North West America* crew to be placed aboard the *Columbia* for transport to China. Shortly, while in Clayoquot Sound, Kendrick passed command of the *Columbia* to Robert Gray and himself took over the *Lady Washington*. Gray, then, would take the *Columbia*'s cargo of pelts and the released Britons to China via the Sandwich Islands, while Kendrick, contrary to Spanish expectations, would trade with natives as he cruised along the Northwest Coast in the smaller *Lady Washington*. The cordial and astute Yankees had got along well with the Spaniards. Their countries had been allies during the American Revolution, and Martínez was far more concerned about a possible Russian threat than a small expedition of American traders in Spanish waters.[12]

Chief Mate Robert Duffin, who was blamed by Colnett for most of the *Argonaut*'s troubles, had secretly written letters intended for Meares describing events in Nootka Sound. Duffin had smuggled the letters and his journal to Thomas Barnett, a released British officer sailing to China on the *Columbia* along with the rest of Funter's crew.

In four months, Gray guided the *Columbia* across the Pacific to Hawaii and then China, arriving November 17, 1789.[13] Duffin's letters as well as other reports from the Britons and possibly the Americans aboard the *Columbia* augmented the information Meares had gleaned from Captain Douglas after the *Iphigenia* had anchored at Macao on October 4, 1789. Until Gray's arrival, Meares knew only about Douglas' encounter with the Spaniards, but now there was alarming news that three Associated Merchants' vessels were in Spanish hands. Duffin's letters and other accounts provided by the *Iphigenia* and the *Columbia* crews would be the primary British documentation that sent the government in London into crisis mode.[14]

Colnett's troubles and complaints continued during the voyage south as a prisoner aboard the *Argonaut* and after reaching San Blas in mid-August 1789. His allegations of misconduct against his captors are contained in his journal and in letters he wrote to the Admiralty, the British ambassador in Madrid and to others. Were Colnett's word to be trusted fully, then the Spaniards were indeed tough captors.

Colnett complained of the terrible conditions the Britons had to suffer en route. He revealed that his second mate, James Hanson, cut his own throat in despair six days after reaching San Blas. Month after month, the extreme heat, humidity and pestilence of the coastal rainy season and the monotony of being confined to San Blas among a hostile population took a toll on their health. Colnett noted that "eight" others, including the chief mate of the *Princess Royal* "and my Boatswain" died when their hopes were dashed after assisting the Spanish in putting copper sheathing on the *Argonaut's* hull in the mistaken belief they soon would be permitted to leave the port. The Spaniards, instead, sailed the *Argonaut* to Acapulco to receive armaments.[15]

Colnett was not one to suffer indignities quietly. He used his quill liberally in complaining to Spanish authorities, even the viceroy, of the ill-treatment he and his men were receiving. He said, "deeming us heretics they thought us entitled to no other treatment than Dogs."[16] Many of his men suffered from fever, as did Colnett, and he suspected the Spaniards preferred for them to die rather than recover.

In mid November, the men were moved 60 miles inland to the more temperate and healthful climate at Tepic. The situation otherwise remained unchanged, except a new viceroy for New Spain, the Conde de Revilla Gigedo, had succeeded Flores in 1789. The new authority disapproved of Martínez's extreme measures and, after receiving Colnett's letters, invited the Briton to come to Mexico City to voice his complaints. Colnett set out by horseback with an escort over the hot, dusty mountains to parley with Spain's chief emissary in the New World. Colnett asserted the long horseback ride caused him to suffer from the piles.

Colnett had some knowledge of Spanish, but the language barrier was too great for an intimate exchange, and the viceroy asked him to put his arguments in writing. Colnett complied, again spelling out his complaints and stating that "quitting your dominions . . . would be great Satisfaction." Revilla Gigedo granted the request, and told Colnett to return to the *Argonaut* and prepare to get under way.[17]

In the negotiations, Colnett asked for, among other things, the return of his "Indian" (an Hawaiian who was a member of his crew). At first Revilla Gigedo said he wanted to have him instructed in the Catholic faith and, anyway, he did not belong to the Briton. But finally the viceroy agreed to release the youth who wanted to go with his shipmates.

Colnett also demanded wages for his men for their time in captivity, and asked that his own salary for the period be computed as for a head of an expedition and not just for his naval rank of lieutenant. Revilla Gigedo agreed to pay the sailors at the rate of Spanish sailors in the Pacific, but denied Colnett's request for higher pay. Instead, Colnett received 218 pesos pending a later settlement of affairs. With those matters settled, Colnett began the long journey back to San Blas.

When Colnett received his crew back on July 9, 1790, he refused to reassign Duffin as chief mate apparently not knowing of Duffin's letters to Meares concerning the capture of the *Argonaut*. He also complained the *Argonaut* had been misused by the Spaniards during the months in San Blas. Some sailors (mainly Portuguese) and a half-dozen or more Chinese who had been brought to San Blas had chosen to remain behind; they eventually were assimilated into Mexican life so far as is known. Other Chinese stayed with Colnett's men.[18]

Under terms of the settlement, the *Princess Royal* (called the *Princesa Real* by the Spaniards) was to be transferred by Captain Manuel Quimper to Colnett and Captain Hudson at Nootka Sound. But Quimper and Colnett had many delays while sailing north, Quimper to explore the Strait of Juan de Fuca and Colnett to acquire skins along the coast. At Bodega Bay, Colnett sent seven men in a longboat to seek furs independently. In a remarkable test of seamanship, these men successfully traded northward and weeks later rendezvoused with the *Argonaut* in the Pacific Northwest. Misfortune struck another detachment: in Clayoquot Sound Colnett despatched a small boat under Hudson to sail to Nootka; all seven men aboard died in an autumn storm. Quimper's survey in the strait was thorough and he and his crew are credited with being the first whites to sail to its end, though he failed to find Puget Sound. Quimper, when he finally arrived off Nootka Sound, was delayed in entering by heavy fog. Because supplies were nearly exhausted, he gave up after six days and sailed south to Monterey. When Colnett finally arrived at Nootka, the *Princesa Real* was nowhere in sight.

When the viceroy learned that the two vessels had missed meeting in Nootka Sound, he ordered Quimper to take the *Princesa Real* to Manila for transfer to her owners in Macao. While en route, Quimper sailed his little charge into Kailua Bay on Oahu in March 1791, where he traded for supplies and received a feather cape from Chief Kamehameha. The chief asked for, and was given, a musket in return. Here, still smarting from his treatment by the Spaniards, Colnett found his missing ship. He brought the *Argonaut* close alongside and ranged his guns as though to open fire. With Juan Kendrick (Captain John Kendrick's son who had joined the

Spanish service while in Nootka Sound) acting as a go-between, the two captains made peace. After reaching Manila, the *Princess Royal* sailed for Macao under a different crew. There, Colnett and his proprietors decided the little ship had been too heavily damaged and refused to accept her.[19] The Spaniards finally sold her in China for 2,000 Spanish dollars.

When Revilla Gigedo earlier had granted Colnett's request to leave Mexico in the *Argonaut*, he had ordered the British captain to desist from further trade on the Northwest Coast. Colnett, however, amassed 1,200 furs that he took to China. By the time he arrived in Macao, Meares already had left for London without knowledge of Colnett's tribulations in captivity. But Colnett sent the information by letter to the Admiralty and various officials.[20] What use, if any, London made of this information during the stormy argument with Spain is not revealed in official British documents in the Public Record Office or the British Library.

Notes

1. "Copies of Letters from Mr. Duffin to Mr. Meares" [July 12, 1789], Appendix No. XIII, in John Meares, *Voyages Made in the Years 1788 and 1789, from China to the Northwest Coast of America* (London: Logographic Press, 1790) [also in Meares' *Memorial* to Parliament, April 30, 1790].
2. Warren L. Cook, *Flood Tide of Empire: Spain and the Pacific Northwest, 1543-1819* (New Haven, CT, and London: Yale University Press, 1973), 161-62, 165-68. In his narrative, Colnett claimed Hudson's letter, which had been left in Spanish hands, gave no inkling of trouble. However, even though Hudson said Colnett would be treated well by Martínez, he did provide a subtle alarm: "Should you go into the Port I am confident the Commodore would order you every assistance in his power as he has done me . . . I am sorry to add that Captain Douglas has left the Coast and Mr. Funter's schooner is taken"; see "Copy of Captain Hudson's Letter, *Princess Royal* off Nootka, 3rd July, 1789," in *The Journal of Captain James Colnett aboard the "Argonaut" from April 26, 1789, to Nov. 3, 1791*, ed. with intro. and notes by Frederick W. Howay (Toronto: Champlain Society, 1940), 55.
3. Ibid., 57.
4. Ibid., 58-59.
5. Cook, *Flood Tide of Empire*, 171-72. For the instructions from "Messrs. Etches, Cox, and Co." to Colnett, see "Copy of a Letter from Mr. Meares to Captain Colnett, Dated 17th April, 1789," Appendix No. II [4 pages], in Meares, *Voyages* [also in Meares' *Memorial* to Parliament, April 30, 1790].
6. Cook, *Flood Tide of Empire*, 171. Colnett claimed the parchment was signed by King George III, but declined to let Martínez read it. Martínez said, "it was imperative that he should show me these papers, as well as the invoice of his cargo, so that I could obtain complete information and comply with my sovereign's orders"; Howay, ed., *The Journal of Captain James Colnett*, 59-60, 311.
7. Cook, *Flood Tide of Empire*, 173n. José Mariano Moziño gathered testimony about this incident in 1792, concluding: "It is likely that the churlish nature of each one

precipitated things up to this point, since those who sailed with both complained of them equally and condemned their uncultivated boorishness."

8. Spanish accounts of the arrest of Colnett are from Martínez's *Diario*, page 86, and other documents. See Cook, *Flood Tide of Empire*, 172-73, for both the Spanish and American descriptions. Colnett's and Martínez's journal accounts are in Howay, ed., *The Journal of Captain James Colnett*, 60, 312.

9. "Copies of Letters from Mr. Duffin to Mr. Meares" [July 12, 13 and 14, 1789], Appendix No. XIII, in Meares, *Voyages* [also in Meares' *Memorial* to Parliament, April 30, 1790]. "Martínez instructed Mondofía to put the English seamen to the sword without quarter if resistance were offered, in which case Colnett and Hudson would also be hanged"; Cook, *Flood Tide of Empire*, 179.

10. Cook, in *Flood Tide of Empire,* 180, states: "The weapon misfired. Another seamen, perceiving the intent, raised his gun and shot." This is how it is presented in Martínez's journal, reproduced in F.W Howay, ed., *The Journal of Captain James Colnett*, 317. However, Howay in his *Voyages of the "Columbia,"* 101n, misquotes Martínez and gives the erroneous impression that Martínez admitted firing the fatal shot. Martínez's diary clearly states he did not. In any event, Martínez was fully responsible for the murder.

11. In his *Memorial* to Parliament, page 4, Meares claimed the *Princess Royal* and the *Argonaut* had aboard "seventy Chinese, who intended to become settlers on the American coast, in the service, and under the protection of the associated company."

12. In October 1789, however, the Spanish seized an American vessel, the *Fair American,* when she entered Nootka Sound. The *Fair American* was captained by 18-year-old Thomas Metcalfe and had a four-man crew. Shortly afterward, the *Eleanora,* captained by the father, Simon Metcalfe, was pursued by, but outran, Spanish ships off Vancouver Island. After the *Fair American* was taken to Mexico and then released by the new viceroy, young Metcalfe sailed to the Sandwich Islands where the small vessel met tragedy at the hands of the Hawaiians in early 1790; Cook, *Flood Tide of Empire,* 191-94, 198.

13. Gray states the *Columbia* arrived in Canton on November 17, 1789; Howay, ed. *Voyages of the "Columbia,"* 129. Meares in his *Memorial* to Parliament claims the *Columbia* arrived on November 2, 1789.

14. Duffin was with Meares on the *Felice* in 1788 and attempted the exploration of the Strait of Juan de Fuca in the ship's launch until attacked by hostile tribesmen. The following documents were included among the considerable reports and accounts gathered by Meares in preparation for presenting his charges against the Spanish government: "Copies of Letters from Mr. Duffin to Mr. Meares" [July 12, 13 and 14, 1789], Douglas' "Extract of the Journal of the *Iphigenia,"* and the "Deposition of the Officers and Men of the Schooner *North-West America*" [sworn to, December 5, 1789, in Canton]. These and other pertinent documents were included by Meares in the appendices of *Voyages,* and in his *Memorial* to Parliament. See also Cook, *Flood Tide of Empire,* 182, 185.

15. Howay, ed., *The Journal of Captain James Colnett,* 73, 75, 322.

16. Ibid., 79-80.

17. Ibid., 97, 102. The viceroy instructed Colnett to return to his ship at San Blas and sail as soon as possible, but to take care "not to trade in establishments or coasts of the Spanish nation."

18. Ibid., 322. It is believed that the Spaniards paid the British sailors at a higher scale than Colnett's rate.

19. For a summary of these events, see "The British Prisoners Released," in Cook, *Flood Tide of Empire,* 289-300. See also, Howay, ed., *The Journal of Captain James Colnett,* 213-15.

20. Colnett averred that he wrote letters, dated May 1, 1790, to the British ambassador in Madrid, his mother, Richard Cadman Etches, and Philip Stephens at the Admiralty protesting Spain's "Piracy and ill Treatment to the Subjects of Great Britain." The letter to the ambassador was sent too late to have been included in Meares' *Memorial* to Parliament. See Howay, ed., *The Journal of Captain James Colnett,* 101, 319-21.

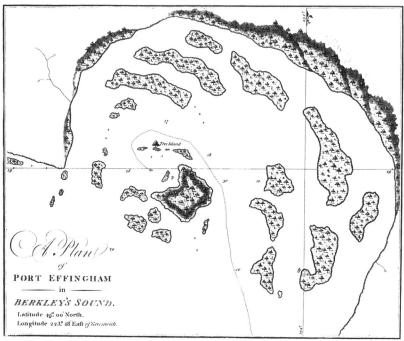

Meares named the port for Thomas Howard, the third Earl of Effingham, Deputy Earl Marshal of England (died November 19, 1791). Mariners named many coastal features after important political figures, financial sponsors and prominent members of society in their home countries. From Meares, *Voyages* (1790).

Chapter Thirteen

Pitt's Pawn: John Meares

T HE CRISIS BETWEEN London and Madrid over the seizure of British vessels in Nootka Sound began before Meares, coming from far-off Macao, had reached his government's offices in Britain. London's first indication that Spain's chief naval representative in Nootka Sound had arrested British sailors and seized "an English" trading ship came in a January 4, 1790, despatch from the British chargé d'affairs in Madrid who learned of the incident from Spanish sources.[1] Shortly Madrid sent an official protest with details about the events on the Northwest Coast.[2] Spain contended British ships had violated Spanish sovereign territory and demanded punishment of the perpetrators and a promise by the British government it would not happen again.

Prime Minister William Pitt (the younger) fired off a testy response on February 26 drafted by Lord Leeds, the secretary of state for foreign affairs. Leeds demanded full information and justification concerning the affair that he deemed was an example of Spanish treachery. Pitt, having long sensed Britain's growing ascendancy on the world scene vis-à-vis the Spanish empire, saw the Nootka incident as an excellent opportunity to undermine the Spanish claim to exclusive sovereignty over the entire Pacific Coast of the Americas. To him, this was more than an insult to the British flag that could be rectified by an apology and the release of British ships and subjects. The solution must at least include equality for ships flying the Union Jack on the sea lanes of the Pacific Ocean and the right to colonize "unoccupied" coasts. In effect, Pitt was trying to establish the principle of freedom of the seas in that part of the world. (The information from Meares when he arrived in London in April 1790 would be invaluable to Pitt and the British crown in the dispute with Spain that would almost lead to war.)

It is obvious Meares was not an eyewitness to the trouble in Nootka Sound. He was in Macao at the time tending to the business of the Associated Merchants' enterprise. The first word about the crisis came with the arrival in Macao of Captain William Douglas in the *Iphigenia* on October 4, 1789, but this information was incomplete. Douglas related how the *Iphigenia* had been detained but then released on condition Douglas would cease trading on the Northwest Coast, a stipulation imposed by the Spanish commandant, Don Estéban José Martínez, which the British captain ignored.[3]

More detailed information followed with the arrival in Macao on November 17, 1789, of the *Columbia Rediviva* under the command of Robert Gray.[4] Aboard the American ship were Captain Robert Funter and the crew of the *North West America*, the little schooner that Meares' men had built in the summer of 1788. The Spaniards had kept the vessel but released the officers and men for transport to China aboard the *Columbia*. Martínez also had sent with Gray 96 sea otter pelts to pay for the passage of the Britons to Macao. The British later maintained that the skins came from 207 pelts taken by the Spaniards from the *North West America*, and that Funter's men were required to stand duty on the *Columbia* en route to China because so many American seamen had been transferred from the *Columbia* to augment the crew of the *Lady Washington* which had remained to trade on the Northwest Coast.[5]

The Britons apprised Meares that the *Princess Royal* under Captain Thomas Hudson also had been threatened and released by the Spaniards. Hudson made the error of returning to Nootka on July 13, 1789, in search of Colnett and had been arrested, his ship seized and later sent to San Blas. The fourth vessel, the *Argonaut,* which was the flagship of the British trading enterprise, had been captured, too, and Captain James Colnett was under arrest. Funter and his men had left Nootka Sound on the *Columbia* the day after Colnett and his crew had departed for San Blas as prisoners aboard their own ship, the *Argonaut.* (Funter, of course, could not know of Colnett's complaints about Spanish ill-treatment of prisoners during the voyage to the Spanish naval base at San Blas and their incarceration there.)

Meares now had the report from Douglas and the testimony of the British officers and men who arrived on the *Columbia*. He also had a journal and several letters (written in secret) from Robert Duffin, Colnett's first mate, concerning Spanish actions. These had been smuggled aboard the *Columbia* by the British officer Thomas Barnett for delivery to Meares.[6] Duffin strongly condemned the actions of Martínez.

Armed with this information, Meares decided he must sail for England and report to his influential friends and the King's government. He was, after all, the chief official of the Associated Merchants and he had to do what he could to right the perceived wrongs to his trading enterprise and to British interests. In Canton on December 5, 1789, Meares had Funter and five other crew members of the *North West America* prepare an affidavit condemning what they regarded as Spanish perfidy. (The affidavit appears as supporting evidence in Meares' *Memorial* to Parliament, as do Duffin's letters and other documents gathered by Meares.)[7]

Meares probably left for London shortly after December 5 because it is known he took the abovementioned affidavit with him. The identity of the ship on which Meares sailed apparently has been lost to history, but it is known from his own records that he spent a few days in the Philippines and engaged in spying on Spanish fortifications, apparently in case war should erupt.[8] Peter Henry, a former crewman on the *North West America*, probably accompanied Meares in returning to England.[9] No doubt Meares began preparing a deposition of the facts and organizing his journal and documents on the voyage home around the Cape of Good Hope.

Meares arrived in London in mid-April and contact was made with influential associates and the government.[10] Pitt, seeing the advantages to be gained from Meares' testimony,[11] ordered him to complete a "Memorial" as soon as possible and apparently assigned William Coombe, a professional writer, to assist in the project.[12] Even before Meares' *Memorial* was presented to Parliament on May 13 and distributed to the British people,[13] Pitt used Meares' information to incite his cabinet to request King George III to authorize a mobilization for war. That Meares' report now formed the foundation for England's claims against Spain was made clear in the minutes of that cabinet meeting on April 30, 1790:

> Upon consideration of the information which has been received from Mr. Meares of the detention and capture of several British vessels at Nootka Sound, on the coast of America, and of the circumstances of that transaction [plus information from Madrid]. . . Your Majesty's servants have agreed humbly to submit to Your Majesty their opinion that Your Majesty's minister at the Court of Madrid should be instructed to present a memorial demanding an immediate and adequate satisfaction for the outrages committed by Monsieur de Martinez; and that it would be proper, in order to support that demand and to be prepared for such events as may arise, that Your Majesty should give orders for fitting out a squadron of ships of the line.

"A View of the City of Macao," in *Voyages*. After returning to Macao in the *Felice* on December 5, 1788, Meares resided in China for a year as the chief agent of the Associated Merchants enterprise.

Present at that meeting and signatories to the submission were the Lord Chancellor, Lord Privy Seal, Duke of Richmond, Duke of Leeds, Lord Chatham, William Pitt and Lord Grenville.[14]

King George acquiesced to Pitt's wishes and war clouds gathered as British preparations went forward to ready ships and impress and recruit sailors for duty during "the Spanish Armament." The British treasury assigned £1,000,000 for military expenditures. Spain also began to mobilize and called on France for support under the so-called Bourbon Family Compact, but France, now in the beginning toils of revolution, hesitated to give assistance. Spain would be left without her key ally if France declined to pledge to aid the Spanish navy. Both Spain and Britain assigned ships and fleets at sea and sent despatches to far-scattered foreign stations ordering arrangements be readied for war. The Prime Minister was gambling that Spain would not be willing to fight over such a remote corner of the globe, but many in the British government thought otherwise. To the English populace a clash at sea appeared just days, sometimes only hours, away.

Propaganda reached a feverish pitch in government announcements, parliamentary and public oratory, newspapers and other publications. In addition to Meares' *Memorial*, presented to the House of Commons on May 13 and immediately released to the public (see Appendix II for the complete text), influential persons in and out of government promoted the printing of other florid pamphlets by such writers as the Etches brothers and Sir James Bland Burges, the undersecretary of foreign affairs.

Meanwhile, Meares personally addressed the Privy Committee for Trade on May 27, 1790, to outline the importance of the fur trade in the commerce between America and China. He also continued his collaboration with William Coombe in preparing the narrative of his exploits, which was much anticipated by the public. Meares' connections at this time to individuals at the highest levels of British society and government are evident in the List of Subscribers who supported the publication of *Voyages*. Nearly 350 names are listed; a veritable who's who in British administration, commerce, banking, finance and the military, in England, Ireland and China. At the head of the constellation of names was "His Royal Highness the Prince of Wales" followed by such active and prominent persons as the Duke of Leeds, the Earl of Effingham, Sir Joseph Banks ("President of the Royal Society"), Evan Nepean ("Under Sec. of State"), J. Henry Cox and Daniel Beale (residents of "*China*"), Alexander Dalrymple (the great proponent of a Northwest Passage), the Etches brothers (John, William, and Richard Cadman) and many others. Lewis W. Meares, Esq., possibly a brother, also is included. A good number of booksellers on the list preordered multiple copies of *Voyages* for their shops. The illustrious subscribers' list guaranteed wide distribution of Meares' narrative when it came out at the end of the year.[15]

Some historians have blamed Meares personally, because of the nature of his trading firm and his later reports about its aims and travails, for deliberately provoking Spanish territorial sensitivities and unscrupulously intensifying the international dispute for his own benefit. This is unfair. Clearly, Meares' main interest and that of his associates was for their captains, as traders/explorers, to develop a lucrative commercial venture in a remote part of the world where interference was not expected from any maritime power. Meares and the other captains felt England had legitimate claims to the region based on the explorations of Cook and the British coastal traders, thus they had a right to establish a factory there. The primary initiative for the Nootka crisis came from Spanish directives and particularly Martínez who likewise felt Spain's claim of sovereignty was legitimate, but he overplayed his authority in seizing British ships. Meares himself was in far off China and never met Martínez. Often overlooked is the fact that the Spanish commodore's wrath caused serious losses in seized ships, men and equipment and revenue for Meares and the Associated Merchants. Meares' displeasure with the Spanish authorities is understandable.

Critics also have accused Meares in his dealings with Pitt's government of distortion and dishonesty in covering up that he had earlier sailed under Portuguese colors and had formed illegal partnerships to avoid the restrictions of the South Sea and East India companies. This charge, too, is wrong. Meares, himself, described the Portuguese connection in his *Memorial*. Despatches from Madrid to London prominently mentioned "Portugueze" ships from Macao as having been detained in Nootka Sound, i.e., Meares' vessels. With the intense scrutiny that any information about Nootka Sound was receiving during the crisis, Pitt and his government must have known about Meares' Portuguese ruse in 1788. (By May 1790, Captain Charles Barkley had told the Spanish ambassador about it, too.[16]) Regarding Meares' flouting of the authority of the South Sea and East India firms, many high-level mercantile and government interests had come to realize the counterproductive nature of these monopolies in the evolution of British trade, commerce and settlement in the Pacific region. The reality was that change had long been needed. Meares' aversion to the monopolies might not be condoned, but it certainly was understandable, and consequently was mostly dismissed as an issue by Pitt.

A case can be made that the cover-ups and exaggerations for which Meares has been accused actually were largely the doing of Pitt and his advisers. In the highly nationalistic discussions with Spain over the rights of "British" vessels at sea, it was in the interest of English negotiators to dismiss or underplay Meares' "Portuguese" connections as well as his flouting of the authority of the monopolies. Meares and Coombe did likewise when preparing the *Memorial* and *Voyages* for publication. In discussions with Spain, Pitt also intentionally made it appear that the captured vessels were naval ships and not trading vessels and he emphasized that Meares' factory at Yuquot was a legitimate British merchants' enterprise. Meares' status as a lieutenant in the Royal Navy (though in reserve) also was given prominence. The reality was that the geopolitical situation in the Pacific was ripe for change, to Spain's detriment. Spain could no longer maintain the fiction that the Pacific was a private Spanish lake. Meares was Pitt's pawn for establishing British rights to trade and colonize there.

With every diplomatic exchange with Madrid, Pitt drew the noose tighter. A strongly worded memorial was addressed to the Spanish crown denouncing the "outrages" committed by the Spaniards. The memorial identified the *Princess Royal* and the *North West America* as naval ships, which they were not, and demanded their return. Pitt demanded punishment "of the officers in question" for their "direct infractions both of the existing treaties between the two crowns and of the general principles of Justice & the Law of Nations."[17] Spain demurred as both navies expanded and readied their fleets. A bloody conflict that could engulf the major nations of Europe seemed imminent. And all over a small harbor on the far-distant shore of Northwest America.

Notes

1. The English chargé d'affairs' information, acquired from his contacts at the Spanish seat of government, is fairly accurate with the exception of an erroneous report of a Russian ship being involved. Letter from Arthur Merry, chargé d'affairs at the court of Madrid, to the Duke of Leeds, January 4, 1790, in Sir James Bland Burges, *A Narrative of the Negotiations Occasioned by the Dispute between England and Spain, in the Year 1790* (London: 1791), 1-3: "Accounts have just been received here from Mexico, That one of the small Ships of War on the American Establishment, commanded by a Subaltern Officer of the Name of Martinez, has captured an English Vessel in the

Port of Nootka, (called by the Spaniards San Lorenzo) in Latitude 50 North of the Coast of California. There are different Relations of this Event. Some of them state, That the Vice-Roy of Mexico, having had Notice that the English were forming an Establishment at the above-mentioned Place, ordered a Ship there to take Possession of it: That M. de Martinez found in the Port Two American Vessels, a Portugueze from Macao, a Russian from some Port of Her Imperial Majesty's Eastern Dominions, and an English one, which had come direct from a Port of Great Britain, with People and Necessaries on Board, to form a Settlement: That the American, Portugueze and Russian Ships were suffered to depart, it appearing that they had only gone there to trade for Furs; and that the English one alone had been detained. Other Accounts mention, That the Spanish Ship had sailed from St. Blas on a Voyage, which, it is said, is annually performed, to reconnoitre the North-West Coast of the Continent: That, when she put into Port Nootka, the English Vessel was not yet arrived: That the latter was seized as soon as she appeared: That the Russian and Portugueze Ships were also captured; and that only the American were suffered to go away. The name of the English Vessel, or of the Master, is not mentioned in any of the Statements of the Transaction which I have yet been able to see; but they all say, that she had been fitted out by a Company of Merchants in London, for the Purpose of forming a Settlement; and that it had been discovered that she was to be followed by Two others. The different Accounts also add, that she had been manned with Spanish Seaman, and dispatched with the News to the Viceroy of Mexico."

2. "Madrid's protest, requesting punishment for those responsible, contained a fairly accurate account of the incident"; Warren L. Cook, *Flood Tide of Empire: Spain and the Pacific Northwest, 1543-1819* (New Haven, CT, and London: Yale University Press, 1973), 205.

3. With the release of the *Iphigenia*, Robert Haswell, second mate of the *Columbia*, in his final log entry had thought the controversy between the Spaniards and Britons was over: "every thing being settled thus Captain Douglas sailed for China." However, after the *Iphigenia* sailed, new trouble broke out between the Spanish and English in Nootka Sound. F. W. Howay, ed., *Voyages of the "Columbia" to the Northwest Coast, 1787-1790 and 1790-1793* (Boston: Massachusetts Historical Society, 1941; Portland: Oregon Historical Society Press, 1990), 101.

4. This was a charge Meares presented in his *Memorial* to Parliament. Robert Gray, in a letter to Bodega y Quadra dated August 3, 1792, confirmed that the *Columbia* took the crew of the *North West America* to China after she was seized by the Spaniards. He also stated the *Columbia* carried "one hundred sea otter skins" valued at $4,875. "These were delivered to Mr. Meares, and were, we suppose, his property"; Howay, ed., *Voyages of the "Columbia,"* 474-79. Other sources put the number of pelts at 96. Meares' *Memorial* to Parliament claimed the total amount of skins seized by Martínez from the *North West America* totaled 207, a number which is repeated by Barry M. Gough in *The Northwest Coast: British Navigation, Trade, and Discoveries to 1812* (Vancouver: University of British Columbia Press, 1992), 133.

5. Whether or not Robert Gray and the Americans provided Meares with information concerning the Nootka affair is uncertain. In a letter to his sponsors in Boston, Gray gives his arrival date as November 17, 1789; Howay, ed., *Voyages of the "Columbia,"* 129. However, Meares claims the *Columbia* entered port on November 2, 1789; see *Memorial* to Parliament, 11.

6. "Copies of Letters from Mr. Duffin to Mr. Meares" [July 12, 13 and 14, 1789], Appendix No. XIII, in John Meares, *Voyages Made in the Years 1788 and 1789, from*

China to the Northwest Coast of America (London: Logographic Press, 1790) [also in *Memorial* to Parliament, April 30, 1790].

7. "Deposition of the Officers and Men of the Schooner *North-West America,*" Appendix No. X, in Meares, *Voyages* [also in Meares' *Memorial* to Parliament, April 30, 1790]. The affidavit, various letters, logs, journal entries and other items served as supporting documentation both in the *Memorial* to Parliament, published in May 1790, and in *Voyages,* published in November 1790 and reprinted in subsequent editions in English, French, Italian, German, and Swedish.

8. A letter from Meares to the Admiralty reports on his observations of Spanish fortifications in the Philippines. The memo, dated Sunday, May 16, 1790, is in the miscellaneous file of the Foreign Office (FO 95/7/3), Public Record Office, Kew, England. The date would indicate Meares wrote it upon his return to London.

9. After returning to Britain, Peter Henry was pressed into service aboard the HMS *Hebe.* In a letter to the Admiralty, Meares asked that Henry be protected so he could testify; FO 95/7/5, Public Record Office, Kew, England. Possibly other *North West America* crewmen returned to London, too, but there appears to be no documentation for this being the case.

10. Warren L. Cook in *Flood Tide of Empire,* 210, claims "The audience that he secured among highly placed figures in the government came about through the merger of his interests with those of the powerful 'King George's Sound Company,' in which men of considerable fortune and influence were involved." In Cook's estimation, Meares' "arrival in London . . . aggravated the situation to a marked degree."

11. According to Sir James Bland Burges, the arrival of Meares "contributed to throw many new Lights upon the Subject, and which proved the Conduct of the Spaniards to have been infinitely more hostile and injurious towards His Majesty, than . . . [we] had given Reason to imagine"; *A Narrative of the Negotiations Occasioned by the Dispute between England and Spain, in the Year 1790* (London), 23.

12. Northwest historian Murray Morgan contends a "ghost writer," William Coombe, worked with Meares in preparing his *Memorial* and journal for publication; see "Exploring the Northwest with a Ghost Writer," *American Bookman* [New York City], September 9, 1991. The Oregon Historical Society Library index indicates Coombe compiled *Voyages* from Meares' notes. Regarding Meares' *Voyages,* Cook states in *Flood Tide of Empire,* 210: "published in 1790 in a deluxe edition on fine paper and accompanied by numerous elegant maps and engravings, this volume is tangible evidence of affluent sponsorship." Indeed, the volume included several pages listing the names of prestigious "subscribers."

13. John Meares, *Authentic Copy of the Memorial to the Right Honourable William Wyndham Grenville, One of His Majesty's Principal Secretaries of State, by Lieutenant John Mears, of the Royal Navy; Dated 30th April, 1790, and Presented to the House of Commons, May 13, 1790. Containing Every Particular Respecting Capture of the Vessels in Nootka Sound* (London: J. Debrett, 1760 [*sic,* 1790]).

14. Minutes of the cabinet meeting, April 30, 1790, are in the miscellaneous file of the Foreign Office (FO 95/7/3), Public Record Office, Kew, England; also quoted in William R. Manning, "The Nootka Sound Controversy," *Annual Report of the American Historical Association* (1904), 376.

15. Shortly, after the release of *Voyages* in November 1790, the so-called pamphlet war between Dixon and Meares, too, occurred. The honors and attention Meares received from the British government and London society no doubt did little to ease Dixon's ill will toward Meares.

16. In May 1790, the Spanish ambassador in London sought out Captain Charles Barkley for personal information about Meares and his activities on the Northwest Coast. In a subsequent report to Spain's chief negotiator, Floridablanca, the ambassador claimed Meares "had no property or even a share in the outfitting" of the captured vessels "because he doesn't have even a house or a home." The ambassador said Meares had been paid a few guineas to make the protest for the Associated Merchants; translated from the Spanish by Cook, *Flood Tide of Empire,* 219. Barkley's services recently had been terminated by the Associated Merchants and he was disgruntled at the firm's directors; see Appendix I, Mrs. Barkley's Case Against John Meares.

17. The handwritten document (in FO 95/7/3) demanded "adequate satisfaction for these outrages," including restitution of the *Princess Royal* and *North West America*, their crews and property "if not already done." No mention was made of the *Iphigenia* and *Argonaut.* The *Iphigenia*, of course, had been released early by Martínez and possibly word had reached Pitt that the *Argonaut* was being freed by the viceroy of Mexico. The Spanish had rebuilt the *North West America* and she was never returned, but supposedly her value was part of the eventual settlement.

REMARKS ON THE VOYAGES

OF

JOHN MEARES, Efq.

IN A LETTER TO THAT GENTLEMAN,

BY

GEORGE DIXON,

LATE COMMANDER OF THE QUEEN CHARLOTTE,
IN A VOYAGE ROUND THE WORLD.

LONDON:
PRINTED FOR THE AUTHOR, AND SOLD BY JOHN STOCKDALE, PICCADILLY;
AND GEORGE GOULDING, JAMES STREET, COVENT GARDEN.
M,DCC,XC.

[PRICE TWO SHILLINGS AND SIXPENCE.

AN

A N S W E R

TO

MR. GEORGE DIXON,

LATE COMMANDER OF THE QUEEN CHARLOTTE,

IN THE SERVICE OF

MESSRS. ETCHES AND COMPANY;

BY

JOHN MEARES, Esq.

IN WHICH THE REMARKS OF MR. DIXON ON THE VOYAGES TO THE NORTH WEST
COAST OF AMERICA, &c. LATELY PUBLISHED, ARE FULLY CONSIDERED AND REFUTED.

LONDON:
PRINTED AT THE Logographic Prefs;
AND SOLD BY J. WALTER, N° 169, PICCADILLY, OPPOSITE OLD BOND STREET.

With the appearance of *Voyages* in late 1790, George Dixon immediately published an attack on Meares initiating a "pamphlet war" in London. Dixon's *Remarks,* dated December 1, 1790, was shortly followed by Meares' *Answer,* January 1, 1791, discounting Dixon's accusations. Dixon responded with *Further Remarks* on February 12, 1791, claiming it was a *"Decisive Refutation"* of Meares' *Answer.* Meares chose not to publish a rebuttal. The title pages of two of the pamphlets are depicted here.

Chapter Fourteen

Not a Shot Was Fired

THE CONTROVERSY BETWEEN London and Madrid that John Meares helped to provoke continued through the summer and into autumn until King Carlos IV, new to Spain's throne, realized he would have no major ally in a war with Britain because of the revolution in France. He ordered his chief negotiator, the Conde de Floridablanca, to accede to nearly all of Pitt's demands. This despite the urging of a junta of advisors that Spain go to war if necessary to preserve claims in Northwest America. If hostilities had ensued it well could have developed into a world war in Europe and overseas with the Triple Alliance (Britain, The Netherlands and Prussia) opposing Spain and her allies.[1]

On October 28, 1790, at the Escorial Palace near Madrid the two nations agreed to the first of three treaties (the Nootka Conventions) that settled, without a shot being fired, the dramatic confrontation arising over control of a harbor half-a-world away. In the end, the actions of Don Estéban José Martínez, which he believed were necessary to protect Spain's interests in the North Pacific, turned out to be the beginning of the end of Spanish pretensions there.

In the First Nootka Convention, signed October 28, 1790, Spain agreed to release British ships and seamen (if this already had not occurred). The tract of land in Nootka Sound that Meares claimed he had purchased from the natives and on which he had erected a building was to "be restored to the said British subjects." The agreement also gave Britain an equal right with Spain to navigate, trade and fish (whaling) "in the Pacific Ocean or in the South Seas" and to establish settlements on lands not occupied by Spain. Britain considered this to include the Pacific Coast from San Francisco north to the Russian claims in Alaska.

The second convention, after extensive negotiations, was signed on February 12, 1793. It provided for an indemnity to be paid by Spain— 210,000 piasters against Meares' claim for $653,433—for damages suffered by Meares and his partners.

The third convention, signed January 11, 1794, called for the mutual abandonment of Nootka Sound, which would be left to the natives. The sound would remain open to ships of any nation, except none could build a permanent base there.

While the Pitt government had established Britain's right to commercial freedom in the eastern Pacific, the treaty seemed not all that negative to Spain at the time. Madrid yet believed its vast empire had the resources to occupy the Northwest Coast. In the years immediately following, England evidenced little interest or desire to take special advantage of her diplomatic victory, probably because of political events in Europe and because the Northwest Coast was very far away. Both monarchies were uneasy allies for a time against revolutionary France, but in 1796 Madrid joined Paris in declaring war against Britain citing controversy over the Nootka Convention as one of the primary causes.

Spain's claim of sole dominion over the entire West Coast of America was curbed; she would have to share Northwest waters and harbors with British ships which continued to come to trade for sea otter pelts on the coast. But soon American vessels dominated the trade. Spain's decline in the North Pacific did not happen all at once. The Spanish struggled to maintain a foothold at Nootka Sound for a time and sponsored eight expeditions of discovery between 1790 and 1793 along the coast from San Francisco Bay to Cook Inlet. Nevertheless, Spain's 300-year old claim to exclusive sovereignty over the eastern Pacific Basin had approached its end.[2]

Disagreement over the size and value of the tract of land that Meares claimed he had bought from Maquinna in 1788 remained a contentious point with Spanish negotiators and Meares' detractors. In his *Memorial,* Meares noted "That your Memorialist, immediately on his arrival in Nootka Sound, purchased from Maquilla [Maquinna], the Chief of the district contiguous to and surrounding that place [Friendly Cove], a spot of ground, whereon he built a house for his occasional residence, as well as for the more convenient pursuit of his trade with the natives, and hoisted the British colours thereon; that he also erected a breast work, which surrounded the house, and mounted one three-pounder in the front."[3]

Meares further contended that he had acquired land and trading rights from Chief Wicananish at Clayoquot Sound, and similar trading rights, through Robert Duffin, from Chief Tatoosh on the Olympic Peninsula. Meares' assertion he had acquired "a spot of ground" at Nootka was supported and expanded on by Robert Duffin, who had been the chief mate on the *Felice* in 1788.

In 1792, Duffin returned to Nootka Sound as the de facto captain of a British brig, the *São José o Fénix,* sailing under the old ruse of flying Portuguese colors from Macao.[4] In meeting with Vancouver, who was in the harbor to negotiate with Spanish officials over this and other Nootka Convention particulars, Duffin prepared an affidavit that went further than even Meares' assertions by indicating the purchase from Maquinna and Callicum included "the whole of the Land which forms Friendly Cove for 8 or 10 Sheets of Copper and several other trifling articles."

But the Spanish authorities in the sound contended Meares' "spot of ground" was only a small tract adjacent to Yuquot on which the house had been built. When the affidavit Duffin gave to Vancouver shortly after was translated to Maquinna, the chief adamantly denied he had sold land to Meares and used the words "aita, aita," considered to mean Meares was a "liar."[5] (Robert Gray, who was in Nootka Sound during much of the controversy in 1788, but not at the moment when Meares acquired the building site, said he knew of no purchase of land by Meares.[6]

Each perspective might be correct in the eyes of the individual stating his view. Meares may have thought he was by oral agreement (through translation) obtaining title to Indian land. Maquinna, not used to the white man's concept of land ownership, may have thought something completely different. That Maquinna, four years later, did understand private ownership is clear in his admission to his questioners that he had sold land to Captain John Kendrick in 1791. Unlike Meares, Kendrick obtained written "deeds" for his land purchases with the "Xs" of several chiefs affixed as signatures.[7] Certainly, at the least, Maquinna and his chiefs had to have granted permission for the British to build their structure.

The type of building Meares had his men erect also became controversial. Robert Gray, the Boston captain who saw the structure in 1788, described it as modest, little more than a hut. His second mate, Robert Haswell, thought it a more substantial structure. Meares himself said the "house" was not an "architectural beauty," but it served its purpose well and was regarded with amazement by the natives who had helped build it.[8] In any event, the structure was torn down by Captain Douglas after Meares had gone in 1788.[9]

During the discussions in Europe between Britain and Spain, agreement had not been reached regarding the size and boundaries of Meares' tract of land. With this issue undecided, the Admiralty had despatched George Vancouver in 1792 with two warships plus a supply vessel to negotiate final terms on the spot with the Spanish commandant at Nootka Sound, Juan Francisco de la Bodega y Quadra. Vancouver, having little in the way of instruction, pictured the site as quite extensive, possibly including all the shoreline of Nootka Sound. Lacking proof for Vancouver's claim, Bodega y Quadra in the end offered to yield up only a small tract in Friendly Cove, the same "spot of ground" Meares had claimed. After several weeks of negotiation, the two decided they could not settle the controversy themselves. Vancouver dispatched two officers by different routes to London. Lt. William Broughton left on a Spanish ship for Mexico, where he crossed overland to the east coast and from there to England. Lt. Zachary Mudge left by sea for Macao on the *São José o Fénix* commanded by Duffin, and from thence to Europe to notify the British government an agreement could not be reached. Vancouver requested further instruction which he never received.[10]

Bodega y Quadra had twice before been on the Northwest Coast and had been thoroughly briefed by Mexico's new viceroy, the highly capable Conde de Revilla Gigedo, as to Spain's objectives. Despite believing Pitt had no real case, the new viceroy had decided to yield Nootka Sound for several reasons: the base was unproductive, difficult to protect and a drain on the treasury.[11] However, Bodega y Quadra held firm against Vancouver's position that a large portion of the sound should be assigned to the British unless Vancouver could provide proof that Meares had established ownership. Meanwhile, Revilla Gigedo decided that Spanish military forces in the region should move to a new base, known as Núñez Gaona (Neah Bay) inside the entrance to the Strait of Juan de Fuca. Construction began at the site in 1792 under Salvador Fidalgo. After a brief period of occupation, the base was abandoned due to the stalemate in the negotiations between Vancouver and Bodega y Quadra and because the harbor was believed to be too exposed to stormy weather.

By 1794 the two nations had signed the third Nootka treaty and all was settled. In 1795, with attention diverted to other issues, Britain and

Spain appointed emissaries to meet at Nootka to conclude the controversy ceremoniously. Pitt selected a lieutenant of marines, Thomas Pearce, and Spain named a general, José Manuel de Álava, as chief representatives. Pearce proceeded to San Blas and then Monterey on Spanish ships. Pearce and Álava then sailed together to Nootka Sound where, on March 16, 1795, the general ordered the dismantling of the Spanish installation. The formal restitution to Great Britain of Meares' "spot of ground" was now at hand. The Spanish flag was lowered and the Union Jack raised on March 28 "in token of possession" by Great Britain. Then the flag was lowered. The commissioners departed Nootka in accordance with terms of the settlement that neither nation would attempt to make a permanent base there again, and they would jointly ensure that no other power could try to establish such a post either. Before leaving, Pearce presented the Union Jack to Maquinna in final assurance that the natives were once again in charge of their own land.[12]

Notes

1. If war had erupted French naval assistance would have been crucial to Spain in helping to protect her overseas colonies from predation by British naval forces. The network of international alliances existing at the time could have resulted in a global conflict pitting Spain, France, Austria, Denmark, Russia and possibly the United States against the coalition of Great Britain, the Netherlands, Prussia, plus perhaps Sweden, Poland and Turkey; Warren L. Cook, *Flood Tide of Empire: Spain and the Pacific Northwest, 1543-1819* (New Haven, CT, and London: Yale University Press, 1973), 217.

2. Freeman M. Tovell, "The other Side of the Coin: The Viceroy, Bodega y Quadra, Vancouver, and the Nootka Crisis," *BC Studies* 93 (Spring 1992), 3. Spanish texts of the three Nootka Conventions can be found in Cook, *Flood Tide of Empire*, Appendix B, 544-47. English texts are in the Public Record Office, Kew, England, and William R. Manning, "The Nootka Sound Controversy," *Annual Report of the American Historical Association* (1904), 454-56, 467-70. According to Manning: "It marked the end of Spain's new brief period of national greatness, which had resulted from the wise reign of Carlos III. It was also the beginning of the collapse of Spain's colonial empire"; 285.

3. Meares, *Memorial* to Parliament, 2.

4. In 1792, Francisco José Viana likewise returned to Nootka Sound as the captain of Meares' former ship, the *Felice*, which still was under Portuguese colors. Others returning to Nootka in 1792 who had witnessed or been involved in the events of 1787-88 included Robert Gray in the *Columbia*, Joseph Ingraham in the *Hope*, the Barkleys in the *Halcyon*, as well as other British and Spanish officers in various ships. This remarkable reunion of individuals meant that Bodega y Quadra and Vancouver had numerous unexpected witnesses to question regarding the past controversy. Cook, *Flood Tide of Empire*, 357-58, 379-80.

5. Duffin claims "the Natives were fully satisfied with their agreement"; quoted in Ibid., 138, 380.

6. See J. Richard Nokes, *Columbia's River: The Voyages of Robert Gray, 1787-1793* (Tacoma: Washington State Historical Society, 1991), chapter 9, for a discussion of the Americans' role during the controversy in Nootka Sound. Gray and Kendrick arrived after Meares acquired the tract of land and the "house" had been constructed.

7. Copies of the deeds obtained by John Kendrick from native chiefs are on file in the Library of Congress. See report of Rep. Alpheus Felch, S526, 32d Congress, 1st session. Kendrick had the original deeds filed in Canton and provided copies to Thomas Jefferson, then the U.S. secretary of state. The originals never have been found. See report of Benjamin Joy, "Columbia's River," 293: "there were regular deeds drawn up, and signed by a number of Indian chiefs." In a letter from Hong Kong Island dated March 11, 1793, Kendrick advised Jefferson that he was enclosing copies of the deeds "to remain in the Department of State" as permanent records. Kendrick hoped that some day he or his heirs might profit from the tracts. That did not come to pass. See *Columbia's River*, 244-45 for text of the letter. The document establishes that the *Lady Washington* was the first American ship to visit Hong Kong.

8. In *Voyages,* 115-16, Meares described the house erected on the site as spacious enough to contain all of the party remaining behind at the factory in Nootka Sound. The ground floor provided work space for coopers, sail makers and other artisans, and for the stores. Blacksmiths were accommodated in an annex to the main building, while the upper floor was for dining and sleeping quarters. The sketch of the building in Meares' *Voyages* makes the structure seem less commodious.

9. Nokes, *Columbia's River,* 103.

10. Cook, *Flood Tide of Empire,* 379, 388, 393, 427; Derek Pethick, *Nootka Connection,* p. 203. Lt. William Broughton was captain of the HMS *Chatham,* the first ship to sail a hundred miles up the Columbia River in 1792. He was relieved of command so he could carry Vancouver's report across Mexico to London.

11. "The cost of defending it was no longer commensurate with its importance for reasons of prestige or trade"; Tovell, "The other Side of the Coin," 8.

12. Cook, *Flood Tide of Empire,* 421-22.

The trading songs of the coastal tribes were appealing to European and American mariners. This one from Alaska's Alexander Archipelago appears in George Dixon, *A Voyage Round the World* (1789). Meares noted the plaintive voices exerted "a solemn and pleasing effect upon our minds."

Chapter Fifteen

Afterword

With the final agreement between Spain and England, none of the maritime powers tried again to establish a base in the sound. The Spanish claim to Nootka Sound and Vancouver Island was eliminated by 1819 through diplomatic means, and Russian pretensions there ended by the mid 1820s. After the international boundary was established between British and American territory in 1846 by the Treaty of Oregon, the Crown Colony of Vancouver Island was created in 1849 (it soon included the Queen Charlotte Islands, too). This insular entity would eventually become part of the larger Colony of British Columbia, which was formed in 1858 at the time of the Fraser River gold rush. British Columbia became a province in the new Canadian confederation in 1871.

Today Nootka Sound is under the control of the Mowachaht Band of the Nuu-cha-nulth Nation. Any visible vestiges of the Spanish settlement are essentially gone. Only a few buildings of more recent vintage stand on the site of the native village of Yuquot, which has been declared a Canadian National Heritage Site. The sound itself is still primitive, although there have been extensive clear cuts of the great forest that so impressed early mariners. A pulp mill on Muchalat Arm near Gold River is visited by ocean-going vessels. A lighthouse on an island near where Fort San Miguel once stood guards the entrance to the sound. Boats and seaplanes carry anglers and tourists to Tahsis village in the arm of the sound where John Kendrick moored his ship two centuries ago.

Where once there was conflict between two great powers of Europe, today there is quietude. The British and Americans who once coveted Nootka as a base for exploitation of the fur trade in this new land, the Pacific Northwest, later moved their focus for other kinds of economic opportunity to the Columbia River and to ports inside the Strait of Juan de Fuca.

⚓

Like many a historical figure before and since, John Meares' time in the limelight was brief. While he served Pitt's purpose perfectly well in the campaign to curtail Spanish domination in the Pacific, and to gain freedom of the seas, he soon was forgotten as other crises in Europe engaged British attention during the Napoleonic era.

Not much is known of Meares' life after the settlement of the Nootka controversy. He must have engaged in other seagoing activities, because that was the life that he chose. He eventually returned to his first love, active duty in the Royal Navy. In 1794, he applied for funds from the Admiralty because of the final settlement of the Nootka question. He was rewarded for his role by promotion to the rank of commander, effective February 26, 1795, which meant a considerable increase in pay, but so far as is known he received none of the Spanish indemnity money. He also was honored by the Crown with the title of baronet, which entitled him to be addressed as Sir John Meares.

On May 12, 1796, he wrote to Evan Nepean, secretary to the British Admiralty, saying that he had recovered from an injury sustained while on "impress duty" in Ireland, and requested assignment to active duty.[1] Records show that he died in Bath, January 29, 1809, probably at the age of 53, but of what cause is not revealed.

Meares apparently considered Bath his lifetime home, and according to his "last will and testament" he owned property in Jamaica. The value of his estate when probated was estimated to be under £7,500. His will listed no spouse or child, but a brother and sister, unnamed, are among the beneficiaries. The brother could have been Lewis W. Meares, Esq. At least that name appears among the many distinguished subscribers of Meares' *Voyages* in 1790. Several friends in Bath are mentioned as beneficiaries and executors.[2] It could be that his wife, the former Mary Ann Guilliband, whom he married in 1796, already was deceased.

The will also listed parties that Meares said owed him money. Among them were James Drummond of South Audley Street, London, £10,873, and Daniel Beale & Co., £21,600 "under an arbitration." These sums obviously were not considered in the valuation of Meares' overall worth by the clerk of the Prerogative Court of Canterbury where the will was proved April 19, 1809.

Some historians and critics have condemned Meares for claiming damages of $653,433 in the Nootka negotiations for himself and the Etches company, contending losses caused by the Spanish seizure of his ships were not that great.[3] But Meares not only was seeking actual damages for the loss of his ships, equipment, and the framework for a schooner contained within the hull of the *Argonaut* that was to be built at Nootka, but also for the ruination of his dream of a permanent fur trading enterprise between the Northwest Coast and China. Even today, plaintiffs in legal actions regularly ask for punitive damages far above the amount of their actual losses. It is likely that the amount on which Britain and Spain eventually settled in 1793 (210,000 Spanish dollars) was close to the mark.

It is known that the crew members of the *Argonaut* and the *Princess Royal* received compensation from the Viceroy of New Spain (of approximately $40,000) when released from captivity in San Blas.[4] It is not clear that Meares was compensated after J. Woodford for Great Britain signed a receipt for "210,000 piastres" from Spain, according to a document on file in the Public Record Office in Kew.[5] Another memo shows that Meares felt he might have been victimized by the Etches sponsors in the settlement. He warned the Admiralty during negotiations that he still had outstanding claims against that enterprise.

Meares did make several enemies among his contemporaries, especially George Dixon and the Barkleys, as noted in earlier chapters. Whatever his sins of omission and commission, Meares deserves a prominent place in the history of the Pacific Northwest. He was among the earliest explorers on the Northwest Coast, he was the first to attempt to found a fur trading empire in the region, and he tried to carry timbers from the magnificent virgin forests to the Orient, and thus founded an export activity important to this day. (Bad luck hounded him here, too. Most or all of the timbers had to be jettisoned from the *Felice* during a storm.) Meares made several important discoveries (but missed other opportunities, such as finding the mouth of the Columbia River); he did use his own information and that provided by others, whom he properly credited, to chart routes across the Pacific and to delineate features along the coast from Alaska to Oregon. His ships carried the first Chinese to Hawaii and the Northwest Coast, and he signed on Hawaiian, Lascar and Filipino crew members. He established the first factory and built the first ship ever constructed on the Northwest Coast. His attempt to initiate a permanent fur trading enterprise launched a series of developments that ultimately led to Spain's voluntary withdrawal from the North Pacific and Northwest America.

Today the journal of his adventures, published in November 1790, is found in the rare book sections of many historical libraries. It was reprinted in several languages, including German, Swedish, Spanish and French, and was republished in English in London in 1791 in two volumes. The original journal and notes which Meares and Coombe used in preparing *Voyages* appear to have been lost or the location of the materials remains unknown. The text of Meares' famous *Memorial* to Parliament has been included as an Appendix in this volume.

Meares must be ranked well below Cook, England's most famous navigator, and George Vancouver, who explored and charted the Northwest coastline. But no student of the early maritime history of the Pacific Northwest can overlook Meares' contributions to exploration and trade and to Spain's later decision to abandon the northern coast. It was Meares' *Memorial* to Parliament in 1790, following the capture of his ships by the Spaniards in Nootka Sound, that provided Prime Minister Pitt with a perfectly tailored cause to face down the Spanish negotiators at the Escorial Palace in Madrid and win equal rights for Britain in the Pacific.

Professor Edmund S. Meany of the University of Washington, a prominent early-20th-century Northwest historian, has noted: "John Meares, a retired lieutenant of the British navy, was the most unconventional and interesting personality of all those figuring in these early marine annals. He sailed under double colors, he succeeded as fur hunter and geographer, he was the pioneer of two great industries, he sought to plant a colony of Chinese men with Kanaka wives, he wrote a book, he precipitated a quarrel between England and Spain which came near embroiling also the new republic of the United States into a serious war. There was nothing dull about John Meares."[6]

Notes

1. Letter, John Meares to Evan Nepean, secretary to the British Admiralty, May 12, 1796, ADM 1/2132 xc 9159, Public Record Office, Kew, England.
2. The "last will and testament of one John Meares of the City of Bath in the County of Somerset" is on file in the Public Record Office in London. It lists in addition to a brother and sister the names of several beneficiaries including: Valentin Jones of Ballbrook House, Somerset County; William Hollings of Calcutta; Thomas Bailey of Bath; Richard Lambert of Bristol; and their heirs and assigns. The latter four were named executors. In addition he made provision for James Read of Bath. The document is not in Meares' hand but that of a clerk in the probate department in an old-fashioned and elaborate style of handwriting.

3. For example, Nellie B. Pipes, ed. of Meares' *Memorial* (Portland, OR: Metropolitan Press, 1933).
4. James Colnett discussed negotiations with the Viceroy of New Spain over the payment of salaries for the crew members and himself. Colnett was to receive lieutenant's pay, not that of a head of an expedition as he requested. As noted earlier, the Spanish pay scale for the South Seas was higher than that of the Meares' enterprise; *The Journal of Captain James Colnett aboard the "Argonaut" from April 26, 1789, to Nov. 3, 1791,* ed. with intro. and notes by Frederick W. Howay (Toronto: Champlain Society, 1940), 108-12 *passim.*
5. Authorization for payment of "deux cens dix mille piastres" was signed by representatives of Spain and Great Britain and a receipt for the same was signed by "J. Woodford for Great Britain, 12 February 1792" as indemnity for the vessels captured by Martínez, in Nootka Sound in 1789. A notation was included that this "constitutes the compensation and indemnification entire and complete"; FO 93/99, Public Record Office, Kew, England.
6. Edmond S. Meany, *History of the State of Washington* (New York: Macmillan, 1924), 25; also quoted in Lewis A. McArthur, compiler, *Oregon Geographic Names* (Portland: Koke-Chapman, 1928), 56.

Mrs. Barkley's Case Against John Meares

A FTER MEARES PUBLISHED *Voyages* late in 1790, chief among his critics was Frances Hornby Barkley, the young wife of the English mariner Charles William Barkley who is credited with being the modern discoverer of the Strait of Juan de Fuca in 1787. She was aboard the *Imperial Eagle* with her husband when the sighting occurred.

On December 30, 1941, in an address before the Pacific Coast Branch of the American Historical Association in Eugene, Oregon, the Canadian historian W. Kaye Lamb summarized and assessed the few remaining key fragments of Mrs. Barkley's two diaries (i.e., four excerpts; two dating from July 1787, and one each from 1788 and August 1792) and her complete *Reminiscences* (written much later in 1836 when she was 66 years-of-age). Over the years, her diary of the voyage of the *Imperial Eagle* apparently had been the only surviving source kept by the Barkleys themselves that documented the discovery of the Strait of Juan de Fuca in 1787. (Her second diary pertained to the voyage of the *Halcyon* to Alaska in 1792.)

On November 22, 1909, Mrs. Barkley's two diaries and other papers were destroyed in a fire at a descendant's home at Westholme, Vancouver Island. Mrs. Barkley's complete *Reminiscences* remains, but it only briefly and unsatisfactorily covers the voyage of the *Imperial Eagle*. However, a researcher, John T. Walbran, fortunately had written down the four select and important passages (and a few notes of lesser import) from Mrs. Barkley's diaries in the years before they were consumed by flames.

From these few remaining key excerpts, and her *Reminiscences* and other brief documentation including entries from the Dixon and Colnett narratives, W. Kaye Lamb produced an account of Barkley's voyage from

England to the Northwest Coast of America and to China more than 200 years ago.[1]

Like Meares, Charles William Barkley (1759-1832) was a trader and not an explorer. From London, Barkley was engaged surreptitiously by certain East India Company entrepreneurs of Calcutta, China, and England to take a sizable ship to the Northwest Coast to obtain sea otter and other pelts from the natives and peddle them in China. (Thus, his business arrangements were quite similar to those of Meares in 1786-88.) Like his father, Barkley had been in East India Company service, but at age 26 resigned from the firm to undertake this venture. The contract called for Barkley to make three trading voyages to the Northwest Coast that could take up to 10 years to complete. As did many captains in this period, Barkley invested his own capital, perhaps up to £3,000, in the effort. His large ship, the 400-ton, 20-gun *Loudoun*, renamed the *Imperial Eagle*, was outfitted in the Thames River and sailed from Ostend, Belgium, November 24, 1786, with his new bride, the 17-year-old Frances Hornby Trevor, aboard.

Mrs. Frances Barkley (1769-1843) was destined to be the first white woman to visit Hawaii and the Northwest Coast, and to circumnavigate the globe, not only once but twice. The *Imperial Eagle* sailed under the banner of Austria (the vessel had been renamed in recognition of the national symbol of that country). This dodge was to avoid the licensing requirements of the East India and South Sea companies which held monopolies on the Pacific trade. The ruse was "a common subterfuge of the time," Lamb pointed out, and he also said: "It is clear that not even Captain Barkley took the change very seriously, for he kept the vessel's records in the name of the ship *Loudoun,* and Mrs. Barkley likewise refers to her as the *Louden* in her diaries and reminiscences."

Barkley arrived in Nootka Sound in June 1787 and successfully traded with Chief Maquinna's people. James Colnett in the *Prince of Wales* and Captain Duncan of the *Princess Royal,* who were properly licensed traders, arrived a few weeks later. They cordially interacted with the *Imperial Eagle's* captain and crew while noting that Barkley, who was essentially unlicensed, had ruined their trade. (In two years, Colnett would become closely allied with Meares in the Associated Merchants venture.) Barkley then sailed down the west coast of Vancouver Island and explored Clayoquot Sound, naming it "Wickaninnish's sound" for the local chief of that name. Mrs. Barkley later wrote that the *Imperial Eagle* was the first ship ever to enter that harbor. After more trading, they continued south and entered another major inlet that the captain named for himself, "Barkley sound," while "Frances Island" and "Hornby peak" were named for his wife, and "Cape Beale" for the purser who later was killed by natives. From here the plot thickens.

In a statement in *Voyages*, published in 1790, Meares gives full credit to Barkley for discovering and naming Barkley Sound and for the first sighting of the Strait of Juan de Fuca:

> The *Imperial Eagle*, Captain Barclay [*sic*; misspelled not only by Meares, but by Etches and Dixon, too], we believe, sailed from Europe the beginning of the year 1787 [actually, November 24, 1786]; and not only arrived at Nootka Sound in August [actually mid June], but explored that part of the coast from Nootka to Wicaninish, and so on to a Sound to which he gave his own name. The boat's crew, however, was dispatched, and discovered the extraordinary straits of John [Juan] de Fuca, and also the coast as far as Queenhythe;—when, after the fatal catastrophe which happened to some of them [six sailors were massacred near Destruction Island], this ship quitted the coast, and proceeded to China; having performed the whole of the voyage in twelve months, which employed the *King George* and *Queen Charlotte* [Portlock's and Dixon's ships] upwards of two years. The *Nootka* [in the same year] made no other discovery but that of distress and misfortune.[2]

In several other shorter passages in *Voyages*, Meares again credits Barkley for his discoveries and accomplishments.[3] In Meares' statement there are a few minor errors (as indicated above), but these obviously are of an insignificant nature. Lamb, however, inexplicably claims this very same passage "is filled with inaccuracies." Meares likely first gleaned at least some of the information about Barkley from word of mouth while in China. Meares was in Macao or Canton when Barkley arrived there from Hawaii and the Northwest Coast in December 1787 with the Hawaiian woman, Winee, aboard. She shortly afterward boarded Meares' *Felice* in January 1788.[4] Before setting sail, one of the partners gave Meares a chart derived from Barkley's explorations from Nootka Sound south to 47° north latitude, and, as was customary, Meares had gained other similar information from other explorer/traders.[5] (Also, apparently after Meares' last voyage to the Northwest Coast, many of Barkley's own records would be turned over to Meares by the trading entrepreneurs who acquired them when Barkley's service was terminated sometime later in 1788.[6])

Were Meares' statements in *Voyages* fulsome enough recognition of Barkley's discovery of the Strait of Juan de Fuca? Mrs. Barkley and a number of latter-day historians have thought not.

In a fragment of her diary for "July, 1787" quoted by Lamb, Mrs. Barkley wrote: "In the afternoon, to our great astonishment, we arrived off a large opening extending to the eastward, the entrance of which appeared to be about four leagues wide, and remained about that width as far as the eye could see, with a clear westerly horizon, which my husband immediately recognized as the long lost strait of Juan de Fuca, to which he gave the name of the original discoverer, my husband placing it on his chart."

What is left of her records makes no comment about whether or not the *Imperial Eagle* entered the strait or if the ship's boat explored into the waterway. Captain John T. Walbran, the researcher who studied Mrs. Barkley's diaries and documents before they were destroyed by fire, wrote in an article in the Victoria *Colonist,* March 3, 1901, that the *"Imperial Eagle* did not go up the Strait, but kept along the ocean coast."[7]

It so happened that after this profitable voyage, Barkley, then sailing under the Portuguese flag, was relieved of command in 1788 by his sponsors who were East India Company personnel. They became alarmed that the company was acquainted with their ruse and they took steps to disassociate themselves from the project. The *Imperial Eagle* was sold and Barkley lost most of his investment in the ship's stores and equipment. (He later in 1792 took the ship *Halcyon,* again with Mrs. Barkley aboard, to Alaska and the Northwest Coast on another long trading venture. One of their two young children died at sea after several weeks.)

One can certainly understand the Barkleys' bitter disappointment at the partners' arbitrary termination in 1788 of a long-term business arrangement that had promised to be lucrative for the young couple. In her accounts, Mrs. Barkley waxes eloquent in denunciations of her husband's employers, and says Meares, who was part of the same enterprise, obtained Barkley's charts, journal, nautical instruments, stores and other equipment acquired by her husband.[8] Barkley later received the sum of £5,000 through arbitration. (Charles Barkley, too, apparently later made disparaging remarks about Meares to the Spanish ambassador in May 1790 during the international crisis.[9])

Mrs. Barkley wrote: "Captain Meares . . . with the greatest effrontery, published and claimed the merit of my husband's discoveries . . . besides inventing lies of the most revolting nature tending to vilify the person he thus pilfered. No cause could be assigned, either by Capt. Barkley or myself for this animosity, except the wish of currying favor with the late agents and owners of the *Loudin* . . . these persons having quarrelled with Captain Barkley in consequence of his claiming on his discharge a just demand."[10]

However, upon close examination of *Voyages*, Meares does not therein "vilify" Barkley, nor does he castigate him in any manner, but, rather, credits Barkley for conducting a fruitful voyage in 1787. And, Meares does not appear to have claimed any discoveries made by Barkley. If anything, Meares' widely distributed *Voyages* provided contributing documentation at an early date (1790) further confirming Barkley's sighting of the Strait of Juan de Fuca and other discoveries of 1787. "Berkley's Sound" always appears where appropriate on Meares' charts and maps in *Voyages*.

Meares did make some ambiguous comments that have led to criticism. These are generally outlined by Lamb who states unequivocally, "most of the references in . . . [Meares'] text are deliberately misleading," yet the complaints actually make for a surprisingly short list which can rather easily be discounted. For example, in *Voyages,* Meares referred to the strait "which we shall call by the name of its original discoverer, John de Fuca." What was Meares' meaning? Was he trying to imply he was the discoverer? Hardly, he made it plain that Barkley was there a year earlier, and the *Imperial Eagle*'s boat "discovered the extraordinary straits of John de Fuca." Meares did name a promontory on Vancouver Island "Cape Beale" apparently for his sponsor of that name, but Barkley also earlier gave it the same name (for his purser, who was killed by Indians on the Olympic Peninsula). In publishing *Voyages,* Meares may have made use of Barkley's chart of "Port Effingham" for his own purposes, but the map had become company property and in the caption Meares clearly indicates the port was "in Berkley's Sound."

Some of Meares' ships sailed under the Portuguese flag, for which he has been criticized. In maritime annals, this was not unusual. A number of ships sailed under false colors (including Barkley's, under two different flags), and many captains from all nations frequently renamed landmarks, too. The early logs, journals and charts are replete with examples. For instance, regarding Bruno de Hezeta's names for the Columbia River landmarks "Cabo San Roque" and "Cabo Frondoso," Meares changed the former to "Cape Disappointment" and the American Robert Gray changed the latter to "Point Adams." In 1792, the Royal Navy's William Broughton tried to rename the "Columbia River" (the name bestowed by its discoverer Captain Gray in the same year, replacing "Río de San Roque") as the "Oregon River." And, regarding "Cape Beale," Barkley and Meares conveniently ended up honoring two men with the same name.

Meares' faults were no more, nor less, than many another mariner of this period. Given the evidence at hand, it is difficult to understand why some historians have perpetuated adverse criticisms of Meares. Perhaps, some have been unduly swayed by the persuasive power in a woman's pen, unique to maritime annals. Frances Hornby Barkley makes for an especially appealing heroine, bravely standing at her husband's side in hazardous, desolate seas during long voyages to the ends of the earth.[11] George Dixon's allegations against Meares in the two pamphlets published in 1790-91 also may have exerted influence on such respected historians as F.W. Howay.

Notes

1. Lamb's paper later was published; see W. Kaye Lamb, "The Mystery of Mrs. Barkley's Diary: Notes on the Voyage of the 'Imperial Eagle,' 1786-87," *British Columbia Historical Quarterly* 6 (January 1942), 31-59. Lamb was the Provincial Librarian and Archivist of the Province of British Columbia (1934-40), Librarian of the University of British Columbia (1940-48), Dominion Archivist (1948) and National Librarian (1953). Among his other historical contributions, he edited a monumental four-volume edition of Captain George Vancouver's journal for the Hakluyt Society, London.

2. John Meares, "Observations on the Probable Existence of a North West Passage, Etc.," lv, in *Voyages Made in the Years 1788 and 1789, from China to the North West Coast of America* (London: Logographic Press, 1790). In addition to crediting Barkley in this section, Meares gives recognition to the essential discoveries made by Hanna, Strange, Laurie, Guise, Portlock, Dixon, Duncan, Douglas and the American captains of the *Columbia* and *Washington* in the years 1785-88.

3. Ibid., lxiii; "I bring the authority of Captain Barclay's officers, &c. who saw every particular which I declare to have seen,—having surveyed these parts in a boat,—though he himself [Barkley] did not go within some leagues of the strait." See examples of other similar statements giving recognition to Barkley on pages 124, 169, and 172 in Meares' *Voyages*.

4. In London, on July 29, 1788, the prominent director of Northwest Coast trading operations, Richard Cadman Etches, had a conversation "with some of the People that belong'd to the *[L]ouden,* Cap. Barclay." The information gleaned by Etches about Barkley's venture, the discovery of the strait and its geographical implications regarding the possibility of a Northwest Passage basically parallels information gained by Meares. See Frederick W. Howay, ed., "Four Letters from Richard Cadman Etches to Sir Joseph Banks, 1788-92," *British Columbia Historical Quarterly* 6 (April 1942): 135-36.

5. Frederick W. Howay, ed., *The Dixon-Meares Controversy* (Toronto: Ryerson Press, 1929), 29-30, 65-66.

6. As Lamb points out, these materials did not include the *Imperial Eagle*'s first log book, which was retained by Barkley (and now is in the holdings of the British Columbia Archives). This first log begins with the ship's departure from Europe in late 1786, and ends on June 11, 1787, just before Barkley made his first landfall on the Northwest Coast at Nootka Sound. Meares, not having access to the first log, may not have had any direct evidence that the *Imperial Eagle* departed Ostend on November 24, 1786. Thus in his statement in *Voyages* he instead gave a best estimate that Barkley had left Europe in early "1787." It appears only those portions of the *Imperial Eagle*'s

records pertaining directly to the Northwest Coast and the fur trade were demanded by the partners in closing their arrangements with Barkley in 1788. It was these charts and materials, and including a second log apparently beginning on June 12, 1787, that then were assigned to Meares in addition to Barkley's stores and equipment. Since it appears that Meares was on his second, and last, Northwest Coast voyage when Barkley's services were terminated, it is possible Meares acquired the documents sometime after he returned to Macao on December 5, 1788. It is unknown if these documents remain in existence today. During the "pamphlet war" in 1790-91, the information also came out that Meares was provided with a chart derived from Barkley before Meares left on his second cruise to North America in early 1788. This apparently occurred before Barkley was dismissed.

7. J.T. Walbran was captain of the Canadian government ship *Quadra* from 1891 to 1903, and author of *British Columbia Coast Names, 1592-1906* (Ottawa: Government Printing Bureau, 1909). In addition to the four main excerpts from Mrs. Barkley's diaries noted by Lamb, Walbran also recorded a few other brief statements and references from Mrs. Barkley's *Louden* diary for inclusion in *British Columbia Coast Names, 1592-1906.*

8. Barry M. Gough in *The Northwest Coast: British Navigation, Trade, and Discoveries to 1812* (Vancouver: University of British Columbia Press, 1992), 89, agrees that Meares obtained "Barkley's charts, journals, and private stores."

9. After meeting with Captain Barkley, the Spanish ambassador reported on May 28, 1790, that Meares "had no property or even a share in the outfitting" of the captured ships "because he doesn't have even a house or a home" and claimed Meares was being paid a few guineas by the Associated Merchants who needed to remain anonymous because of their connections to the monopolies; translated from the Spanish by Warren L. Cook, *Flood Tide of Empire: Spain and the Pacific Northwest, 1543-1819* (New Haven, CT, and London: Yale University Press, 1973), 219.

10. Mrs. Barkley also claimed: "Capt. Meares got possession of my husband's Journal and plans from the persons in China to whom he was bound under a penalty of £5,000 to give them up for a certain time for, as these persons stated, mercantile objects, they not wishing the knowledge of the [Northwest] Coast to be published." Lamb, "The Mystery of Mrs. Barkley's Diary," 50-51.

11. Regarding Mrs. Barkley's charges, John T. Walbran states: "It is impossible at this day [1909] to say, in the absence of Captain Meares' account of the dispute, what grounds there were for the accusation, but it may be stated that he obtained the journals, &c., through the agents of the *Imperial Eagle*"; *British Columbia Coast Names, 1592-1906*, 34.

Appendix II

Meares' Memorial to Parliament

COPY OF THE MEMORIAL

Presented to The House of Commons, *May* 13, 1790 :—
Containing every Particular respecting the Capture of the Vessels
in Nootka Sound.

THE Memorial of *John Meares*, Lieutenant in his Majesty's Navy, most humbly sheweth,—That early in the year 1786, certain merchants residing in the East Indies, and under the immediate protection of the Company, desirous of opening a trade with the North West Coast of America, for supplying the Chinese market with furs and ginseng, communicated such design to Sir John Macpherson, the governor-general of India, who not only approved of the plan, but joined in the subscription for its execution; and two vessels were accordingly purchased, and placed under the orders and command of your Memorialist.

That in the month of March your Memorialist dispatched one of the said vessels, which he named The *Sea Otter*, under the command of Mr. Tipping, to Prince William's Sound, and followed her in the other ship, which he named The *Nootka*.

That on your Memorialist's arrival in Prince William's Sound, in the month of September, he found the *Sea Otter* had left that place a few days before; and, from intelligence he has since received, the ship was soon after unfortunately lost off the coast of Kamtschatka.

That your Memorialist remained in Prince William's Sound the whole of the winter; in the course of which time he opened an extensive trade with the natives; and having collected a cargo of furs, he proceeded to China, in the autumn of 1787.

That in the month of January 1788, your Memorialist having disposed of the *Nootka*, he, in conjunction with several British merchants residing in India, purchased and fitted out two other vessels, named the *Felice* and *Iphigenia;* the former your Memorialist commanded, and the latter he put under the direction of Mr. William Douglas. That your Memorialist proceeded from China to the Port of Nootka, or King George's Sound, which he reached in the month of May, and the *Iphigenia* arrived in Cook's River in the month of June.

That your Memorialist, immediately on his arrival in Nootka Sound, purchased from Maquilla, the chief of the district contiguous to, and surrounding that place, a spot of ground, whereon he built a house for his occasional residence, as well as for the more convenient pursuit of his trade with the natives, and hoisted the British colours thereon; that he also erected a breast-work, which surrounded the house, and mounted one three-pounder in front; that having so done, your Memorialist proceeded to trade on the coast; the *Felice* taking her route to the Southward, and the *Iphigenia* to the Northward, confining themselves within the limits of 60° and 45° 30' minutes North, and returned to Nootka Sound in the month of September; that on your Memorialist's arrival there, his people, whom he had left behind, had nearly compleated a vessel, which, previous to his departure, he had laid down; and that the said vessel was soon after launched by your Memorialist, and called the *North-West America*, measuring about forty tons, and was equipped with all expedition to assist him in his enterprizes.

That, during the absence of your Memorialist from Nootka Sound, he obtained from Wicananish, the chief of the district surrounding Port Cox and Port Effingham, situated in the latitude of 48° and 49°, in consequence of considerable presents, the promise of a *free and exclusive trade with the natives of the district*, and also his permission to build any storehouses, or other edifices, which he might judge necessary; that he also acquired the same privilege of exclusive trade from Tatootche, the chief of the country bordering on the Straits of John De Fuca, and purchased from him a tract of land within the said strait, which one of your Memorialist's officers took possession of in the King's name, calling the same Tatootche, in honour of the chief.

That the *Iphigenia*, in her progress to the Southward, also visited several ports, and in consequence of presents to the chiefs of the country, her commander had assurances given to him of not only a free access, but of an exclusive trade upon that coast, no other European vessel having been there before her.

That your Memorialist, on the 23d of September, having collected a cargo of furs, proceeded in the *Felice* to China, leaving the *Iphigenia* and the *North-West America* in Nootka Sound, with orders to winter at the Sandwich Islands, and to return to the coast in the Spring. That your Memorialist arrived in China early in the month of December, where he sold his cargo, and also the ship *Felice*.

That a few days after your Memorialist's arrival in China, the ships *Prince of Wales* and *Princess Royal*, fitted out from the Port of London by Messrs. John and Cadman Etches and Co. came to Canton from a trading voyage on the North West Coast of America; and your Memorialist finding that they had embarked in this commerce under licenses granted to them by the East India and South Sea Companies, which would not expire until the year 1790, and apprehending at the same time that the trade would suffer by competition, he and his partners associated themselves with the said Messrs. Etches and Co. and a formal agreement was executed in conference between your Memorialist and Mr. John Etches, then supercargo of the two ships, making a joint stock of all the vessels and property employed in that trade; and under the firm they purchased a ship, which had been built at Calcutta, and called her the *Argonaut*.

That the *Prince of Wales* having been chartered to load teas for the East India Company, soon after returned to England; and the *Princess Royal* and *Argonaut* were ordered by your Memorialist to sail for the coast of America, under the command of Mr. James Colnett, to whom the charge of all the concerns of the company on the coast had been committed.

Mr. Colnett was directed to fix his residence at Nootka Sound, and, with that view, to erect a substantial house on the spot which your Memorialist had purchased in the preceding year; as will appear by a copy of his instructions hereunto annexed.

That the *Princess Royal* and the *Argonaut*, loaded with stores and provisions of all descriptions, with articles estimated to be sufficient for the trade for three years, and a vessel on board in frame, of about thirty tons burthen, left China accordingly in the months of April and May, 1789. They had also on board, in addition to their crews, several artificers of different professions, and seventy Chinese, who intended to become settlers on the American coast, in the service, and under the protection of the associated company.

That on the 24th of April, 1789, the *Iphigenia* returned to Nootka Sound; and that the *North-West America* reached that place a few days after: that they found, on their arrival in that port, two American vessels, which had wintered there; one of them was called the *Columbia*, the other the *Washington*: that on the 29th of the same month, the *North-West America* was dispatched to the northward to trade, and also to explore the Archipelago of St. Lazarus.

That on the 6th of May, the *Iphigenia* being then at anchor in Nootka Sound, a Spanish ship of war, called the *Princessa*, commanded by Don Stephen Joseph Martinez, mounting twenty-six guns, which had sailed from the Port of San Blas, in the Province of Mexico, anchored in Nootka Sound, and was joined on the 13th by a Spanish snow of sixteen guns, called the *San Carlos*, which vessel had also sailed from San Blas, loaded with cannon and other warlike stores.

That from the time of the arrival of the *Princessa* until the 14th of May, mutual civilities passed between Captain Douglas and the Spanish officers, and even supplies were obtained from Don Martinez for the use of the ship; but on that day he, Captain Douglas, was ordered on board the *Princessa*, and, to his great surprize, was informed by Don Martinez, that he had the King's orders to seize all ships and vessels he might find upon the coast, and that he, the Commander of the *Iphigenia*, was then his prisoner: that Don Martinez thereupon instructed his officers to take possession of the *Iphigenia*, which they accordingly did, in the name of his Catholic Majesty, and the officers and crew of that ship were immediately conveyed as prisoners on board the Spanish ship, where they were put in irons, and were otherwise ill-treated.

That as soon as the *Iphigenia* had been seized, Don Martinez took possession of the lands belonging to your Memorialist, on which his temporary habitation before mentioned had been erected, hoisting thereon the standard of Spain, and performing such ceremonies as your Memorialist understands are usual on such occasions; declaring, at the same time, that all the lands comprized between Cape Horn and the sixtieth degree of North latitude did belong to his Catholic Majesty; he then proceeded to build batteries, storehouses, &c. in the execution of which he forcibly employed some of the crew of the *Iphigenia*, and many of them who attempted to resist were very severely punished.

That during the time the commander of the *Iphigenia* remained in captivity, he had frequently been urged by Don Martinez to sign an instrument, purporting, as he was informed, (not understanding himself the

Spanish language) that Don Martinez had found him at anchor in Nootka Sound; that he was at that time in great distress; that he had furnished him with every thing necessary for his passage to the Sandwich Islands; and that his navigation had in no respect been molested or interrupted: but which paper, on inspection of a copy thereof, delivered to Mr. Douglas, and hereunto annexed, (No. II.) appears to be an obligation from him and Mr. Viana, the second captain, on the part of their owners, to pay on demand the valuation of that vessel, her cargo, &c. in case the Viceroy of New Spain should adjudge her to be lawful prize, for entering the Port of Nootka without the permission of his Catholic Majesty: that Captain Douglas, conceiving that the port of Nootka did not belong to his Catholic Majesty, did frequently refuse to accede to this proposal; but that Don Martinez, partly by threats, and partly by promises of restoring him to his command, and of furnishing him with such supplies of stores and provisions as he might stand in need of, ultimately carried his point; and having so done, he, on the 26th of the same month, was restored to the command of the *Iphigenia*, but restrained from proceeding to sea, until the return of the *North-West America;* insisting that he should then dispose of her for 400 dollars, the price which one of the American captains had set upon her.

That during the time the Spaniards held possession of the *Iphigenia*, she was stripped of all the merchandize which had been provided for trading, as also of her stores, provisions, musical instruments, charts &c. and, in short, every other article (excepting twelve bars of iron) which they could conveniently carry away, even to the extent of the master's watch, and articles of cloathing.

That the commander of the *Iphigenia*, finding himself thus distressed, applied for relief, and after much solicitation obtained a trifling supply of stores and provisions, for which he was called upon to give bills on his owners. The articles so supplied were charged at a most exorbitant price, and very unequal in quality or quantity to those which had been taken from him.

That notwithstanding what had been insisted on by Don Martinez, respecting the sale of the *North West America*, he had constantly refused to dispose of that vessel on any ground, alleging that, as she did not belong to him, he had no right to dispose of her; that the *North-West America* not returning so soon as was expected, he, Capt. Douglas, was told by Don Martinez, that on his ordering that vessel to be delivered to him for the use of his Catholic Majesty, he should have liberty to depart with the *Iphigenia;*

that he accordingly, on the first of June, wrote a letter to the master of the *North-West America*, but cautiously avoided any directions to the effect desired, (vide *Iphigenia's* Journal) and availing himself of Don Martinez's ignorance of the English language, he instantly sailed from Nootka Sound, though in a very unfit condition to proceed on such a voyage, leaving behind him the two American vessels which had been suffered to continue there unmolested by the Spaniards, from the time of their first arrival; that the *Iphigenia* proceeded from thence to the Sandwich Islands, and after obtaining there such supplies as they were enabled to procure with the iron before mentioned, returned to China, and anchored there in the month of October, 1789.

Your Memorialist thinks it necessary upon this occasion to explain, that in order to evade the excessive high port charges demanded by the Chinese from all other European nations excepting the Portuguese, that he and his associates had obtained the name of Juan Cawalho to their firm, though he had no actual concern in their stock; that Cawalho, though by birth a Portuguese, had been naturalized at Bombay, and had resided there for many years, under the protection of the East India company, and had carried on an extensive trade from thence to their several settlements in that part of the world.

That the intimacy subsisting between Cawalho and the governor of Macao had been the principal cause of their forming this nominal connection; and that Cawalho had in consequence obtained his permission that the two ships above mentioned, in case it should be found convenient so to do, should be allowed to navigate under, or claim any advantages granted to the Portuguese flag.

That this permission had answered the purpose of your Memorialist, so far as respected the port charges of the Chinese, until the return of the *Iphigenia;* but the Portuguese Governor dying soon after her departure, and Cawalho becoming a bankrupt, his creditors demanded his interest in that ship; that your Memorialist having resisted their claim, an application was made by them to the succeeding governor for possession of the ship; that the governor had, in consequence, investigated the transaction, and finding that Cawalho had no actual concern or interest in the property, obliged her to quit the port; that this proceeding had subjected the *Iphigenia* at once to the increased port charges, which were instantly demanded by, and paid to, the Chinese.

Your Memorialist has stated this transaction thus fully, in order to shew that the *Iphigenia* and her cargo were actually and *bonâ fide* British property, as well as to explain the occasion of the orders which were given to her commander, extracts of which accompany this, and are referred to in the journal of that ship, having been under the inspection of Don Martinez.

Your Memorialist further begs leave to state, that after the departure of the *Iphigenia*, Don Martinez became apprized of the purport of the letter with which he had been furnished; and that, on the return of the *North-West America* off the port of Nootka, on the 9th of June, she was boarded and seized by boats manned and equipped for war, commanded by Don Martinez; that he did tow and convey the said vessel into the Sound, and anchoring her close to the Spanish ships of war, did then take possession of her in the name of his Catholic Majesty, as good and lawful prize; that the above mentioned vessel was soon after hauled alongside of the Spanish frigate; and that the officers and men, together with the skins which had been collected, amounting to 215, of the best quality, and also her stores, tackle, and furniture, articles of trade, &c. were removed on board the Spanish frigate; that the commander of the *North-West America*, his officers and men, were accordingly made prisoners, and Mr. Thomas Barnett, one of the officers of that vessel, and some of her men were, as appears in the affidavit of William Graham, one of the seamen belonging to that vessel, hereunto annexed, (No. IV.) afterwards put in irons.

That the *Princess Royal* arriving a few days after the seizure of the *North-West America*, and being allowed by Don Martinez to depart, the skins collected by the last mentioned vessel (excepting twelve of the best quality, which Don Martinez thought fit to detain) were returned to the master, and, with permission of Don Martinez, were shipped on board the *Princess Royal*, for the benefit of the owners; and that ship, as appears by her Journal, put to sea on the 2d of July, to pursue the trade upon the coast.

That Don Martinez, after seizing the *North-West America* in the manner and under the circumstances above stated, employed her on a trading voyage, from which she returned after an absence of about twenty days, with seventy-five skins, obtained by British merchandize, which had either been found in the vessel at the time of her capture, or had been taken from the *Iphigenia;* and that the value of the furs collected cannot, upon a moderate calculation, be estimated at less than 7,500 dollars, and which Don Martinez had applied to his own advantage.

That the *Argonaut* arrived off the Port of Nootka on or about the 3d of July, 1789. That Don Martinez, on observing her in the offing, boarded her in his launch, and with expressions of civility, promised Mr. Colnett, her commander, every assistance in his power; that before the *Argonaut* entered the Sound, Mr. Thomas Barnett (who had belonged to the *North-West America*, and who was then a prisoner) came off in a canoe, and informed Mr. Colnett of the proceedings which had taken place, and of the danger to which he was exposed; but that, under the assurances given by Don Martinez, that the *Argonaut* should remain unmolested, and being in want of refreshments for the crew, Mr. Colnett proceeded into Nootka Sound.

That, notwithstanding the assurances given by Don Martinez, he, on the next day, sent the first lieutenant of the *Princessa*, with military force, to take possession of the *Argonaut;* and that ship was accordingly seized in the name of his Catholic Majesty, the British flag was hauled down, and the Spanish flag hoisted in its stead.

That on the seizure of the *Argonaut*, her officers and men were made prisoners; and Mr. Colnett was threatened to be hanged at the yard arm, in case of his refusing compliance with any directions which might be given to him.

That on the 13th of July, the *Princess Royal*, as is stated in her Journal, again appeared off the Port of Nootka; that her commander approaching the Sound in his boat, in expectation of finding there the commander the expedition, (from whom he was desirous of receiving instructions for his future proceedings) was seized and made prisoner by Don Martinez, and under threat of hanging him at the yard-arm, forced him to send orders to his officers to deliver up the *Princess Royal* without contest.

That a Spanish officer was dispatched into the offing with these orders; and that the vessel was accordingly seized in the name of his Catholic Majesty, and brought into port; that her crew were in consequence made prisoners; and that her cargo, consisting of 473 skins, including 203 which had been put on board her from the *North-West America*, as appears by the inclosed receipt, (No. V.) was seized.

That Mr. Colnett, from the circumstances of his capture, became so deranged, that he attempted frequently to destroy himself; and that, according to the last accounts received, the state of his mind was such as to render him unfit for the management of any business which might have been entrusted to his care; that in this melancholy situation, however, Don Martinez, notwithstanding the vessel and cargo had been formally seized, attempted to procure from him the sale of the copper, of which a principal part of the cargo of the *Princess Royal* had been composed; and that such sale would actually have taken place, had not the other officers of that vessel, seeing Colnett's insanity, prevented it.

Your Memorialist farther begs leave to represent, that the American ship *Columbia* intending to proceed to China, the crew of the *North-West America* were ordered by Don Martinez on board her; principally, as your Memorialist understands, for the purpose of assisting her in her navigation to China, the greater part of her own crew, as well as of her provisions; having been previously put on board the *Washington*, in order that she might be enabled to continue on the coast.

That the *Columbia* having reduced her provisions considerably from the supplies she had spared to her consort, was furnished from the *Argonaut*, by order of Don Martinez, with what was necessary for her voyage, said to be intended, however, for the supply of the *North-West America;* that previous to the departure of the *Columbia*, ninety-six skins were also put on board her, as appears by the paper hereunto annexed, (No. VI.) to defray the wages of the officers and crew of the *North-West America*, under a supposition that their late employers would be unable to liquidate their demands; first deducting, however, thirty per cent. from the sales, which Don Martinez had agreed should be paid for the freight on the said skins to the American commanders.

That the *Columbia*, thus supplied, left Nootka Sound accordingly, and proceeded to the Southward; that a few days after she entered Port Cox, where she was joined by her consort the *Washington*, from whom she received a considerable number of skins, conceived to be the whole, excepting the ninety-six before mentioned, which had been collected by the Americans and Spaniards, as well as by the British traders; and with which, after sparing a further quantity of provisions to the *Washington*, the *Columbia* proceeded to China, where she arrived on the 2d of November, and landed the crew of the *North-West America*.

That the crew of the *North-West America*, previous to their leaving Nootka Sound in the *Columbia*, saw the *Argonaut* proceed, as a prize, to San Blas; and that her officers and men, who were Europeans, were put on board her as prisoners; and that the *Princess Royal* was shortly to follow, with her crew in confinement in the same manner. The *Washington*, on joining the *Columbia* in Port Cox, gave information that the *Princess Royal* had also sailed for San Blas.

That Don Martinez had thought fit, however, to detain the Chinese, and had compelled them to enter into the service of Spain; and that, on the departure of the *Columbia*, they were employed in the mines, which had then been opened on the lands which your Memorialist had purchased.

Your Memorialist begs leave to annex a deposition of the officers and crew of the *North-West America*, together with an extract of the Journal of the *Iphigenia*, and also some letters which he has received from Mr. Duffin, second officer of the *Argonaut;* which papers will serve to throw considerable light on the several transactions alluded to in this Memorial: He also has subjoined a statement of the actual as well as the probable losses which he and his associates have sustained from the unwarrantable and unjustifiable proceedings of Don Martinez, in open violation of the treaty of peace subsisting between this country and the Court of Spain, and at times and in situations where, according to the common laws of hospitality, they might have expected a different conduct.

Your Memorialist therefore most humbly begs leave to submit the case of himself and his associates to the consideration of Government, in full confidence that the proper and necessary measures will be taken to obtain that redress, which he and his associates have, as British subjects, a right to expect.

(Signed) JOHN MEARES

London, 30th of April, 1790

Your Memorialist also begs leave to annex an acknowledgment given by Don Martinez, of his having obtained possession of the *North-West America*. (No. XI.) J.M.

Meares' *Memorial* to Parliament was dedicated "To the Right Honourable William Wyndham Grenville, One of His Majesty's Principal Secretaries of State" and included "14 Inclosures." An annex to the *Memorial* and *Voyages* lists actual losses (wages, skins, etc.) at 153,433 Spanish dollars, and probable losses (vessel in frame aboard the *Argonaut*, loss of future cargo, etc.) at 500,000 Spanish dollars.

[Source: Appendix, in John Meares, *Voyages Made in the Years 1788 and 1789, from China to the North West Coast of America* (London: Logographic Press, 1790).]

Who Were the First Europeans to Visit Hawaii?

W HEN WILLIAM DOUGLAS, captain of Meares' consort, the *Iphigenia*, anchored in Kealakekua Bay off the island of Hawaii in December 1788 and again in July 1789, he believed he was the first European captain to arrive there since the visit of James Cook and the *Discovery* and *Resolution* in early 1779. Douglas was mistaken. Captains Portlock and Dixon in the *King George* and *Queen Charlotte* were there ahead of the *Iphigenia* by a year, and Captain James Hanna may have preceded them, though that is uncertain. Douglas also believed, as have most mariners and historians ever since, that Cook was the European "discoverer" of the islands in 1778. Douglas may have been wrong on that score, too.

Recent challenges to this belief have arisen. In February 1996, the Marine Option Program of the University of Hawaii and the Hawaiian Maritime Center hosted a symposium on early Hawaiian history in which learned papers were presented contending that a Spanish mariner, and not Cook, was the first European captain to bring a ship to the islands. Speculation concerning Spanish arrivals as early as 250 years before Cook is not new. The possibility has often been mentioned in historical works based on Hawaiian legends, but the theory generally has been discounted. A book written by Eric W. Dahlgren in 1916, heretofore considered the definitive work on the subject, concluded that no proof existed that any other mariner preceded Cook. This conclusion has been supported by other Hawaiian historians but now should be considered in doubt.[1]

Major contributors to the symposium included Alan Lloyd, a national director of the U.S. Navy League and a retired engineer for the Hawaiian Electric Company; Richard W. Rogers; and Steve Gould, a staff member of the Maritime Center. Each contributed data supporting the Spanish discovery theory. (Important information on this topic also comes from the writings of artist/historian Herb Kawainui Kane of Captain Cook, Hawaii.[2]) Lloyd reported on his study of 16 ancient charts and 2 old globes which depict a group of islands in the same latitude as the Hawaiian chain, but approximately 1,000 miles too far to the east. Rogers' and Gould's reports covered their extensive research into logs and documents that seem to provide evidence that Spanish mariners sighted and/or visited the islands before Cook's arrival. Kane contends in his book *Voyagers* that Spaniards could have visited Hawaii two centuries before Cook, but because storms, currents and a lack of accurate timepieces prevented them from determining the accurate longitude, they charted the islands ten degrees too far east.

People from distant Pacific islands, of course, reached Hawaii centuries before the first white men. Hawaiian historians such as Ralph S. Kuykendall and Herb Kane place the arrival of the earliest colonists at 1,500 to nearly 2,000 years ago. After two or more waves came from the Marquesas and Tahiti, voyaging in twin-hull canoes from far-off islands, contact with the outside ceased long ago and Hawaii became isolated. The early Polynesians guided their vessels by wave patterns, currents, the stars and the paths of birds and were the real discoverers of Hawaii. One historian identifies the Tahitian demi-god Hawaii Loa as the first to arrive.

Should Cook at least be recognized as the practical discoverer of the Sandwich Islands, which he named for his benefactor, the Earl of Sandwich, First Lord of the Admiralty? Legends of earlier European arrivals have long existed, but Dahlgren in 1916 seemed to put the question to rest. Dahlgren's conclusion was that Cook should receive the credit. A Spanish shipwreck may have left sailors stranded on shore, but, if so, none returned to Spain to tell the tale. Dahlgren was supported by John F.G. Stokes in 1939. Terence Barrow also has written that no evidence has been found confirming early Spanish arrivals.[3]

Cook was on his way to the Northwest Coast when he happened upon the Sandwich Islands early in 1778. His journal states his vessel, the *Resolution,* arrived off an island on the morning of January 18, 1778, which must have been today's Oahu. He sailed on by and on the 19th reached Kauai, where he went ashore at Waimea Bay the following day. His two ships continued on to the Northwest Coast in an unsuccessful search for a Northwest Passage, which took the expedition as far north as the icy Arctic before returning to Hawaii to spend the winter. In Kealakekua Bay he was treated as a great chief or the god Lono. But when he went ashore to attempt to regain a boat stolen from the *Discovery*, he was struck down and killed by natives on February 14, 1779.

Cook's journal in 1778 lends some validity to the claims that he was preceded by Spanish mariners. He noted: "The only iron tools or indeed pieces of iron seen among them, which they were supposed to have before our arrival, was a piece of iron hoop about three inches long, fited into a wooden handle in the same manner as their stone adzes and a nother edge tool which was supposed to have be[en] made of the point of a broad sword. This, and their knowing the use of iron made some immagine that we were not the first Ships that had been at these islands, on the other hand the very great surprise they shewed at the sight of the ships and their total ignorance of fire arms seemed to prove the contrary."[4]

However, the contention that Cook himself knew he was not the first European to see the islands are rebutted by his last remarks written in 1779 just before his death:

"Perhaps there were few on board who now lamented having failed to find a northwest passage homeward last summer. To this disappointment we owe our having in our power to enrich our voyage with a discovery which, though the last, seemed in many respects to be the most important that had hitherto been made by Europeans through the extent of the Pacific Ocean."[5]

Were there Spaniards unknown to Cook who had laid eyes on these islands centuries before him? Modern researchers say yes. Beginning in the 16th century, Spanish galleons carried Mexican silver from Acapulco to Manila, and brought back Asian goods prized in Spain. Their course generally was 300 nautical miles south of Hawaii on the western leg, and 1,000 miles north on the eastern track following prevailing currents.

While Cook believed he was the actual discoverer of the Sandwich Islands, one of his officers, James Burney, wrote that he and others had seen natives brandishing iron skewers "we supposed to have come from the Spaniards." According to Rogers and Gould at the 1996 symposium, Cook's subordinate captain on the *Discovery*, Charles Clerke, also had noted several iron objects and entertained ideas that Europeans had been in the islands prior to their own expedition.

The argument goes like this: 16th century Spaniards saw a group of islands in the vicinity of the 20th parallel of latitude, where the Hawaiian chain lies, but they mistakenly located them 10 or 20 degrees east of the actual longitudinal position later established by Cook. The information in some way reached Europe and was placed on new charts in Spain and elsewhere. In 1743, the British mariner George Anson in the *Centurion* captured the *La Nuestra Señora de Covadonga* and obtained a chart of the Spanish route to Manila showing the Los Monges group.

A map in Cook's possession based on Anson's chart located the Los Monges islands far east of the Sandwich Islands. When a cartographer, Lieutenant Roberts, drafted the chart of Cook's voyage, Cook instructed him to include La Mesa, La Vicina and La Desgraciada at those positions even though Cook had never sighted them.

At the 1996 maritime symposium, Alan Lloyd testified that he had knowledge of, and had investigated, 16 charts and 2 globes, most of which dated prior to Cook's explorations. They showed an island group often called Los Monges, with individual islands named La Mesa, La Desgraciada, and La Vicina (various spellings). La Mesa (Spanish for table) appears to be the largest and lies in the same latitude as the island of Hawaii on which Mauna Loa is located, a mountain with a table-like appearance.

The globes were created by Jodocus Hondius and Adrian Veen of Amsterdam in 1613, and by Peter Anichs in 1757. The Hondius globe is in the National Maritime Museum in Greenwich, England, and the Anichs globe is in the Landeskundliches Museum in Innsbruck, Austria. Most of the 16 charts were drawn up between 1572 and the time of Cook's expedition. A few others with similar inclusions of the Los Monges group were drafted after Cook's voyage.

Although these globes and charts portray the islands, this did not mean that each indicated a new sighting of the isles by mariners. Early cartographers often repeated information contained on earlier charts (which could include erroneous as well as accurate information).

Who supposedly made these early sightings? Modern researchers advance several possibilities. Rogers and Gould list them:

> 1527: Spanish sailors under the command of Admiral Saavedra see the islands of Hawaii and Maui amid a great eruption and named them Los Bolcanes. Saavedra himself was unconscious at the time because of an injury occurring in a storm. (There are several variations of this account.)
>
> 1542: Juan Gaitano with the fleet of Villalobos visits Oahu and names it Anabluda. His journal was published in Italy.

1565-70:   Someone revisits these islands and renames them La Mesa, La Desgraciada and La Vicina.
1574-86:   A vessel wrecks on one island, probably Maui.
1624 or earlier: Someone sees the Island of Hawaii and names it Uloa.
Late 1600s: Someone sees Kauai and names it La Maria Laxeria.
1693-1705:   A vessel wrecks on the Island of Hawaii.
1778:   Cook arrives and names the Sandwich Islands.

Historian Mary Charlotte Alexander, in her book *The Story of Hawaii*, published in 1912, related that in the early 16th century, a ship wrecked at Keei, south of Kealakekua Bay on the Island of Hawaii. A large man with a sword at his side, and a woman identified in legend as his sister, struggled ashore and fell on their knees in prayer. Natives who watched called the place "Kuloa," which means "to kneel." The duo were fair-skinned. Alexander identified the incident with a known flotilla of three ships dispatched by the Spanish conquistador Hernando Cortés from San Blas, Mexico, to determine a course to the Philippines. Cortés in a letter to Philip V of Spain in 1526 recounted that he was about to dispatch such a flotilla to conquer the Spice Islands. The ships were the *Florida*, *Espíritu Sanctu* and the *San Iago* under the command of Admiral Álvaro de Saavedra.[6]

The *Florida* is the only one of the three ships known to have survived the voyage. Conceivably, a storm could have driven one of the other two on the rocks in Hawaii. The two refugees were befriended by the natives and lived out their lives in the islands. Alexander supports her tale, which she derived from "meles" (chants), with a sketch in her book of a crudely carved image that she believes is of a Spaniard, complete with ruff and pigtail, of that period. It was uncovered by a German scientist in the 19th century and shipped to a Berlin museum. Later a plaster copy of the statue was made and sent to the Bernice Pauahi Bishop Museum in Honolulu. It is known there as the "Manoa Image."[7]

The burden of proof that Spaniards were in the islands before James Cook remains with those engaged in this research. The Marine Option program of the University of Hawaii plans to conduct further research including electronic probes into Kealakekua Bay in the hope of finding Spanish ship wreckage.

It may well be that the French maritime explorer, Jean Francois Galaup, Comte de la Pérouse, was correct when he wrote in 1786: "In the charts [of the Pacific Ocean] might be written: Sandwich Islands, surveyed in 1778 by Captain Cook, who named them, but anciently discovered by the Spanish navigators."

This fact was evident to the 19th century residents of Hawaii. In the October 21, 1856, edition of *The Friend*, a newspaper published in Honolulu, the editor quoted from Pérouse's account: "It appears certain [that the islands were] discovered for the first time by Gaitán in 1542." Gaitán sailed from La Navidad in Mexico "at 20 degrees north latitude and stood west and ran 900 leagues" (without changing latitude). He "fell in with a group of islands inhabited by savages almost naked." The islands were surrounded by coral. Gaitán noted coconut and other fruits, but the islands had no gold nor silver, which were coveted by the Spanish. Gaitán named them the "King's Islands." But, Pérouse noted, the account erred in placing Gaitán's islands between 9 and 10 degrees north latitude instead of between the 19th and 21st degrees where the Hawaiian Islands are situated; he concluded this was "an error of the press."

If *The Friend* editor (relying on Pérouse) and the modern advocates of Spanish discovery are correct, Captain Cook was not the first European to visit the islands. That honor may rightfully belong to Juan Gaitán or some other Spaniard, but the British hero must at least have credit for bringing them to the world's ken and thus changing the history of the Pacific.[8]

Notes

1. Eric W. Dahlgren, *The Discovery of the Hawaiian Islands: Were the Hawaiian Islands Visited by Spaniards before Their Discovery by Captain Cook in 1778?* (Stockholm: Ahlmquist and Wicksells Boktryckeri, 1916), 2; see also, John F.G. Stokes, "Hawaii's Discovery by the Spaniards: Theories Traced and Refuted," *Hawaiian Historical Quarterly* [Honolulu], 1939.
2. See especially, Herb Kawainui Kane, *Voyagers* (Bellevue, WA: Whalesong Press, 1991).
3. Terence Barrow, *Captain Cook in Hawaii* (Norfolk Island, Australia: Island Heritage, 1962); see also Barrow's introduction, *Hawaiian Historical Legends* (William D. Westervelt, reprint, 1996): "The truth is, no scholar has succeeded in establishing any historical evidence for a Spanish discovery prior to that of Captain Cook."
4. James Cook journal, quoted from A. Grenfell Price, ed., *The Explorations of Captain James Cook in the Pacific As Told by Selections of His Own Journals, 1768-1779* (New York: Dover 1971), 225.
5. This was James Cook's final journal note before his murder. Subsequent entries were made by Lt. James King.
6. Hubert Howe Bancroft, in *History of Mexico*, Vol. X (Vol. II, 1521-1600) (San Francisco: Bancroft, 1883), named the vessels and confirmed that they sailed from San Blas in October 1527. They were the *Florida, Espíritu Santo* and *Santiago* under the command of Álvaro de Saavedra Ceron. Two ships became separated and were never seen again. A copy of Mary Charlotte Alexander's book, *The Story of Hawaii,* is in the

Waikiki-Kapahulu branch of the Hawaii State Library. The Berlin museum she mentions as the home of the original carving of the "Spanish sea captain" is the Museum fur Velkerunde.

7. The copy statue was seen and photographed by this author in an obscure corner of a warehouse at the Bishop Museum in 1997.

8. A copy of *The Friend* account, the volume of letters from Cortés to Philip V of Spain and a copy of Bancroft's *History of Mexico* (Vol. X) are in the private collection of Francis S. Murphy of Portland, Oregon.

Documents

No. 1

Passing Certificate for Commission of John Meares

September 17, 1778

In pursuance of 16 Sep 1778 we have examined Mr John Meares who by Certificate appears to be more than Twenty-two years of age and find he has gone to Sea more than six years in the ships under mentioned Viz:

Cruizer -captain['s cabin boy] & able [seaman] 7 mos 1 day
Cruizer -mid[shipman] 3 wks 5 days
King Fisher -able 10 mos
King Fisher -mid, 4 mos 1 - 3 [1 wk 3 days]
Torvey -mid 1 yr 9 - 1 - 1
Captain -mid 3 - 3 - 2
Torlay -able 1 - 2 - 1
Triton -mid 1 - 11 - 2 - 4
[total] 6 - 10 - - 11 [6 years 10 mos 1 day]

He produceth Journals kept by himself in the *Torvay* & *Triton* and certificates from *Capn* of his intelligence & etc and is qualified to do the duty of an able Seaman and Midshipman. [Dated the] 17 Sept 1778 [Signed by] Ch Middleton Ed Le Cras and Capn Abraham North

[Source: ADM 107/7, folio 59, Public Record Office, Kew, England.]

No. 2

Minutes of Cabinet Meeting

April 30, 1790

Whitehall 30 April 1790: Present the Lord Chancellor and other lords & dukes, Mr. Pitt and Mr. Grenville:

> Upon consideration of the information which has been received from Mr. Meares of the detention and capture of several British vessels at Nootka Sound, on the coast of America, and of the circumstances of that transaction . . . Your Majesty's servants have agreed humbly to submit to Your Majesty their opinion that Your Majesty's minister at the Court of Madrid should be instructed to present a memorial demanding an immediate and adequate satisfaction for the outrages committed by Monsieur de Martinez; and that it would be proper, in order to support that demand and to be prepared for such events as may arise, that Your Majesty should give orders for fitting out a squadron of ships of the line.

Present at the cabinet meeting were the Lord Chancellor, the Lord Privy Seal, the Duke of Richmond, the Duke of Leeds, Lord Chatham, William Pitt and Lord Grenville. As a result, a strong protest was sent to Spain over "these repeated outrages." The letter demanded "restitution of the said vessels [named were the *Princess Royal* and the *North West America*], their crews & the property belonging to them . . . and the officers in question be punished for their direct infraction both of the existing treaties between the two crowns and of the general principles of Justice & the Law of Nations" and that "such reparation shall be made to the persons who have suffered on this occasion, as may indemnify them for the Costs which they have sustained."

[Source: FO 95/7/3, Spain and Spanish America 1790 April-June, Public Record Office, Kew, England.]

No. 3

Excerpts from Third Nootka Convention between
Great Britain and Spain

Signed at Madrid, January 11, 1794.

Their Brittannick and Catholick Majesties . . . being desirous to remove
and obviate all Doubt and Difficulty relating to the execution of the First
Article of the Convention concluded between their said Majesties on the
Twenty eighth of October One Thousand Seven Hundred and Ninety—
have resolved [and sent to their officers to carry out] . . .

In the shortest time—after their arrival at Nootka they shall—meet together at or near the buildings which were formerly occupied by the Subjects
of His Brittannick Majesty . . . [where they shall exchange declarations:]

I, N. . . . N. . . . [by order of His Catholick Majesty] . . . restore to N
. . . . N . . . . the Buildings and Districts of Land situated on the Coast of
North America or on the Islands adjacent thereto . . . of which the Subjects
of His Brittannick Majesty were disposessed about the month of April
[1789] by a Spanish officer . . .

I, N. . . . N. . . . [by order of His Brittannick Majesty] declare that
[the buildings and lands] . . . have been restored to me by N . . . . N . . . .
which restitution I declare to be full and satisfactory . . .

That the British officer shall then cause the British flag to be hoisted
on the Land thus restored . . . the officers of the two Crowns shall respectively withdraw their people from the said Port of Nootka.

Their Majesties have farther agreed that it shall be free for the Subjects of both Nations to frequent occasionally the aforesaid Port and to
construct there temporary Buildings . . . But that neither One nor the
Other . . . shall make any permanent Establishment . . . or claim there any
Right of Sovereignty or Territorial Dominion to the Exclusion of the Other
. . . [and to assist each other] to maintain to their Subjects free Access to
the said Port of Nootka against any other Nation which should attempt to
establish there any Sovereignty or Dominion . . .

[Signed:] Lord St Helens and the Duque de la Alcudia, done at Madrid
the Eleventh Day of January One Thousand Seven Hundred and Ninety Four.

Written in English and Spanish side by side.

[Source: FO 93/99/5B, Public Record Office, Kew, England.]

No. 4

Meares' Request to the Admiralty for Reassignment to Naval Duty
Letter to Evan Nepean, Secretary to the British Admiralty

May 12, 1796

Sir,

I beg you will be pleased to inform their Lordships, that since my return from Ireland, for the recovery of my health, after receiving an hurt there, when Employed on the Impress Service, I am now quite recovered, and am ready, and desirous to Serve, wherever their Lordships may think proper to Employ me.

I am, sir, your most obed. & very able Servt.

Jno. Meares

[Source: ADM 1/2132, Public Record Office, Kew, England.]

No. 5

Excerpts from the Last Will and Testament of John Meares

January 19, 1809

This is the last will and testament of Mr John Meares of the city of Bath in the County of Somerset Esquire—Whereas there is due to me from James Drummond of South Audley Street London Esquire the sum of ten thousand eight hundred and seventy three pounds Sterling and also there is due to me from Daniel Beale & Co. London who under an arbitration twenty one thousand six hundred pounds Sterling out of which said cost Sum I so order and direct that all my Just Debts, Funeral Expenses and the costs of proving this my will be paid and discharged . . . [I] give devise and bequeath unto my friend Valentin Jones of Ballbrook House of the County of Somerset Esquire William Hollings now of Calcutta in Bengal Esquire Thomas Bailey of the City of Bath hatter and hosier and Richard Lambert of the City of Bristol merchant and the Survivors and Survivor of those his Heirs, Executors advisors and assigns all that my freehold Estate in Jamaica . . . [I] hold the same and every part thereof unto them the said Valentin Jones William Hollings Thomas Bailey and Richard Lambert their heirs and assigns forever upon trusteeship that they my said trustees and the survivors and survivor . . . administrators or assigns shall and do immediately sell and convert the same into Money for the best price or prices that can be reasonably had or gotten for the same and the money arising from sale therof be considered as part of my personal estate . . . I have a patent under the Crown of nine hundred pounds per annum payable at the Irish Treasury upon which there will be about four thousand pounds in arrear and due to me which I also give to my aforesaid trustees and to the Survivors and Survivor of them his Executors and advisors . . . to form part of my personal Estate and be disposed of . . . I give devise and bequeath unto James Read all those my six [holdings?]. . . in the Swansea Council . . . I give and bequeath unto the said Valentin Jones William Hollings Thomas Bailey and [blank] . . . the full sum of four thousand pounds of lawful British money . . . [from the liquidation of the estate] or other inventions as they may think most singular. [Thirty thousand rupees were claimed owed by] My good friend . . . William Hollings of Calcutta . . . as will appear by the [arrangement?] between us . . . Now I so honor give and bequeath the said Debt or Sum of thirty thousand rupees and every part thereof, unto the said James Read of the City of Bath to hold the same and every part thereof, unto the said James Read his Examiners advisers and assigns to and for his own benefit and disposal forever . . .

Further instructions were given to Thomas Bailey concerning distribution of proceeds from the estate to James Read and to his "Brother and Sister" (unnamed) in equal proportions and smaller sums to others including the children of Thomas Bailey. The will is dated January 19, 1809, and was witnessed by Benjamin Atkinson, Brandy Browrandt(?) (of Bath), John Bowers (bookseller, Bath) and Luke Evill(?) (attorney, Bath). The will was "proved at London" April 19, 1809, before the "surrogate of the Right Honourable Sir John Driscoll" in the prorogation court of Canterbury.

The dates reveal that Meares probably filed his will in recognition of the fact he did not have long to live. The dates also confirm that he died in 1809 as recorded by David Syrett and R.L. DiNardo, *The Commissioned Sea Officers of the Royal Navy, 1660-1815* (London: Scolar Press, Navy Records Society, 1994). The records of Bath Abbey date his death as January 29, 1809. Despite the listing of substantial amounts owed Meares from various sources and claimed property holdings, a notation on the recorded copy of the will shows the estate was valued by the court at "less than £7,500."

[Source: Public Record Office, London, London.]

Select Bibliography

Unpublished Primary Sources

British Admiralty (Royal Navy), original letters, despatches, documents, etc., Public Record Office, Kew, England.

British Foreign Office (John Meares and the Nootka controversy), original letters, despatches, documents, etc., Public Record Office, Kew, England.

Carrington, (Arthur) Hugh. "Nootka Meares," typescript manuscript, 1964, British Library, London.

Meares, John. "Last Will and Testament of John Meares," Public Record Office, London.

Published Primary Sources

"Argonaut" [probably John or Richard C. Etches]. *An Authentic Statement of All the Facts Relative to Nootka Sound; Its Discovery, History, Settlement, Trade, and the Probable Advantages To Be Derived from It; in an Address to the King.* London: J. Debrett, 1790.

Colnett, James. *The Journal of Captain James Colnett aboard the "Argonaut" from April 26, 1789, to Nov. 3, 1791,* ed. with intro. and notes by Frederick W. Howay. Toronto: Champlain Society, 1940.

Dixon, George. *Further Remarks on the Voyages of John Meares, Esq. in Which Several Important Facts, Misrepresented in the Said Voyages, Relative to Geography and Commerce, Are Fully Substantiated. To Which Is Added, a Letter from Captain Duncan, Containing a Decisive Refutation of Several Unfounded Assertations of Mr. Meares, and a Final Reply to His Answer.* London: J. Stockdale and G. Goulding, 1791. [Reprinted in Howay, Frederick W., ed. *The Dixon-Meares Controversy.* Toronto: Ryerson Press, 1929.]

_____. *Remarks on the Voyages of John Meares, Esq. in a Letter to That Gentleman.* London: J. Stockdale and G. Goulding, 1790. [Reprinted in Howay, Frederick W., ed. *The Dixon-Meares Controversy.* Toronto: Ryerson Press, 1929.]

_____. [Assisted by William Beresford]. *A Voyage Round the World; But More Particularly to the North-West Coast of America: Performed in 1785, 1786, 1787, and 1788, in the "King George" and "Queen Charlotte," Captains Portlock and Dixon.* London: G. Goulding, 1789. [Reprinted by Da Capo Press, New York, 1968.]

Douglas, William. "Extract of the Journal of the *Iphigenia*" [April 20-June 2, 1789], in Meares, *Voyages . . . 1790.*

_____. "Voyage of the *Iphigenia*, Capt. Douglas, from Samboingan, to the North West Coast of America," in Meares, *Voyages . . .* 1790.

Haswell, Robert. "A Voyage Round the World Onboard the Ship *Columbia-Rediviva* and Sloop *Washington,"* and "A Voyage on Discoveries in the Ship *Columbia Rediviva."* MS, Massachusetts Historical Society, Boston. [Text in Howay, Frederick W., ed. *Voyages of the "Columbia" to the Northwest Coast, 1787-1790 and 1790-1793.* Boston: Massachusetts Historical Society, 1941; Portland: Oregon Historical Society Press, 1990.]

Hoskins, John Box. "John Hoskins' Narrative of the Second Voyage of the 'Columbia.'" MS, Massachusetts Historical Society, Boston. [Text in Howay, Frederick W., ed. *Voyages of the "Columbia" to the Northwest Coast, 1787-1790 and 1790-1793.* Boston: Massachusetts Historical Society, 1941; Portland: Oregon Historical Society Press, 1990.]

L., C. *A Voyage Round the World, in the Years 1785, 1786, 1787, and 1788. Performed in the "King George," Commanded by Captain Portlock; and the "Queen Charlotte," Commanded by Captain Dixon.* London: R. Randal, 1789.

Meares, John. *An Answer to Mr. George Dixon, Late Commander of the "Queen Charlotte." In the Service of Messrs. Etches and Company. by John Meares, Esq. in Which the Remarks of Mr. Dixon on the Voyages to the North West Coast of America, &c Lately Published, Are Fully Considered and Refuted.* London: Logographic Press, 1791. [Reprinted in Howay, Frederick W., ed. *The Dixon-Meares Controversy.* Toronto: Ryerson Press, 1929.]

_____. *Authentic Copy of the Memorial to the Right Honourable William Wyndham Grenville, One of His Majesty's Principal Secretaries of State, by Lieutenant John Mears, of the Royal Navy; Dated 30th April, 1790, and Presented to the House of Commons, May 13, 1790. Containing Every Particular Respecting Capture of the Vessels in Nootka Sound.* London: J. Debrett, 1760 [*sic*, 1790] [also contained as an addendum to Meares' *Voyages . . .*]. [Recent editions are by Nellie B. Pipes, ed. and notes, Metropolitan Press, Portland, OR, 1933, and Glen Adams, ed., Ye Galleon Press, Fairfield, WA, 1985.]

_____ [Assisted by William Coombe]. *Voyages Made in the Years 1788 and 1789, from China to the North West Coast of America. To Which Are Prefixed, an Introductory Narrative of a Voyage Performed in 1786, from Bengal, in the Ship "Nootka"; Observations on the Probable Existence of a North West Passage; and some Account of the Trade between the North West Coast of America and China; and the Latter Country and Great Britain.* London: Logographic Press, 1790. [Reprinted by Da Capo Press, New York, 1967.]

Portlock, Nathaniel. *A Voyage Round the World; But More Particularly to the North-West Coast of America: Performed in 1785, 1786, 1787, and 1788, in the "King George" and "Queen Charlotte," Captains Portlock and Dixon.* London: J. Stockdale and G. Goulding, 1789. [Reprinted by Da Capo Press, New York, 1968.]

Other Sources

Anderson, Bern. *Surveyor of the Sea: The Life and Voyages of Captain George Vancouver.* Seattle: University of Washington Press, 1960.

Annual Register for the Year 1790. London: J. Dodsley, 1793.

Bancroft, Hubert Howe. *History of the Northwest Coast, 1543-1846,* 2 vols. San Francisco: Bancroft Company, 1884.

Barrow, Tui Terence. *Captain Cook in Hawaii.* Norfolk Island, Australia: Island Heritage, 1962.

Beaglehole, John C., ed. *The Journals of Captain James Cook on His Voyages of Discovery,* 3 vols. Cambridge, England: University of Cambridge Press for the Hakluyt Society [1955-74].

Beals, Herbert K., trans. and annotation. *For Honor and Country: The Diary of Bruno De Hezeta.* Portland: Western Imprints, Oregon Historical Society, 1985.

_____, trans. and annotation. *Juan Perez on the Northwest Coast: Six Documents of His Expedition in 1774.* Portland: Oregon Historical Society Press, 1989.

Bell, William (Edward). Extracts from the MS "Journal of William Bell on Board the HMS *Chatham* during Vancouver's Voyage, 1792-1794." Archives of Hawaii, Honolulu; hand-copied from the original in the Alexander Turnbull Library, Wellington, NZ.

Boit, John, Jr. "Remarks on the Ship *Columbia*'s Voyage from Boston, (on a Voyage, round the Globe.)" MS, Massachusetts Historical Society, Boston. [Text in Howay, Frederick W., ed. *Voyages of the "Columbia" to the Northwest Coast, 1787-1790 and 1790-1793.* Boston: Massachusetts Historical Society, 1941; Portland: Oregon Historical Society Press, 1990.]

Buck, Peter H. (Te Rongi Hi Roa). *Explorers of the Pacific: European and American Discoveries in Polynesia.* Honolulu: Bernice P. Bishop Museum, 1953 [#43, printed by the Honolulu Star-Bulletin, 1953].

_____. *Vikings of the Pacific.* Chicago: University of Chicago Press, 1959.

Bulfinch, Thomas. *Oregon and Eldorado: or, Romance of the Rivers* [Columbia and Amazon rivers]. New York: J.E. Tilton, 1866.

[Burges, Sir James Bland.] *Letters Lately Published in The Diary, on the Subject of the Present Dispute with Spain. Under the Signature of Versus.* London: G. Kearsley, 1790.

_____. *A Narrative of the Negotiations Occasioned by the Dispute between England and Spain, in the Year 1790.* London: n.p., 1791.

Cape Meares State Park. Salem: State of Oregon Park Service, 1991.

Chickering, William Henry. *Within the Sound of These Waves: The Story of the Kings of Hawaii Island.* Westport, CT: Greenwood Press, 1971.

Cohen, J.M., ed. and trans. *The Four Voyages of Christopher Columbus.* Bungay, Suffolk, England: Penguin Books, Chaucer Press, 1969.

Colnett, James. *A Voyage to the South Atlantic and Round Cape Horn into the Pacific Ocean . . . by Captain James Colnett, of the Royal Navy, in the Ship "Rattler."* London: W. Bennett, 1798.

Cook, Warren L. *Flood Tide of Empire: Spain and the Pacific Northwest, 1543-1819*. New Haven, CT, and London: Yale University Press, 1973.

Davis, Felix G. *Captain Robert Gray: Tiverton's Illustrious Son*. Tiverton, RI: Tiverton Historical Society, 1945.

Denton, V.L. *The Far West Coast*. Toronto: J.M. Dent and Sons, 1924.

Dmytryshin, Basil. *Russian Penetration of the North Pacific Ocean, 1700-1797: A Documentary Record*, vol. 2, with Thomas Vaughan and E.A.P. Crownhart-Vaughan. Portland: Oregon Historical Society Press, 1988.

Elliott, T.C. "John Meares' Approach to Oregon," *Oregon Historical Quarterly* 29 (1928).

Fornander, Abraham. *An Account of the Polynesian Race: Its Origins and Migrations, and the Ancient History of the Hawaiian People to the Times of Kamehameha I*. Rutland, VT: Charles P. Tuttle, 1982 [4th printing].

Fuller, George W. *A History of the Pacific Northwest, with Special Emphasis on the Inland Empire*, vol 1. New York: Alfred A. Knopf, 1946, 2d ed. rev.

Gibson, Kenneth. "My Discovery of Historical Fort Defiance." Unpublished paper, dated 1985, MS 2212, British Columbia Archives.

Godwin, George. *Vancouver: A Life, 1757-1798*. London: Philip Allan, 1930.

Gough, Barry M. *Distant Dominion: Britain and the Northwest Coast of North America, 1579-1809*. Vancouver and London: University of British Columbia Press, 1980.

_____. "India Based Expeditions of Trade and Discovery in the North Pacific in the Late Eighteenth Century," *Geographical Journal* 155 (July 1989) [Royal Geographic Society reprint].

_____. *The Northwest Coast: British Navigation, Trade, and Discoveries to 1812*. Vancouver: University of British Columbia Press, 1992.

Gray, William P. *Voyages to Paradise: Exploring in the Wake of Captain Cook*. Washington, DC: National Geographic Society, 1981.

Hawthorne, Julian, and G. Douglas Brewerton, eds. *History of Washington, the Evergreen State*, vol. 1. New York: American Historical Publishing Company, 1893.

Hayes, Edmund. "Gray's Adventure Cove," *Oregon Historical Quarterly* 68 (1967).

_____, ed. *Log of the "Union:" John Boit's Remarkable Voyage to the Northwest Coast and around the World, 1794-1796*. Portland: Oregon Historical Society, 1981.

Holbrook, Stewart H. *The Columbia*. New York and Toronto: Rinehart, 1956.

Howay, Frederick W., ed. *The Dixon-Meares Controversy*. Toronto: Ryerson Press, 1929.

_____, ed. "Four Letters from Richard Cadman Etches to Sir Joseph Banks, 1788-92," *British Columbia Historical Quarterly* 6 (April 1942).

_____, ed., intro. and notes. *The Journal of Captain James Colnett aboard the "Argonaut" from April 26, 1789, to Nov. 3, 1791*. Toronto: Champlain Society, 1940.

_____, ed. and comments. *A List of Trading Vessels in the Maritime Fur Trade, 1785-1825*, ed. by Richard A. Pierce. Kingston, Ontario: Limestone Press, 1973 [reprint].

_____, ed. *Voyages of the "Columbia" to the Northwest Coast, 1787-1790 and 1790-1793.* Boston: Massachusetts Historical Society, 1941; Portland: Oregon Historical Society Press, 1990.

Holm , Don. *Pacific North.* Caldwell, ID: Caxton, 1969.

Inglis, Robin., ed. *Spain and the North Pacific Coast: Essays in Recognition of the Bicentennial of the Malaspina Expedition, 1791-1792.* Vancouver, BC: Vancouver Maritime Museum, 1992.

Innes, Hammond. *The Last Voyage: Captain Cook's Lost Diary.* New York: Alfred A. Knopf, 1979.

Janson, A.P. *The Olowalu Massacre and other Hawaiian Tales.* Norfolk Sound, Australia: Island Heritage, 1977.

Joesting, Edward. *Hawaii: An Uncommon History.* New York: W.W. Norton, 1972.

Kamakau, S.M. *Ruling Chiefs of Hawaii.* Honolulu: Kamehameha Schools Press, 1961.

Kane, Herb Kawainui. *Voyagers.* Bellevue, WA: Whalesong, 1991.

Krauss, Bob. *Next Wave.* Honolulu: Honolulu Advertiser, 1995.

Kuykendall, Ralph S. *The Hawaiian Kingdom, 1778-1854,* vol. 1. Honolulu: University of Hawaii Press, 1980 [6th printing].

_____, and A. Grove Day. *Hawaii: A History from Polynesian Kingdom to American Statehood.* Englewood Cliffs, NJ: Prentice-Hall, 1970 [8th printing].

Lamb, W. Kaye. "The Mystery of Mrs. Barkley's Diary: Notes on the Voyage of the 'Imperial Eagle,' 1786-87," *British Columbia Historical Quarterly* 6 (January 1942).

_____, ed. *The Voyages of George Vancouver, 1791-1795,* 4 vols. Cambridge, England: University of Cambridge Press for the Hakluyt Society, 1967.

Ledyard, John. *Journal of Captain Cook's Last Voyage,* ed. by James K. Mumford. Corvallis: Oregon State University Press, 1963.

Lee, W. Storrs, comp. *Washington State: A Literary Chronicle.* New York: Funk and Wagnalls, 1968.

Lowe, C.H. *The Chinese in Hawaii: A Bibliographic Survey.* Taipei, Taiwan: China Printing, 1972.

Lyman, William Denison. *The Columbia River: Its History, Its Myths, Its Scenery, Its Commerce.* New York: G.P. Putnam's Sons; New York and London: Knickerbocker Press, 1917; 3d ed.

Manning, William R. "The Nootka Sound Controversy," *Annual Report of the American Historical Association,* 1904 [281-478].

Marshall, James Stirrat, and Carrie Marshall, annotation. *Pacific Voyages: Selections from Scots Magazine, 1771-1808.* Portland, OR: Binfords and Mort, 1960.

McArthur, Lewis A. *Oregon Geographic Names.* Portland: Koke-Chapman, 1928.

McClellan, Edwin N. "Winee of Waikiki," *Outrigger Forecast Magazine,* April 1950.

Mc Donald, Lucile. *Search for the Northwest Passage.* Portland, OR: Binfords and Mort, 1958.

Meares Island, Protecting a Natural Paradise. Tofino and Vancouver, BC: Friends of Clayoquot Sound, Western Canada Wilderness Committee, 1985.

Menzies, Archibald. *Hawaii Nei: 128 Years Ago*, ed. by W.F. Wilson. Honolulu: New Freedom Press, 1920.

Miller, David O. "Kaiana, the Once Famous 'Prince of Kauai,'" *Hawaiian Journal of History* 22 (1988).

_____. "Notes and Queries," *Hawaiian Journal of History* 23 (1989).

Morgan, Murray. "Exploring the Northwest with a Ghost Writer [William Coombe]," *American Bookman* [New York City], September 9, 1991.

Nokes, J. Richard. *Columbia's River: The Voyages of Robert Gray, 1787-1793*. Tacoma: Washington State Historical Society, 1991.

_____. "Patriot or Scalawag? John Meares' Exploits on the Northwest Coast," *Columbia: The Magazine of Northwest History*, Fall 1990.

Nouvelle Biographie Generale . . . xxxiv (Mar-Mer). Paris: Firmin Didot Freres, 1861.

Official Papers Relative to the Dispute between the Courts of Great Britain and Spain, on the Subject of the Ships Captured in Nootka Sound, and the Negociation that Followed Thereon. London: J. Debrett, 1790.

Oliver, Douglas L. *The Pacific Islands*, rev. ed. Garden City, NY: Doubleday, 1962.

Parrish, Philip H. *Before the Covered Wagon*. Portland, OR: Metropolitan Press, 1931.

Pethick, Derek. *The Nootka Connection: Europe and the Northwest Coast, 1790-1795*. Vancouver, BC: Douglas and McIntyre, 1980.

Price, A. Grenfell, ed. *The Explorations of Captain James Cook in the Pacific: Selections of his Own Journals, 1768-1779*. New York: Dover, 1971.

Ronda, James P. *Astoria and Empire*. Lincoln and London: University of Nebraska Press [1990].

Sahlins, Marshall. *How "Natives" Think: About Captain Cook for Example*. Chicago: University of Chicago Press, 1995.

Schwantes, Carlos, and Katherine Morrisey, David Nicandri, and Susan Strasser. *Washington: Images of a State's Heritage*. Spokane, WA: Melior, 1988.

Shrapnel, G.S. *Suppressed Naval History of British Columbia*. Victoria: Diggon-Hibben, n.d.

Speck, Gordon. *Northwest Explorations*, ed. by L.K. Phillips. Portland, OR: Binfords and Mort, 1954.

Stephen, Leslie, ed. *Dictionary of National Biography*, vol. 13. London: Smith, Elder [1885-1901].

Strange, James. *James Strange's Journal and Narrative of the Commercial Expedition from Bombay to the North-west Coast of America: Together with a Chart Showing the Tract of the Expedition*, intro. and ed. by A.V. Venkatarama Ayyar. Madras: Government Press, 1929.

Syrett, David, and R.L. DiNardo. *The Commissioned Sea Officers of the Royal Navy, 1660-1815*. London: Scolar Press, Navy Records Society, 1994.

Tovell, Freeman M. *The Heceta-Bodega Voyage of 1775: Its Significance for Spain's Presence in the Pacific Northwest*. Victoria, BC: Terra Incognita, 1995.

_____. "The other Side of the Coin: The Viceroy, Bodega y Quadra, Vancouver, and the Nootka Crisis," *BC Studies* 93 (Spring 1992).

Vancouver, George. *A Voyage of Discovery to the North Pacific Ocean, and Round the World*, vol. 1. London: G.G. and J. Robinson and J. Edwards, 1798.

Vaughan, Thomas, and Bill Holm. *Soft Gold: The Fur Trade and Cultural Exchanges on the Northwest Coast of America*. Portland: Oregon Historical Society Press, 1982.

Viola, Herman J., and Carolyn Margolis, eds., assisted by Jan S. Danis. *Magnificent Voyagers: The U.S. Exploring Expedition, 1838-1842*. Washington, DC: Smithsonian Institution Press, 1985.

Wagner, Henry R. *Spanish Explorations in the Strait of Juan de Fuca*. Santa Ana, CA: Fine Arts Press, 1933.

Walbran, John T. *British Columbia Coast Names, 1592-1906*. Ottawa: Government Printing Bureau, 1909.

Ward, Robert. "Lost Harbour Found: Where Sir Francis Drake Really Went in the Pacific." Unpublished typescript, dated 1987, Essex, England.

Index